Necrologies

Necrologies

A BOOK OF
WELSH OBITUARIES

MEIC STEPHENS

seren

s

Seren is the book imprint of
Poetry Wales Press Ltd.
57 Nolton Street, Bridgend, Wales, CF31 3AE
www.seren-books.com

The right of Meic Stephens to be identified as
the author of this work has been asserted in accordance
with the Copyright, Designs and Patents Act, 1988.

© Meic Stephens, 2008

ISBN 978-1-85411-476-1

A CIP record for this title is available from the British Library.

The publisher acknowledges the financial assistance of the Welsh Books
Council.

Printed in Plantin Light by Bell & Bain Ltd.

Contents

Introduction

Obituaries are about life, not death. They celebrate human character and achievement in all their myriad forms. Obituarists, in the first instance, note the bare facts of the deceased's life – place and date of birth, occupation, spouse's name, number and gender of children, date and place of death – and these are often printed for quick reference in italic or bold type at the head or foot of the column. Whether the piece is read or skipped often depends on this synopsis, and on the strap-line under the subject's name, because some of us may have no interest in, say, estate agents however distinguished. Then, since an obituary is something more than a *Who's Who* entry or an undertaker's announcement, the life has to be described and put into some sort of context, so that even if the reader did not know the lately departed, which is more than likely, the additional facts and opinions about him or her will give a more rounded picture of the full human being. The obituarist's function is to praise the dead and comfort the living, for the living like reading about their dead, and to inform and engage the interest of the wider public. The Gazette pages of our major newspapers, which have their own ways of recording engagements, marriages and births as well as deaths, as part of the life-cycle, are one reason why so many readers are loth to change their daily reading habits.

In fact, as aficionados of the genre well know, obituaries are not about death at all, and so there is nothing macabre or morbid about writing or reading them. Death hardly enters into it. Certainly, 'the obituary aesthetic' requires that, unless the deceased suffered bravely for many years or met a violent end, or died young, the ghastly cause and grisly details are not given. Although we in Britain have taken up some of the funeral customs of other countries in recent years – flowers at the roadside, clapping the hearse, wreaths made to look like rugby balls, favourite pop-songs played during the service, and so on – we have yet to follow the American example in the writing of obituaries: Americans are less squeamish in the face of death and yet more deferential and bland about the life; and we do not yet have conferences of obituary-writers as they do in the United States.

The only convention almost universally observed is that nothing should be said, or left unsaid, in ways that might be construed by grieving relatives and friends as criticism of the person they loved.

Indeed, *de mortuis nil nisi bonum* is still the working motto of all necrologists – unless, of course, the deceased was, say, a Chicago gangster or a Nazi war-criminal or the commandant of a Soviet gulag. Even so, for more humdrum lives there are circumlocutions and euphemisms which convey a flavour of the subject's character and behaviour: 'he was very good company late at night' usually means the chap was merry in his cups; 'she was a vivacious woman who turned many a head' may signify that the lady had scores of lovers; 'he was a canny Scot' is perhaps a reference to the man's tight-fistedness; 'he never married' is accurate but delicious enough to invite speculation; and so on. Skeletons in the family cupboard, or sexual preferences, or the whiff of marital scandal, are revealed only if they have some direct bearing on the deceased's life and work, and preferably with the consent of the bereaved. Yet such references, if included at all, may add interest and colour to what might otherwise be in danger of resembling those cold-hearted tributes sometimes paid by clergymen over the coffins of people whom they never knew, so a fine line has to be trod. There should be, moreover, no recourse to such awful clichés as Abraham's Bosom, the Grim Reaper, the Final Curtain, the Pearly Gates, Joining the Majority, the Great Committee Room in the Sky, a Good Innings, the Elysian Fields or Crossing the Styx. It is, too, the height of bad manners when the writer draws attention to himself or claims too large a part in the deceased's success. As in so much else in life, common sense and tact, as well as as getting the facts right, are paramount when treating of a person's last end, and self-effacement on the obituarist's part is to be preferred to self-advertisement.

Best of all are the obituaries which mix fact and opinion with anecdote and yes, even a little humour, though sepulchral levity and lachrymose sentimentality are always misplaced. For there comes a moment in most obituaries, as in most memorial services, when someone tells a faintly amusing story about the deceased: how she was fond of multicoloured hats, perhaps, or what he once said to his overbearing boss at a Christmas party or what she did with back-issues of *Vogue*. It is at that moment we know fond memories are being evoked, tears are giving way to smiles and life is thus being reaffirmed. 'A good obit,' wrote Marilyn Johnson in *The Dead Beat*, her book about the writing of obituaries, 'is an act of reverence, a contemplation of a life that sparked and died.' The truth of this observation is often borne out by the gratitude of the bereaved or by the appreciative comments made by friends and colleagues, which is reward enough for the several days' work that has gone into writing the piece. It is also heartwarming to know that obituaries are often cut out and, if of an author, are sometimes to be found tipped inside his or her books where they serve a purpose far better than any blurb.

The function of the obituary has another, wider and less personal dimension. To read, as many do, the daily Obituaries page in any of 'the major four' – *The Times, The Daily Telegraph, The Guardian,* and *The Independent* – all of which regard the writing of obituaries as examples of 'the higher journalism', is to be informed about a wide range of specialist subjects and about people from all over the world who have distinguished themselves in one way or another, and about whom the reader might not otherwise have heard. To understand the allusions they contain goes to the making of a well-furnished mind which takes a lively interest in the contemporary world and its recent history. The several anthologies of obituaries taken from *The Times, The Daily Telegraph, The Guardian,* and *The Independent* make for fascinating reading for this very reason. The obituary, therefore, is life-enhancing even as valedictions are being made to the dead.

I am not sure Quentin Crisp was wholly right when he wrote in *The Naked Civil Servant,* 'An autobiography is an obituary in serial form with the last instalment missing', but I can see what he was driving at. Rather, I would agree with those who think an obituary is the first draft of biography. In this important regard the London dailies, as newspapers of record, have served a very useful purpose ever since the *Gentleman's Magazine,* the first English periodical to carry obituaries, began doing so in the mid-eighteenth century. It is regrettable that no newspaper in Wales in recent times has given regular space to obituaries and that our radio and television programmes, especially those in English, often overlook the passing of even our most distinguished people.

Although I have written a few obituaries for *The Times* and *The Guardian,* most of my pieces have been for *The Independent.* I prefer the paper's house-style and, as with *The Guardian,* its requirement that obituaries should be signed, for I like to know whose opinions I am reading. It is usually the first of all the London papers to carry an obituary, often at the rate of four a day and, impressively, on the day after the death, to be followed some time later by other papers which lift the basic facts (and sometimes more) to fill their pages. I began writing for *The Independent* in January 1995 when I sent in an obituary of my late friend Harri Webb, and have gone on, under the expert guidance of the paper's first Obituaries Editor James Fergusson and, after his leaving the paper in 2007, under that of his successor Diana Gower and her deputy Sarah Quarmby, to contribute eight or nine a year. All of the seventy-two obituaries in this book were first published in *The Independent* and are reprinted here with that paper's kind permission.

For the purposes of this book I have taken the opportunity of correcting a few small mistakes which crept into the newsprint versions, since even the most careful obituarist, in the rush to file copy, sometimes gets things not quite right; a slightly wrong emphasis or misunderstanding can lead to errors that are not revealed until spotted by relatives whose sensibilities are still raw after the loss of their loved one. If only for this reason, the writing of obituaries is always, in James Fergusson's phrase, 'an especially exacting form of news-gathering'. There is less risk of error if the piece can be honed over several days and then filed months and perhaps years in advance of the subject's death – it is no secret, after all, that that is how most obituaries are written. I am indebted to the relatives of many of the people whose lives are described in this book for their help at the time of their bereavement. For any factual mistakes or infelicities which may remain I apologise unreservedly.

I have added nothing with hindsight but a number of minor blemishes have been silently removed. I have also restored a few sentences that were excised by the Editors so that the piece could be fitted on the page. There is never any shortage of copy for the Obituaries page and the regular contributor soon learns that each piece has to be succinct but not lapidary, comprehensive but not too detailed, lively but not whimsical, and he or she must be ready to accept editorial cuts. Another way in which the necrologies reprinted here differ from the versions published in the paper is that I have restored the full names of the people who have died, or sometimes called them by their first name, especially if I knew them well. This seems to me preferable to the use of surnames alone, which to my ear smacks of the English public school and the British armed forces. I find it difficult referring to Kyffin Williams, for example, as Williams, particularly as he was known throughout Wales as Kyffin.

A large part of my intention in writing about Welsh people for a London paper is to convey a sense of Welsh society that cannot always be taken for granted in England. In this respect I consider myself as much 'a foreign correspondent' as, say, James Kirkup, who lives in Andorra, when he writes about Catalan, French, or Spanish writers and film-makers. Many of the lives I have attempted to describe were not well known outside Wales but *The Independent* has never declined my offers to write about such people. In this way I have tried to foster an awareness of some of our more eminent compatriots, and a little about our culture, beyond our borders. Readers in Wales are therefore asked to bear in mind that all these valedictions were originally written for a readership elsewhere for whom some things needed to be elucidated, and some more than once. There was, alas, a need for a quick gloss on such references as Owain Glyndŵr, Pantycelyn, National Eisteddfod, Saunders Lewis, Penyberth, Cymdeithas yr Iaith Gymraeg, The Merthyr Rising, Eifionydd, and Yr Academi Gymreig, among others. There is, therefore, some repetition when such references occur.

Even so, I have chosen to write about people – among them politicians, civil servants, boxers, soldiers, and so on – whose lives, for the most part, were spent in Wales and whose work was done here. They illustrate the cultural life of Wales in the latter half of the twentieth century and the beginning of the twenty-first, though the present selection is necessarily confined in that it concentrates, for the most part, on writers, artists, historians, journalists, academics, broadcasters, musicians, and actors.

Friends sometimes ask me what my criteria are for deciding about whom I am going to write an obituary in *The Independent*. Well, the first is that I should be acquainted with the deceased, if not intimately at least well enough to write cogently about his or her life and work; I have only once written about someone I had never met, and that was at the request of a relative and the piece is not included here. Second, he or she must have made a significant contribution to the public life of Wales, and third, the difficult question must always be asked, 'Why will this person be remembered?' or, put another way, 'Why does he or she deserve to be remembered?' Above all, the man or woman must in some way be interesting to others or the work notable. Describing what he or she was like as a person is easy compared to any attempt at answering such questions. Fortunately, *The*

Independent is different from *The Times* (for long 'the only paper to seen dead in'), and from *The Daily Telegraph* into which so many of the pinstriped – majors, Home Office mandarins, landowners, bishops, Tory grandees, and the like – seem to be admitted, in that it is more open-minded and gladly finds room for people who might best be described as the quirky, the outrageous, the quietly courageous, and those for whom the local was the real. As *The News of the World* used to say of itself in another context, 'All human life is there'.

So I repeat: there can be nothing gloomy about the writing or reading of obituaries. Death for the obituarist is merely a cue for composing a small biography of a person who has been admired, liked or found interesting. Only once have I written about a person I heartily disliked, and the reader of this book will have no difficulty spotting the exception to the general rule. Perhaps I ought not to have written with such animus, but at the same time I should say the man's passing was noted in much the same way in other papers. Be that as it may, an obituary should be a celebration of a life, however diminutive in the larger scheme of things and however obscure it may seem to the movers and shakers. It is, if you like, a last fanfare, something between eulogy and elegy, for a person who has helped us to understand better what it means to be human.

This book is published in the year I achieve what we call in Welsh *oed yr addewid*, the psalmist's promise of 'threescore years and ten'. In 2005 the National Eisteddfod offered a prize for the writing of an obituary 'in the style of a quality newspaper'. I thought it might be fun to see what would happen if I sent in, under the pseudonym Taphos, an obituary of one Meic Stephens. The adjudicator, a woman not known for writing obituaries, but perhaps a keen reader of them, thought the entry, although one of the best three entered in the competition, did not provide enough information about its subject, which was a slap on the wrist for me, and besides, rather more hearteningly, 'Meic Stephens still has a few years ahead of him in which he might continue to make a contribution to the literature of Wales' – perhaps she had in mind that the psalmist goes on to say, 'or even by reason of strength fourscore'. Anyway, the prize was withheld on the grounds that no entry was worthy of it. So perhaps I shall rejig and translate my piece, and send it off, *mutatis mutandis*, to *The Independent* to file against the time when it can be used; such things have not been unknown. Unless, that is, someone, somewhere, has already beaten me to it and is even now writing my obituary. If so, just one word of advice to whoever it was enquiring about the state of my health the other day: don't forget to double-check your facts and, as Glyn Jones used to say about the writing of his poems and stories, remember to burnish your copy with a final 'huh-huh'. As for the rest, my only regret is that I shan't be around to read it.

Meic Stephens
Whitchurch, Cardiff
May 2008

Harri Webb

Poet and Welsh Republican

Few poets in recent times have achieved the popularity of Harri Webb. Shortly after the opening of the Severn Bridge in 1966, his "ode" to the new edifice was to be heard quoted widely throughout South Wales:

> Two lands at last connected
> Across the waters wide,
> And all the tolls collected
> On the English side.

The squib was stamped on a thousand T-shirts and, for a while, lorry drivers coming out of Wales, with the rhyme emblazoned on their chests, would shout it at the imperious attendants who took their money.

Harri Webb wrote mostly in English, but another of his poems, in Welsh, "*Colli Iaith*" ("Losing a language"), exquisitely rendered by the folk singer Heather Jones, became that rare thing – a song by a living poet that was generally thought to be traditional. He was delighted when it was incorporated into the annual ceremonies of the National Eisteddfod, where its blend of poignancy and defiance had enormous appeal.

Born into a working-class home in the docklands of Swansea in 1920, Harri was educated at Magdalen College, Oxford, where he read Medieval and Modern Languages, specialising in French and Spanish. In 1941 he joined the Navy and served as an interpreter with the Free French in the Mediterranean, and also saw action in the North Atlantic, an experience which was to affect his nervous make-up.

Demobilised at Largs, in Scotland, five years later, he wandered in Scotland for a while, without any sense of personal direction. The discovery of Hugh MacDiarmid's writing at this point in his life proved decisive. Like the Scot, Harri was "always where extremes meet", and he learnt his Nationalism, which was left-wing and inclined to the quixotic, from the writer and political activist who was to become his hero. He then decided to return to Wales and throw himself into the political fray.

Harri began his career with the Republicans, a small group who enlivened the Welsh political scene of the 1950s by the burning of Union Flags in the towns of South Wales and the handling of dynamite up in the hills. After the movement's demise in 1959, he was for a while a member of the Labour Party, but then – appalled by its attitude to the question of self-government for Wales – joined Plaid Cymru. He edited the party's newspaper and stood as its candidate at Pontypool in the general election of 1970.

Harri Webb was a vivid platform speaker, reserving his most scathing invective for his erstwhile comrades in the Welsh Labour Party, though capable of being equally trenchant about Plaid Cymru when he thought it was failing to give a lead as a movement of national liberation, as at the time of the drowning of the Tryweryn Valley after the building of a reservoir by Liverpool Corporation.

A convivial man, noted for his iconoclastic wit and wide erudition, especially among the young and less abstemious of his compatriots, he earned and enjoyed the status of People's Poet, thinking of himself as belonging to the ancient tradition of the Welsh Bard, whose function it was to rally his people against the foe, whether the English invader or the servile, collaborating Welsh.

He came to prominence as a poet during the 1960s, when political Nationalism was beginning to make headway in the industrial valleys of South Wales, and became a regular contributor to my magazine *Poetry Wales*. His reputation as a poet of the Nationalist cause rests on the poems in *The Green Desert* (1969) and *A Crown For Branwen* (1974), which contain his most delicately lyrical work, but also on the rollicking ballads, outrageous epigrams and pint-pot doggerel to be found in *Rampage and Revel* (1977) and *Poems and Points* (1983).

Among his other books were an account of the Merthyr Rising of 1831, published in 1956, a volume of stories for children based on the Mabinogion tales (1984), and a number of television scripts, including *How Green Was My Father* (1976). He also translated Pablo Neruda's epic poem *Alturas de Machu Picchu* into elegantly flowing Welsh, achieving that "sonorous utterance" that was also his aim as both poet and public speaker. The social condition of Wales was the "one theme, one pre-occupation" of all his writing, though he set it in a broad frame of cultural allusion and contemporary significance.

His last years were sad and lonely. After his retirement, his health quickly deteriorated, he was housebound, and saw few of his old friends. He found some solace, however, in the Anglican faith of his boyhood, indulged his passion for the American cinema of the 1940s, and continued to read extensively in the languages at his command. Although his head was turned more than once, he never married.

By profession Harri was a librarian, first in Cheltenham, where he had gone to escape an unhappy relationship with a Cardiff woman, then in the iron town of Dowlais, near Merthyr Tydfil, and latterly at Aberpennar (Mountain Ash) in the Cynon Valley, one of the most socially deprived spots in mid-Glamorgan, where he lived until taken into hospital last summer. But, ever a Swansea Jack, he asked to be moved to his home town in November, wanting, I believe, to die there.

His last public act was to announce, in 1985, that he would write no more in English, adding with characteristic hyperbole that English was "a dying language" and that the only language for a true Welshman was Welsh.

For my part – and I write as his friend of more than thirty years, his literary executor, and the only other person to have read his voluminous journal – I take this to mean that Harri, almost all of whose writing was done in English, had nothing more to communicate, and that this was his way, provocative to the last, of burning Union Flags.

Harri Webb, poet: born Swansea 7 September 1920; died Swansea 31 December 1994.

The Independent (3 January 1995)

Glyn Jones

Poet, prose-writer and chronicler of Anglo-Welsh literature

Poet, short-story writer, novelist, translator, and critic, Glyn Jones was among the most versatile and distinguished of those Welshmen who, in the 1930s, contributed to the emergence and definition of an Anglo-Welsh literature which, although written in English, was specifically Welsh in feeling, style, and subject-matter.

His book *The Dragon Has Two Tongues* (1968) is a largely autobiographical account of how a generation of writers was formed by the religious, political, and educational forces shaping South Wales in the years between the two world wars.

Glyn Jones was typical of them in several crucial respects. Born in Merthyr Tydfil in 1905, into a Welsh-speaking home, he suffered a wholly English education at the Cyfarthfa Grammar School and, after nearly losing his Welsh, had to educate himself in the language and literature of his country. Although he became a fluent Welsh-speaker, and able to render the most technically complex Welsh poetry, almost all his own writing had to be done in English, the language of his schooling, his adolescent reading, and his awakening imagination.

Like so many of his contemporaries – Jack Jones, Rhys Davies, Gwyn Thomas, for example – Glyn Jones was politically of the Left, though never an active member of the Labour Party and always sympathetic to the aims of Plaid Cymru. It was the wretched condition of the industrial valleys of South Wales during the Depression, and later the deprivation he witnessed as a young teacher in a Cardiff slum, which made him a Socialist. At the outbreak of war in 1939 he registered as a conscientious objector on pacifist grounds, a stand for which he was temporarily deprived of his teaching post by the Cardiff Education Authority.

What made Glyn different from his generation, who were for the most part agnostic if not downright hostile to the narrower aspects of Welsh Nonconformity, were his Christian beliefs and practice. Brought up by devout parents, he was a chapelgoer all his life, regularly attending Sunday School and taking a full part in the affairs of Minny Street Congregational Chapel, one of the bastions of the Independent cause in Cardiff. A mild-mannered, diffident man, loth to say anything ungenerous about others, he seemed to have a saintly touch to his character, though there was nothing smug or sanctimonious about him and he had a delicious sense of humour.

Staunch though his political and religious convictions were, little of them was allowed to impinge on his poetry and prose. He was concerned, rather, with the English language and its use as a medium for the depiction of human character in all its astonishing variety. "I fancy words," he wrote in his panegyric to his hometown of Merthyr Tydfil, delighting in a "gift for logopeic dance" which he had learnt from D.H. Lawrence and Gerard Manley Hopkins. The images of his poetry are fresh and bountiful, the words have a shining newness, as though they have just been turned over for the first time like pebbles on a beach. There is something, too, of Welsh prosody in his English, as well as the observations of a painterly eye which he cultivated as a young man.

Glyn Jones's early poems appeared in the *Dublin Magazine* in 1931 but, although poetry remained his first love, his output was comparatively small – there will be about eighty-four poems in the edition of his work which, as his literary executor, I am now preparing for the press. His first volume, *Poems*, published by the Fortune Press in 1939, reflects his fascination with alliteration and copious metaphor, while *The Dream of Jake Hopkins* (1944) includes a long poem for broadcasting which is the most moving ever written about the teaching profession. He continued writing well into his eighties, adding new work to the two volumes of his *Selected Poems* which appeared in 1975 and 1988. A selection of his poems, stories, translations, and critical writings may be found in his last book, *Goodbye What Were You?* (1994).

It was as a short-story writer that Glyn excelled most consistently. Like Dylan Thomas, an early friend who thought highly of his work, he used a boy-narrator for many of the stories in *The Blue Bed* (1937) and *The Water Music* (1944). Almost all are set in the Merthyr of his boyhood or else in the greener landscape of Carmarthenshire, particularly Llansteffan on the Tywi where his people had their roots and which held a special place in his affections.

The middle of Glyn Jones' life was devoted to the novel. His first, *The Valley, The City, The Village* (1956) brims with character, incident, and splendid description of places and people. In *The Learning Lark* (1960) he pilloried the corruption associated with teaching appointments in the Labour-controlled Valleys of South Wales. His most important novel, which has attracted a good deal of interest from academic critics, is *The Island of Apples* (1965), which weaves realism with fantasy in a retelling of the legend of Ynys Afallon, the magic island to which Arthur was carried after being mortally wounded in battle.

The poetic quality of Glyn Jones's prose was vividly demonstrated in 1965 when, in a famous case of plagiarism, it was revealed that Hugh MacDiarmid had lifted verbatim some lines from a short story of his and recast them in a poem, entitled "Perfect", about the wing of a dead pigeon. During the ensuing correspondence in the columns of the *Times Literary Supplement*, in which two opposing camps emerged, Glyn could not bring himself to complain, keeping a typically dignified silence until the Scot's supporters began to claim that he had somehow "improved" the quality of the Welshman's prose. Some twenty years later, over supper at my home, the two poets were able to laugh off the episode, and move on to some splendidly scurrilous gossip about mutual acquaintances among the London literati.

Glyn received several honours during the course of his literary career. He was elected President of the Welsh Academy, the national association of writers in Wales, and was awarded an honorary DLitt by the University of Wales in 1974. He enjoyed his status as the doyen of Welsh writers but was always ready to encourage younger men and women in their literary endeavours, and never sought the limelight. With his wife Doreen, whom he married in 1935 and to whom all his books were dedicated, he kept open house for a wide circle of their friends, whose conversation was the only pleasure he allowed to interrupt his daily writing schedule.

Glyn's last years were marred by the amputation of his right arm, for a writer the ultimate indignity, but his interest in the republic of letters remained vital to the last. Among those who gathered at his bedside during his final illness none was untouched by the serenity of his temperament and his undiminished delight in the world he was about to leave.

Morgan Glyndwr Jones, poet, short-story writer, novelist: born Merthyr Tydfil, Glamorgan, 28 February 1905; married 1935 Doreen Jones; died Cardiff 10 April 1995.

The Independent (11 April 1995)

Lynette Roberts

Poet who came to Wales from Argentina

Lynette Roberts made her reputation in the 1940s when, as the wife of the literary impresario Keidrych Rhys, she was among those writers associated with his combative magazine *Wales*. Having married in 1939, they made their home at Llanybri, a village in south Carmarthenshire not far, across the Taf estuary, from Laugharne. This was Dylan Thomas country and Rhys published and promoted his neighbour's early poems and stories. But Lynette and Keidrych were divorced in 1948 and, a few years later, on becoming a Jehovah's Witness, she gave up writing and retired from the Welsh literary scene. Her last years were spent in a nursing-home at Ferryside, which looks across the Towy to Llanybri.

Very little is known about her background, except that she was born in Buenos Aires, to parents whose origins were partly Welsh, but who had emigrated to Argentina from Australia. Educated in the country of her birth and in England, Lynette Roberts was a *rara avis* among the writers of Wales, but immersed herself in the literature of her husband's country, drawing on Welsh myth and landscape, and on the social life of the district where they had settled. Several of the poems in Rhys's booklet *The Van Pool* (1942) speak of the hardship of their life. In one of her most poignant poems written at this time, "Lamentation", she wrote:

> O the cold loss of cattle
> With their lovely big eyes,
> The emptiness of sheds,
> The rick stacked high.
> The breast of the hills
> Will soon turn grey
> As the dogs that grieve
> And I that fetched them in:
> For the good gates are closed
> In the yard down our way.

The poetry she had begun writing during the late 1930s attracted the attention of T.S. Eliot who published, under the Faber imprint, two volumes of her work, *Poems* (1944) and *Gods with Stainless Ears*

(1951), the second of which is a long heroic poem of some complexity and erudition in the manner of David Jones. She also published, at her husband's Druid Press, a collection of monologues inspired by life at Llanybri, *Village Dialect* (1944), and *The Endeavour* (1954), a reconstruction of Captain Cook's first voyage to Tahiti, New Zealand and Australia, in 1769-71.

Her poems, many of which are modishly experimental in style and recondite in subject-matter, appeared in numerous anthologies and literary journals during the 1940s, in both Britain and the Americas, and she was a frequent contributor to the BBC's Third Programme. After her religious conversion, she put aside a great deal of her writing, including a third collection of poems, a volume of short stories, two verse-plays, a historical novel, and a number of essays on rural themes.

Lynette Roberts received very little critical attention during her lifetime but her collected poems are now being prepared for the press.

Evelyn Beatrice (Lynette) Roberts, poet: born Buenos Aires 4 July 1909; married 1939 Keidrych Rhys (died 1987; one son, one daughter, marriage dissolved 1948); died Ferryside, Carmarthenshire 26 September 1995.

The Independent (28 September 1995)

Gwyn A. Williams

Politically engaged historian and broadcaster

The historian Gwyn A. Williams saw himself as "a people's remembrancer": by which he meant that he chose as his professional role the elucidation and celebration of the Radicalism which he took to be the essence of the Welsh political tradition.

He was unusual among academic historians in that, although meticulous in his scholarship and widely read in the· history of Marxism in Europe, he was able to infuse his writing with a passionate concern about the fate of his own people and to demonstrate, often in a most vivid manner, that Wales – particularly South Wales – was the very anvil on which the progress of the urban working class had first been hammered out.

But he was not content with scholarly exegesis that was not backed up by political engagement. He tried to influence public opinion by presenting the history of Wales in new, sometimes startlingly dramatic ways, whether in his lectures and books or in the many television programmes he made, in both Welsh and English, during the latter part of his career. In all his work the call to action was explicit and unequivocal: the capitalist, centralist, British State (and the English hegemony) had to be undone if the national community of Wales was to survive and prosper.

Although he began, during the heady days of the civil war in Spain, as a Young Communist, and remained an unrepentant Socialist for the rest of his life, Gwyn Alf (as he was known, to distinguish him from several other eminent Welshmen with similar names) was for many years an uneasy member of the Labour Party but eventually found his political home on the left wing of Plaid Cymru. For a while he was a leading member of the editorial board of the magazine *Radical Wales*, and served on the party's Executive Committee. He was, however, never persuaded to stand as a Plaid Cymru candidate, although his oratory (in which he used a slight stammer to excellent effect) made him one of the most effective and popular public speakers in Wales.

Born in the iron town of Dowlais, on the hill above Merthyr Tydfil, the cradle of the Industrial Revolution in Wales, he read History at the University College of Wales, Aberystwyth, and was appointed

Lecturer in Welsh History there in 1954. He was such an entertaining speaker that students from other departments, myself among them, regularly sat in on his lectures, for the sheer excitement of hearing what he had to say about the industrial Wales in which we had grown up, after which we adjourned to the nearest pub, where he would continue to hold forth with the most brilliant dialectic that any of us had encountered.

Gwyn left Aberystwyth to take up a Readership at York and from 1965 to 1974 he held the Chair of History at that university. His doctoral thesis had been published as *Medieval London: from commune to capital*, in 1963, and was followed five years later by *Artisans and Sans-Culottes*, about popular movements in France and Britain during the French Revolution. His European perspective was grounded in these early works and others: *Proletarian Order* (1975), a study of Antonio Gramsci and the history of Communism in Italy, and *Goya and the Impossible Revolution* (1976), as part of the research for which he learnt Italian and Spanish respectively. His wife, Maria, belonged to the community of steelworkers from northern Spain who were long established in Dowlais.

But it was with his books on specifically Welsh subjects that Gwyn made most impact as an historian. Returning to Wales in 1974 as Professor of History at University College, Cardiff, he set about reinterpreting key episodes in Welsh history. His *The Merthyr Rising* (1978) was the first full account of the workers' revolt of 1831 and the execution of Dic Penderyn, one of the earliest martyrs of the Welsh working class.

In *Madoc: the making of a myth* (1979) he examined the evidence for the discovery of America by Prince Madog ab Owain Gwynedd in about 1170 and, in particular, for the existence of a tribe of Indians, known as Mandans, who were said to be his descendants. It was the Welshman John Dee, the magus of his age, who had first claimed the New World for the Queen of England on the basis of this persistent yarn, which was developed by Robert Southey in his long poem *Madoc* in 1805. Gwyn debunked the myth as an imperialist fiction, but showed how it had fired the imagination of Welsh Radicals for centuries thereafter and was comparable, in its patriotic potency, with the English myth of the free-born Saxon living under the Norman yoke.

He returned to these themes and introduced others in *The Welsh in*

their History (1982), a collection of essays which argues for the opening up of new discourses, and in *When was Wales?* (1985), perhaps
his most influential work. The latter was written while he was making
the television series *The Dragon has Two Tongues*, in which he
appeared in bruising confrontation with the rather more cautious
Wynford Vaughan-Thomas; the question of who won this verbal
punch-up, and on how many points, is still hotly debated in Wales
and one by which the sheep and the goats can be separated.

The book concludes with some typically trenchant observations,
not unaffected by the stress of Thatcherism:

The Welsh as a people have lived by making and remaking themselves in
generation after generation, usually against the odds, usually within a British
context. Wales is an artefact which the Welsh produce. If they want to. It
requires an act of choice. Today, it looks as though that choice will be more
difficult than ever before. There are roads out towards survival as a people,
but they are long and hard and demand sacrifice and are at present unthink-
able to most of the Welsh... Some kind of human society, though God knows
what kind, will no doubt go on occupying these two western peninsulas of
Britain, but that people, who are my people and no mean people, who have
for a millennium and a half lived in them as a Welsh people, are now nothing but a naked people under an acid rain.

In 1983 Gwyn took early retirement from his Chair at Cardiff (he
was fond of describing himself as "a redundant historian") and
began making films with Teliesyn, one of the independent companies
on which the reputation of Welsh broadcasting now largely depends.
He moved from Cardiff to the village of Drefach Felindre, in Dyfed,
where he shared a home with Siân Lloyd. Among the people about
whom he made films were James Gillray, Sylvia Parkhurst, Pushkin,
Mary Shelley, and the Welsh writers Saunders Lewis, T.E. Nicholas
and Iolo Morganwg.

His last book, *Excalibur: the search for Arthur* (1994), was a clear-
eyed account of a subject which has confused so many lesser historians, and his last film, *Gwyn Alf – a People's Remembrancer* (1995) a
moving autobiography of a man who chose the hard road to an
understanding of his life and times.

The image of Gwyn Williams which remains in the memory contains his pugnacious but engaging manner and the impish wit with
which he expounded his theses about Wales and the Welsh. A small

man, with a shock of white hair and the Iberian features that seem so typical of the valleys of south-east Wales, he developed a quirky but compulsive television style that had all the immediacy and eloquence of his writing, using the medium unapologetically to put over what he thought the Welsh people needed to know about their own past.

But I am pretty sure that it is for his books he will be remembered. For many of my generation, who were undergraduates in the late 'fifties and early 'sixties, and who participated with him in the political campaigns of the 'seventies and 'eighties, he shares a place with that other great Welsh Socialist, Raymond Williams, as an important influence on the way we now think about our country and people.

Gwyn Alfred Williams, historian: born Dowlais, Merthyr Tydfil, Glamorgan 30 September 1925; Professor of History, York University 1965-74; Professor of History, University College, Cardiff 1974-83; married 1950 Maria Fernandez (one son); died Drefach Felindre, Carmarthenshire 16 November 1995.

The Independent (18 November 1995)

Pennar Davies

Poet, scholar and prose-writer

Pennar Davies was among the most scholarly, religious, and passionate men to have written in the Welsh language during the 20th century. A prolific writer, he combined in his poetry and prose a polymathic command of language, theology, and psychology with a personal tenderness rooted in his Christian faith, which was by turns mystical and practical in its concern for human frailty and the world's suffering.

Whether in his delicately wrought love-poems or in his more contemplative novels and spiritual journals, he laid great emphasis on both *eros* and *agape*, endeavouring always to balance them in a richly complex whole by means of myth, symbol, and a sometimes labyrinthine erudition which few of his readers were able to penetrate without difficulty. There is much self-analysis in his prose works, often of an uncompromising kind and usually illuminative of the cultivated Christian mind under pressure from the barbarities of the modern world but ultimately finding equilibrium in the affirmation of traditional certainties.

William Thomas Davies was born, a miner's son, at Mountain Ash in the Cynon Valley in the old county of Glamorgan, in 1911. He took the name Pennar from Aberpennar, by which the town is known in Welsh, as a sign of his identification with the native culture of Wales. Using the pseudonym Davies Aberpennar, he wrote poems in both Welsh and English up to about 1948 but thereafter he chose Welsh, which he had learnt as a young man, as the medium for almost all his literary work. He was deeply committed to the Welsh language and it, together with his religious convictions, was the bedrock of his Nationalism. During the 1970s, together with two other academics, Ned Thomas and Meredydd Evans, he cut off the power at Pencarreg television transmitter in a campaign for an improved Welsh-language service which led to the establishment in 1982 of S4C, the fourth channel which now broadcasts programmes in Welsh.

Left-wing and pacifist in politics, he stood as Plaid Cymru candidate in the steel town of Llanelli at the General Elections of 1964 and 1966. He was an effective public speaker, though not averse to the loftier manner which his audiences and congregations came to expect of him as a leader of Welsh religious and political life. His winning of the Llanelli seat would have raised the intellectual debate in Wales by several notches above what it was during the 1960s, but it was not to be: he attracted only the more radical sections of the chapel vote and made little dent in the Labour majority.

After a brilliant career at University College, Cardiff, where he graduated in Latin in 1932 and in English the year following, he went on to Balliol and Mansfield Colleges, Oxford, and then to Yale University, where he took his doctorate in 1943. In that year he married Rosemarie Woolff, a refugee from Nazi Germany, who promptly learnt Welsh and made it the language of their home. During the 1940s he was a member of the Cadwgan Group, a small circle of intellectuals who used to meet at the Rhondda home of J. Gwyn Griffiths, later Professor of Classics and Egyptology at University College, Swansea.

Pennar spent three years as a minister with the Independents in Cardiff before his appointment in 1946 as Professor of Church History at Bala-Bangor Theological College, a bastion of the Congregationalist cause in Wales. In 1952 he became Principal of the Memorial College at Brecon, a post in which he remained, after the college's removal to Swansea in 1959, until his retirement in 1981.

Pennar Davies wrote in a variety of literary and scholarly modes. He published, besides a barrage of pamphlets, six volumes of verse, a collection of short stories, six novels, and several works of a theological nature, of which *Y Brenin Alltud* ("The exiled king", 1974), a study of Christ's practical goodness, is perhaps the most mature and rewarding: Some of his poems, which refer as often to Newton and Einstein as to the heroes of the Welsh pantheon, are breathtaking attempts at reconciling the discoveries of science with religious belief. Among the figures from Welsh history to have captured his imagination was John Penry, the Puritan pamphleteer, executed in 1593 on suspicion of being the Martin Marprelate who had dared to attack the institution of episcopacy and lampoon the Church of England.

Some measure of Pennar's wide culture and literary gifts, together with a bibliography of his publications, is to be found in the Festschrift published under the editorship of Dewi Eurig Davies in 1981.

There was something enigmatic in Pennar Davies's personality which some found disconcerting, especially those who saw in him walking proof of the veracity of Benjamin Jowett's boast that the mark of a Balliol man is that he is able to excel so effortlessly. Tall, broad-shouldered, handsome, he might have seemed to many the very type of a muscular Christian, but his beatific smile hinted at a deeper sensibility that was preoccupied, in everything he did, with the revelation of the numinous in humankind.

For myself, I always found him extremely good company, not least during a trip to Finland in 1977, when, on Midsummer's Eve, we found ourselves sitting on an island beach as the sun dipped, but never sank, below the horizon. I shall always remember how Pennar was much taken with the metaphysical implications of the midnight sun, relishing the thought that, albeit temporarily, darkness had been banished from the world.

William Thomas (Pennar) Davies, writer and theologian: born Mountain Ash, Glamorgan 12 November 1911; Professor of Church History, Bala-Bangor Theological College 1946-50; Professor of Church History, Memorial College, Brecon 1950-59, Principal 1952-59; Principal and Professor of Church History, Memorial College, Swansea 1959-81; married 1943 Rosemarie Woolff (four sons, one daughter); died Swansea 29 December 1996.

The Independent (2 January 1997)

Alexander Cordell

Writer of popular historical novels

Alexander Cordell was a popular writer whose novels were read by people who do not usually read novels. He wrote twenty-eight of them, mainly historical romances which came perilously close, in the view of some critics, to bodice-rippers but which, for his many admirers, were exciting and well-researched yarns with a good deal of contemporary social significance. Opinion divides sharply over their literary merit, a consideration to which the author always declared himself deeply indifferent, preferring to point to their large sales in both Britain and the United States and the esteem in which he was held by that most genial section of the book-buying public, the common reader.

He was born George Alexander Graber in Colombo, Ceylon (now Sri Lanka), in 1914, the son of a soldier. Much of his youth was spent in the Far East, particularly China, about which he was to write in *The Sinews of Love* (1965), which is set in Hong Kong, *The Bright Cantonese,* (1967), a spy story, and *The Dream and the Destiny* (1975), about the Long March of Mao Tse-tung. From 1932 he served in the British army and during the Second World War was promoted to the rank of major in the Royal Engineers.

Although he began to write shortly after demobilisation in 1946, his first novel, *A Thought of Honour,* was not published until 1954 and did not attract much public attention. He was, nevertheless, set on becoming a successful novelist and applied himself to the grind of writing with single-minded determination, keeping regular hours and letting nothing interfere with his schedule. Only rarely would he undertake journalistic work, though he was not averse, as his reputation grew, to giving younger writers the benefit of his experience and views, usually expressed trenchantly and with little sympathy for established writers. He was particularly scornful of poets, urging them to tackle "something more substantial" – such as a novel.

Graber first settled in Wales in 1950, working as a quantity survey-or in the western valleys of Monmouthshire. It was there, mainly around the old iron towns of Blaenavon, Ebbw Vale and Tredegar, an area which was one of the cradles of the Industrial Revolution, and now known as Cordell country, that he discovered the grim landscape and Radical politics which he was to make the stuff of his highly coloured novels.

It seems that he was genuinely taken, too, with the democratically minded people whom he encountered while carrying out research for his books, and despite his very aloof, English, military manner, many warmed to him and became his loyal readers. Popular interest in the local history of industrial South Wales was given a huge fillip by the fact that Cordell had brought the past to life in his novels in ways which ordinary people could understand and find useful, whatever professional historians might say about their authenticity.

His best-known novel, and an international best-seller, was *Rape of the Fair Country* (1959), the first of a trilogy about life in early industrial Wales which also included *The Hosts of Rebecca* (1960) and *Song of the Earth* (1969, published in the United States as *Robe of Honor*). These books present romanticised accounts of the struggle for trade-union rights in the ironworks, of the Chartist movement which excited the author profoundly, and of the Rebecca Riots, a major social disturbance in west Wales which broke out in 1839 and took the form of attacks on toll-gates by armed gangs of men dressed as women.

The historical events depicted by Cordell are as vivid as the larger-than-life characters who act out their own personal dramas in his books. They include, for the most part, marginalised people, victims of their time and place, who nevertheless manage to rise above their circumstances and make their mark on the society by which they are oppressed, albeit as part of the anonymous, and unsung, crowd.

What has embarrassed some readers is his insistence on introducing romantic interest into his plots, at which he was not adept, and dialogue which, for Welsh readers in particular, is sometimes excruciating in its inversions, phoney idiom and pseudo-poetic lilt. As with Richard Llewellyn's *How Green Was My Valley* (1939), Cordell's novels were controversial in Wales on account of the picture they gave of local society, morals and way of life, and few have been able to appreciate them for the fiction which they so obviously are.

Cordell was dismissive of any criticism on this score, nurturing an implacable suspicion that there was a conspiracy against him among literary critics in Wales, which extended to the Arts Council and the Welsh Academy (the national society of writers). He made few friends in the republic of letters, largely as a consequence of his opinionated antipathy towards fellow writers and his penchant for self-publicity in the press which endeared him to few.

When in 1971 the Welsh Arts Council invited the playwright Eugène Ionesco to visit Wales and receive its International Writer's Prize, Cordell dashed off a letter to the *Western Mail* complaining that it was scandalous to be giving money to a rich organisation like Unesco when it would have been better spent on writers. His attempts to persuade the Council to establish a prize for novelists, to be named after him, was thereafter given a frosty reception for which he never forgave it.

Nevertheless, such was the success of his Welsh novels that Cordell was encouraged to write a second trilogy dealing with much the same subject-matter. In *The Fire People* (1972), about the Merthyr Rising of 1831, he told the story of Richard Lewis, a young miner known to history by his sobriquet Dic Penderyn, "the first martyr of the Welsh working class", who was hanged in Cardiff for the alleged wounding of one of the soldiers sent to Merthyr to put down the armed insurrection by the town's workers. This second trilogy was completed with the publication of *This Sweet and Bitter Earth* (1977), which deals with the Penrhyn Quarry Lock-outs of 1896-1903 and the Tonypandy Riots of 1910, and *Land of My Fathers* (1983), which revisits South Wales during the Chartist period.

Those who tended to scorn the historical authenticity of Cordell's novels had to pause for reflection with the appearance of *The Fire People*. Dic Penderyn had gone to the scaffold protesting his innocence and there was widespread sympathy for the view that he had been made a scapegoat by the ironmasters. In his novel Cordell revealed details, found in official documents and subsequently confirmed, that some forty years after the rising, a man living in America had confessed to the crime for which Dic had been executed. For this, and for his firm grasp of the political realities of the day, the author earned the warm regard of Gwyn A. Williams, the leading historian of South Wales in its revolutionary heyday. Another historian of the same period, Dai Smith, has compared him with Howard Fast, author of the novel *Spartacus* (1951), in the painstaking detail and swashbuckling sweep of his narratives.

Cordell claimed that in the 1930s he had been a Marxist and he certainly remained on the political left for the rest of his life. A late statement of his Communist sympathies is to be read in *To Slay the Dreamer* (1980), a story set against the background of the Civil War in Spain, although there is ample evidence of his views in almost all his novels, including the trilogy (1971) for younger readers about the 1798 Rebellion in Ireland. His last novel, *Send Her Victorious*, was published last month.

Although he was not active on behalf of any political party, Cordell's long residence in Wales (interrupted only by residence in the Isle of Man during the 1970s) gave him a certain sympathy for the idea of Welsh self-government, and shortly before the general election of May 1997 he announced from his home in Wrexham that he had joined Plaid Cymru, having recognised in Dafydd Wigley MP, the party's President (at last, the cynics sighed), the kind of democratic Socialism in which he had always believed.

The cause of Alexander Cordell's death has not yet been established. His body was found on 9 July in a stream near a disused quarry above Llangollen and is believed to have lain there for a few days; he was clutching family photographs. The police say that foul play is not suspected.

George Alexander Graber (Alexander Cordell), novelist: born Colombo, Ceylon 9 September 1914; married 1937 Rosina Wells (died 1972, one daughter); 1973 Elsie Donovan; died near Llangollen, Denbighshire c.9 July 1997.

The Independent (11 July 1997)

Ron Berry

Novelist who wrote about the Welsh working class

For those who thought that, after *How Green Was My Valley*, the novel of Welsh proletarian life was exhausted, the work of Ron Berry came as something of a surprise.

Although he did not have the lyrical gifts of Richard Llewellyn, nor the power to create a powerful myth about the loss of Eden after the discovery of coal in the South Wales valleys, Ron Berry was able to draw a more authentic picture of working-class life because he was born into it and never left. His six novels are testimony to his deep sympathy with a way of life which, now that only one of the region's pits remains, has virtually come to an end and will soon pass from living memory.

He was born a miner's son in 1920 at Blaen-cwm, which, as its name implies, is at the top end of the Rhondda Fawr, perhaps the most famous of all the coal-bearing valleys of South Wales. Leaving school at the age of fourteen, he worked as a miner in local pits until the outbreak of the Second World War, during which he served in both the Army and the Merchant Navy.

He also played soccer for Swansea Town and, "thick-set, pigeon-toed, and peasant-fisted", took up boxing for a while, a sport celebrated in his penultimate novel, *So Long, Hector Bebb* (1970), which is unusual in that its narrative consists of a series of interior monologues which are as sensitive as they are menacing.

Ron Berry began writing after spending a year at Coleg Harlech, "the College of the Second Chance", the residential college for adult students at Harlech in North Wales, where he read avidly and developed his left-wing political views in endless argument with staff and fellow-students. He was to remain profoundly suspicious of academic exegesis, particularly of the novel, but was able to hold his own in any discussion of the genre. His gruff manner and sometimes contentious views enlivened the correspondence which he kept up with a wide circle of friends and acquaintances.

The Rhondda of Ron Berry's novels is unlike that of any other novelist: it is economically more prosperous (before the closing of the mines), its people more sophisticated and more hedonistic, less concerned with politics and religion than those in the stories of, say,

Rhys Davies or Gwyn Thomas. The main characters in his first novel, *Hunters and Hunted* (1960), are feckless and mainly concerned with boozing, women and drawing the dole. In *Travelling Loaded* (1963) he describes the picaresque adventures of men who work in a steelworks during the winter and spend the summer living rough in the countryside.

Ron Berry once told me that he was trying to recreate a "happier Rhondda" than the one conventionally portrayed in the many novels which have taken the Valleys as their background. His concern that the old communal values were beginning to wither was first expressed in *The Full-Time Amateur* (1966), in which social change proceeds apace as the affluent working class buy cars and televisions, go to bingo and take package holidays abroad.

He saw himself as their chronicler, lovingly but sometimes caustically recording "what remains of the past" before "it sputters out as garbled memory". This threnody for a doomed way of life found its fullest expression in *Flame and Slag* (1968), a novel based on his journal of a dying miner, whose poignant recollection of the old Rhondda is used as counterpoint to the brash rootlessness and incomprehension of his children.

In Ron Berry's novels the working class, for all their shortcomings, adapt, survive and eventually thrive in their new conditions, so that his work is more a warm-hearted affirmation of his belief in them than a rigorous critique. When Dewi Joshua, the hero of *This Bygone* (1996), his last novel, is declared redundant it looks like the end of him and the community of Moel. This novel contains what will almost certainly be the last nostalgic look by a writer with first-hand experience of the mines at the industry which, more than any other, went to the making of South Wales. More than anything, Dewi misses "the togetherness of men underground, the bonding, walking the main, old blokes in the double-parting discussing Moel Exchange events... butties and mates settling down for grub at 11 o' clock, blokes queuing in the lamproom, and collier-boys chin-wagging outside the pay hatch on Fridays".

Despite the fact that five of his books were published in London by such reputable firms as Hutchinson, W.H. Allen and Macmillan, Ron Berry was neglected by metropolitan critics and, in Wales, it was only on the appearance of his last novel that he attracted much attention. This general indifference to his work took its toll and, together with the arthritis which plagued him for more than thirty years, was largely responsible for his rather sour attitude to critics and academics. Usually unemployed and often short of money, he spent a good deal of his time in fly-fishing and bird-watching. One of his books was about the return of the peregrine falcon to his beloved Rhondda.

His financial difficulties were partially relieved in the 1970s when a number of his friends were instrumental in obtaining a Civil List pension for him.

Ronald Anthony Berry, novelist: born Blaen-cwm, Glamorgan 23 February 1920; married Rene Jones (two sons, three daughters); died Pontypridd, Rhondda Cynon Taff 16 July 1997.

The Independent (24 July 1997)

Rhydwen Williams

Poet and novelist who won the Crown on two occasions

Rhydwen Williams was a writer of prodigious, even prodigal talent who, contrary to the Welsh literary stereotype, wrote mainly about industrial and urban South Wales, in particular the Rhondda Valley where he was born, a miner's son, in 1916.

His trilogy of novels, *Cwm Hiraeth*, generally thought to be his finest achievement in prose, is based on the story of his own family over three generations, and has some claim to be the most outstanding example in Welsh of the *roman-fleuve*. The first, *Y Briodas* ("The wedding", 1969) deals with life in the Rhondda in his parents' day, from 1900 to 1915, when the valley was a cauldron of industrial unrest which was to boil over in the Tonypandy Riots of 1910.

In *Y Siol Wen* ("The white shawl", 1970) he described the General Strike of 1926 and in *Dyddiau Dyn* ("A man's days", 1973), the economic depression which ravaged South Wales in the 1930s. These events are seen through the eyes of the author's Uncle Siôn, a poet and thinker who turns against the chapel and the Lib-Labbery of William Abraham (Mabon), the Rhondda miners' leader, to embrace Socialism and the ideals of the South Wales Miners' Federation, only to grow disillusioned and bitterly opposed to the materialism of the Labour Party and the hegemony of its local representatives.

Rhydwen Williams's birth and family background in the Rhondda, the most famous of the coal-bearing valleys of South Wales, marked him indelibly and, although he was to spend the years from 1931 to 1941 away from the Valley, notably at Christleton in Cheshire, to which his parents had moved in search of work and where he was intensely unhappy, it was to the Rhondda that he returned in his imagination and there, in 1941, that he was given his first pastorate – at Ainon, a Baptist chapel in the mining village of Ynys-hir.

His five years at Ynys-hir were the making of him as a poet. Hitherto he had worked at a variety of menial jobs and studied intermittently at the University Colleges of Swansea and Bangor. A conscientious objector on Welsh Nationalist grounds, he had served for a while with a Quaker ambulance-unit during the bombing of Liverpool. Of a rebellious nature, he was often in trouble with his denomination on account of his pacifism, political Nationalism, unorthodox theological views, and Bohemian life-style. He had a fondness for good wine, expensive restaurants, fast cars, the theatre and good company into old age, and his profligate attitude to money was legendary. But the call to the Christian ministry had always been strong in him and, blessed with good looks and a voice that were compared with Richard Burton's, he became a powerful preacher and a gifted reader of poetry on the Welsh Home Service of the BBC.

His development as a poet was encouraged through his friendship with the Cadwgan Circle, a coterie of Welsh writers and intellectuals who included Gareth Alban Davies (later Professor of Spanish at Leeds), J. Gwyn Griffiths (later Professor of Classics and Egyptology at Swansea) and Pennar Davies (later a distinguished theologian and Principal of the Independents' College at Brecon and Swansea). They met at the Griffithses' home at Pentre in the Rhondda, where they discussed contemporary European literature and, in particular, the need to liberate Welsh literature from the puritanical shackles and lyrical niceties imposed on it by the eisteddfodic tradition. What Rhydwen learnt in these discussions was to prove more important to him than the scant formal education he had received. Huxley, Orwell and Auden were among his heroes. He was also a close associate of Kitchener Davies, the dramatist and pioneer of the Nationalist cause in the Rhondda.

Although Rhydwen was always more than a mere eisteddfodic writer, and was usually ready to poke fun at the Eisteddfod's conservative standards and more arcane rituals, it was at the National Eisteddfod that he first came to prominence as a poet. He won the Crown competition in 1946 with his poem *"Yr Arloeswr"* ("The pioneer") and again in 1964 with *"Y Ffynhonnau"* ("The springs"). The second of these, a long poem in the free metres (the Chair is awarded for a poem in the strict metres), is about tradition and its renewal in Rhondda society, and many readers have found it the most moving and memorable of all his works. He published nine volumes of verse, including one in English, and his collected poems appeared in 1991.

Leaving Ynys-hir in 1946, he held pastorates in Resolven and Pont-Iliw in the Swansea Valley for the next thirteen years, and spent another at Rhyl on the coast of North Wales. While at Pont-Iliw he had the pleasure, at a local eisteddfod, of presenting a recitation prize to the young Siân Phillips.

But he then turned his back on the Baptist ministry and accepted an invitation to join Granada Television in Manchester, one of the first ministers to forge a career in the new medium. There, on shoe-string budgets, he produced trail-blazing Welsh-language programmes in which his gifts as impresario and broadcaster were allowed to flower. He also wrote television scripts, one of which, about Dietrich Bonhoeffer, was shown in Germany, the first Welsh-language television play to be broadcast on a foreign network.

Besides his trilogy, Rhydwen published seven other Welsh novels between 1972 and 1988, and one in English, including *Breuddwyd Rhonabwy Jones* ("The dream of Rhonabwy Jones", 1972), a light-hearted send-up of the Gorsedd of Bards of the Isle of Britain, of which he was a life member by virtue of his having won the Crown; *Apolo* (1975), set in the world of television before Cardiff became known as "media city"; *Amser i Wylo* ("A time to weep", 1986, for which he won the Daniel Owen Prize), about the Senghenydd Explosion of 1913, the greatest pit-disaster in the annals of British mining; and *The Angry Vineyard* (1975), a fictional account of the Merthyr Rising of 1831 and the execution of Dic Penderyn, "the first martyr of the Welsh working class".

From 1980 to 1986, despite suffering a stroke in 1981 which physically incapacitated him for the rest of his life, Rhydwen edited the current affairs magazine *Barn* ("Opinion"), bringing to it his journalistic flair, wide reading and keen interest in music and the visual and performing arts. A volume of his autobiography appeared as *Gorwelion* ("Horizons") in 1984.

Robert Rhydwenfro Williams, poet and novelist: born Pentre, Glamorgan 29 August 1916; married 1943 Margaret Davies (one son); died Merthyr Tydfil 5 August 1997.

The Independent (7 August 1997)

Cliff Bere

Author of the Welsh Republican Manifesto

Cliff Bere was a Welsh Republican, one of a small group of militants, mostly ex-servicemen and intellectuals, who enlivened the political scene in Wales during the 1950s in a coalition of left-wingers whose natural homes would otherwise have been in the Labour Party or Plaid Cymru. Prominent among them were the poet Harri Webb and the Labour peer Gwilym Prys Davies.

The movement – it was not a party though it put up a candidate at Ogmore in the general election of 1950 – was hostile to the Labour Party because of its broken promises on self-government for Wales, critical of Plaid Cymru on account of its pacifism and recognition of the Crown, and utterly opposed to the Tories on just about every other count.

Besides heckling speakers from the main parties, at which they were adept, the Republicans went in for painting slogans and burning Union Flags in public places, and holding open-air meetings up and down the industrial valleys of South Wales which sometimes ended in fisticuffs. They also excelled at making scurrilous attacks on prominent Welsh politicians of the day, including Jim Griffiths, later the first Secretary of State for Wales, and Aneurin Bevan, whom they considered to be a lost leader of his class and people.

Cliff Bere was, by common assent, the most single-minded of the Republicans, and the most hard-working. It was he who wrote the movement's manifesto, published in 1948, and held the group together for the eight years of its existence. As a public orator, he was no firebrand but would speak at street-corners with a conviction which never failed to impress his audience. Whenever he spoke in public he addressed his audience as "Welsh men and women . ." rather than as "Ladies and gentlemen".

He seemed to take particular pleasure in "the simple ceremony of burning the English flag" and hearing his record read out by policemen in court. It was his ambition to go to prison and refuse to wear uniform, as a political prisoner, but the nearest he got was when, in the 1970s, he was involved in a series of clandestine acts carried out on the fringe of the Nationalist movement; he was very disappointed to be let off by a judge who had not fully understood the part he had played.

The main work of the Republican movement after 1954 was the publication and distribution of a bi-monthly newspaper, the *Welsh Republican*. It had a circulation of a few hundred copies, many of which were sold in the street by the indefatigable Cliff Bere. The paper was remarkable for its coverage of Welsh current affairs, especially matters relating to the economy of South Wales such as the future of the coal and steel industries and the plight of the Cardiff docks. It also provided a vitriolic commentary on the Labour Party's attitude towards the question of Welsh self-government at a time when no such critique existed.

Many of its articles were written, mostly anonymously, by Cliff. They were sceptical towards the Parliament for Wales Campaign of 1951-55 because it fell short of the republic on which the movement had set its sights. They also deplored the appointment of David Maxwell-Fyfe ("Dai Bananas") as part-time Tory Minister of State for Welsh Affairs and spoke out against military conscription in Wales, though arguing in favour of a Welsh army. Prior to the Coronation of 1953, the paper expressed staunchly anti-royalist views.

Cliff Bere was born of Welsh parents in Burnley, Lancashire, and had learned to speak Welsh as an adult. He studied Law at the University College, Swansea, and at London University, but his studies were interrupted by the Second World War, during which he served in North Africa. It was there he resolved to fight for Wales after the conflict was over. A talented graphic artist, he was employed for ten years at the National Museum of Wales in Cardiff.

He was also an able writer and polemicist. Besides a novel, *I Was a King*, he wrote a memoir of the Welsh Republican Movement, *The Young Republicans* (1996), which is a valuable source of information about politics in Wales during the post-war period, though it is mainly concerned to show the movement in the best possible light and makes no attempt to assess its legacy among the various *groupuscules* which have since laid claim to be its heirs. The truth is that in most of their initiatives the Republicans were unsuccessful and the fire of Republicanism which they hoped for did not materialise. Even the bookshop which Cliff Bere and Harri Webb opened at Bargoed in 1951 did not last the year.

With the movement's demise in 1959, some members went back into the Labour Party. Gwilym Prys Davies, for instance, stood as the

Labour candidate in the Carmarthen by-election of July 1966 at which Gwynfor Evans won the seat for Plaid Cymru; he later became a Labour peer and an opposition spokesman on Northern Ireland. Others withdrew from active politics, while one or two left Wales altogether to pursue distinguished careers overseas. But Cliff Bere threw in his lot with Plaid Cymru, becoming one of its most devoted members with a commitment which few have been able to match.

His private manner was quiet, courteous and rather shy. I never heard him raise his voice and, in conversation, he was reluctant to talk about himself, but his political zeal was always to the fore and his gentleness of spirit disappointed, then impressed many younger people who went to him for guidance and inspiration.

His unusual surname is Anglo-Saxon in origin, but he took great satisfaction from knowing it is also the name of a small castle in Meirionnydd which had been built by order of Llywelyn Fawr in the early 13th century and reinforced by his grandson Llywelyn ap Gruffudd, the last prince of independent Wales. Its significance for him was that Bere was a Welsh castle, built for the defence of Wales rather than for its subjugation, and therefore a worthy name for a Welsh patriot.

He would have been pleased by the result of the referendum announced in the small hours of Friday, while at the same time arguing that the Assembly which Wales is now to have is only "a half-way house" on the road to full self-government. It is fitting that at his funeral today, his coffin will be draped with Y Ddraig Goch, the Red Dragon, the national flag of Wales, a country to which he devoted his life.

Clifford Ifan Bere, political activist born Burnley, Lancashire 1915; married 1949 Eluned Rhys Evans (four sons); died Barry, Vale of Glamorgan 16 September 1997.

The Independent (22 September 1997)

John Elwyn

Painter of rural west Wales

If Kyffin Williams is the most distinguished living painter of the sublimely rugged but largely depopulated mountains of north Wales, it is the work of John Elwyn which most vividly celebrates the gentler hills, and convivial people, of the rural west.

He was a popular painter in the best sense: his canvases are bought for private homes as often as by public institutions, in both his native country and further afield. They are, for the most part, landscapes inspired by the *genius loci* of the villages, orchards, lanes, farmyards and chapels of the south Cardiganshire countryside which he knew and loved, despite his long residence in southern England, and portraits of the people from among whom he had sprung. Retrospective, nostalgic even, and often anecdotal and unashamedly emotive, they are also "landscapes of the mind" which seem to evoke the green arcadies in which so many Welsh people, however long they may have been urbanised, have their family roots.

He was born John Elwyn Davies at Emlyn Mill in the small village of Adpar, a staunchly Welsh-speaking, Nonconformist community consisting mostly of farmers, weavers and craftsmen, across the river Teifi – which is the county boundary hereabouts – from the market-town of Newcastle Emlyn in the old county of Carmarthen.

Many of his paintings draw on a happy childhood which shaped him as both man and artist. He never forgot his Welsh, inheriting from his father, who was something of a local poet, a delight in language and story-telling which served him in good stead when, in later life, he was introduced to the circle of Welsh writers who included Glyn Jones, John Ormond and Leslie Norris, whose portraits he painted.

After spending two years at the Carmarthen School of Art, he went on to the West of England College of Art in Bristol, where he was awarded an Exhibition tenable at the Royal College of Art in London. In his first year there he studied architectural drawing, still-life painting and life-drawing, and enrolled in an evening class at the London College of Printing in order to learn engraving.

His facility for figure drawing attracted the attention of Gilbert Spencer, the Professor of Painting, who described the young

Welshman as one of the best students he had ever had the good fortune to teach. One of the influences on John Elwyn at this time was the Euston Road School of painters; he was also deeply impressed by the Cézanne centenary exhibition of 1939.

His studies were interrupted by the outbreak of war later that year when the Royal College moved to the Lake District. Having already registered as a conscientious objector, he was directed to work in forestry above Pont-rhyd-y-fen in the Afan Valley, where he remained for four years, painting a scarred industrial district dominated by the steelworks of Port Talbot in a Neo-Romantic style which owed a good deal to English artists such as Michael Ayrton and Graham Sutherland. It was not until 1947 that he was able to resume his studies at the Royal College.

From 1948 to 1953 John taught at the College of Art in Portsmouth. His first London exhibition was held at the Paul Alexander Gallery in 1949 and it was at about this time that he began making engravings for *Radio Times*. Encouraged by Winifred Coombe-Tennant, a wealthy landowner and generous patron of young Welsh artists, to paint what he knew most about, he now returned in his imagination to his halcyon childhood in Cardiganshire, finding in it the subject-matter which he was to spend the rest of his career exploring.

When questioned about his passionate interest in farm, barn, meadow, hedgerow, stone wall, mart and chapel, he would often quote Benjamin Britten: "The important things are the local things." For John Elwyn, his native patch was as inspirational as Suffolk had been to Constable or Cookham to Stanley Spencer.

Nevertheless, John Elwyn's vision was universal in its affectionate, though sometimes mischievous evocation of an essentially rural society which seemed timeless in its close links with the seasons and the land, and for this reason his work has sometimes been compared with that of Dylan Thomas, whose poetry prompted several of his paintings.

His sophisticated, sensuous delight in rich tonal values, his technical virtuosity and highly decorative use of broken panes of colour, especially yellow, orange and green, are reminiscent of the work of French painters like Pierre Bonnard and Edouard Vuillard, which he had admired and emulated as a student at the Royal College. They went to the making of some of the most lusciously sunlit canvases ever painted of the Welsh countryside.

One of his most frequent images is that of a leafy lane leading to a white-walled farm set among fields of wheat, which (although he was reluctant to comment on what seemed to be its obvious Freudian symbolism) I take to be his equivalent of Dylan Thomas's "Fern Hill", a reference to his "green and golden" childhood.

In 1953 John Elwyn took up a teaching post at the School of Art in Winchester, where he was to remain until his retirement in 1976. By now, in a post-war Wales slowly awakening to its achievement in the visual arts, largely as a result of stimulation by official bodies, he was recognised as one of the most eminent of contemporary painters, and may honours came his way. He won the Gold Medal for Fine Art at the National Eisteddfod in 1956, held one-man exhibitions at the Leicester Galleries in London and was commissioned to make lithographs by the Curwen Press and to illustrate some of the *Shell Guides to the Countryside*.

A man of eirenic temperament, John Elwyn remained modest and unassuming about his own work and always ready to praise that of others. His retrospective exhibition at the National Library of Wales in 1996 was the final accolade for a Welsh painter who had practised his art with unswerving devotion and great distinction.

John Elwyn Davies (John Elwyn), painter: born Adpar, Cardiganshire 20 November 1916; married 1970 Gillian Butterworth; died Southampton 12 November 1997.

The Independent (25 November 1997)

Kate Bosse-Griffiths

Scholar and writer in her adopted language

The literature and culture of Wales have been enriched by many people born beyond its borders but few have made a contribution as distinguished as that of Kate Bosse-Griffiths. She not only learnt Welsh but made it the language of her home and wrote extensively in it on topics not usually treated by writers for whom it is the mother-tongue.

Born in Wittenberg-am-Elbe, Luther's town, a little to the north of Leipzig, in what was to become East Germany, Käthe Bosse was of partly Jewish parentage but grew up as a member of the Lutheran Church and in a family noted for its high culture and liberal views; her father was an eminent gynaecologist.

After receiving her secondary education at the local Gymnasium and studying at the University of Munich, where she took a doctorate in Classics and Egyptology in 1935, she joined the staff of the Egyptology and Archaeology Department in the Berlin State Museums but was dismissed when it was discovered that her mother was a Jew.

She arrived in Britain in 1936 and found research posts in Egyptology, first at the Petrie Museum at University College London, and later at the Ashmolean Museum in Oxford. It was in Oxford, where she was a senior member of Somerville College, that she met the Welsh scholar J. Gwyn Griffiths.

Their home at Pentre in the Rhondda Valley became the meeting place of the Cadwgan Circle of writers who included Pennar Davies, later Principal of the Independents' Theological College in Swansea, and Rhydwen Williams, the poet and broadcaster. It was largely the initiative of Kate Bosse-Griffiths, who brought a European perspective to its discussions of literature, politics, religion and Welsh society.

The war years were a dark time for her: her mother was to die in the Nazi concentration camp at Ravensbrück; her doctor brother eventually escaped to Sweden. After the war, her husband joined the staff of the Classics Department at the University College, Swansea, where he was to remain for the rest of his career; he is now Professor Emeritus of Classics and Egyptology. Their home in the Sketty district of Swansea again became a meeting place for writers and political activists.

Kate Bosse-Griffiths was as distinguished as her husband (who is also a poet and literary critic in Welsh) in her chosen field. For more than twenty-five years she was Keeper of Archaeology at Swansea Museum, where she gave special attention to the prehistoric and Roman collections and published a booklet, *Twenty Thousand Years of Local History*. In 1971 she was appointed honorary Curator of the Wellcome Museum, formerly in the Department of Classics and Ancient History and now in the Egypt Centre at the University of Wales, Swansea, which is to be officially opened later this year.

It was Kate Bosse-Griffiths who arranged for part of the Egyptian Collection made by Sir Henry Wellcome, the pharmaceutics million-aire, to be taken out of storage and rehoused at Swansea in 1971; she also compiled a catalogue of the 5,000 objects held there. The collection's centrepiece is the magnificently painted wooden coffin of Iw-s-hesw-mwt, a female musician of the 21st Dynasty, which the university acquired from the Royal Albert Museum, Exeter. She also tracked down, in the British Museum and the Brooklyn Museum respectively, a *shabti* figure and the musician's *Book of the Dead* from the Amun-ra temple at Karnak. Among her specialist publications are studies of the coffin, Egyptian amulets and ancient writing, articles in learned journals such as the *Journal of Egyptian Archaeology* and her book *Tywysennau o'r Aifft* ("Ears of corn from Egypt", 1970).

She began writing in Welsh as early as 1942, starting with *Mudiadau Heddwch yn yr Almaen* ("Peace movements in Germany", 1943). It was followed in 1951 by *Bwlch yn y Llen Haiarn* ("A gap in the iron curtain"), which addressed the question of a united Germany at the height of the Cold War, and a travel book, *Trem ar Rwsia a Berlin* ("A glimpse of Russia and Berlin", 1962), in which she gave her clear-eyed impressions of the Soviet Union and her native country. Although of left-wing sympathies, she was highly critical of Stalinism and the Communist regime in East Germany.

Her main contribution to Welsh letters was her two novels, *Anesmwyth Hoen* ("Uneasy colour", 1941) and *Mae'r Calon wrth y Llyw* ("The heart is at the wheel", 1957), and her two collections of short stories, *Fy Chwaer Efa* ("My sister Eva", 1944) and *Cariadau* ("Loves," 1995), published in her 85th year. All her fiction is cosmo-politan in its attitudes and subject-matter, and refreshingly libertarian about sexual matters, although she did not consider herself a feminist.

One of her last books was a study of witchcraft and folk-medicine, *Byd y Dyn Hysbys* ("The world of the wizard", 1977).

Although formidably rigorous and perfectly capable of holding a conversation on the most erudite subjects in her adopted language, Kate Bosse-Griffiths was a woman of vivacious personality and genial disposition who shared her husband's commitment to the cause of Plaid Cymru and was a staunch worker for the party at a local level. Both their sons, Robat and Heini Gruffudd, are notable prose-writers in Welsh; one is a leading publisher of Welsh books and the other a tutor in the Department of Continuing Adult Education at the University of Swansea.

Käthe Bosse, Egyptologist and writer: born Wittenberg-am-Elbe, Germany 16 July 1910; married 1939 J. Gwyn Griffiths (two sons); died Swansea 4 April 1998.

The Independent (10 June 1998)

Tom Richards

Broadcasting executive and writer

The long tradition of journalism in Wales has produced many news-men who have cut their teeth with provincial papers and then gone on to make their mark in London. But Tom Richards, professional to his fingertips, was content to stay at home.

Born in Towyn, Merioneth, in 1909, but brought up in Dolgellau, Tom Richards was the son of a station-master at what is known to English tourists as Dovey Junction. He spoke Welsh as his first lan-guage, and all his creative writing was done in Welsh, but it was in English that he chose to work as a journalist. It was a language that he loved and wrote with precision and panache.

His career began in 1927 when, straight from school, he landed his first job as a reporter with the *Cambrian News*, in Cardiganshire, after which the ink was in his blood. Eight years later he joined the *Western Mail* in Cardiff, a paper then owned by Lord Thomson, and worked there for seven years as a sub-editor.

Exempted from call-up in 1939 because he had lost a leg at the age of fifteen as a result of tuberculosis, he was appointed campaigns officer with the Welsh Region of the Ministry of Information in 1942. Moving to the BBC as publicity officer in 1945, he became an indis-pensable member of its staff at a time when resources were scarce and programmes made on shoestring budgets called for ingenuity and perseverance.

Although later in life he was to regret his lack of higher education and the fact that he had not even trained as a reporter, he was wide-ly read in what he called "an unsystematic and time-wasting way".

In 1952 he was promoted to the post of News Editor at the BBC in Cardiff, where he pioneered both radio and television news. Among the young men he took on as newsreaders was Michael Aspel.

This was a difficult era for the Corporation in Wales. There was growing pressure for better news coverage in both Welsh and English and for a wider variety of programmes. Conservative and Labour allegations of Nationalist bias further complicated an already fraught operation, and Tom Richards was seen as the man who could cast an unbiased eye over Welsh broadcasting, because he kept his politics to himself. Together with his assistants Wyn Roberts (later a Tory Secretary of State for Wales, and now Lord Roberts of Conwy) and John Ormond Thomas, who was to make his mark as a poet and filmmaker, Tom Richards was given the laborious task of working out how many Plaid Cymru members had taken part in talks and discussions in 1955. Several months later, it was announced that of the 360 speakers in that year's programmes, only fifteen were known to be party members.

The Ince Report of 1956, charged with looking into the matter, came to the conclusion that some criticism of a lack of balance over the previous six years was justified, but that "if Nationalism in the widest sense is considered, then it is difficult for the Broadcasting Council in Wales to avoid such charges... as it has the duty 'to pay full regard to the distinctive cultural interests of Our People in Wales.'" The Nats under the Mats scare was over.

Tom took over as the BBC's representative in West Wales in 1963, remaining in that post until his retirement six years later. It was there, at the West Wales branch of the BBC in Alexandra Road, Swansea, that I first met him – a streetwise man with a genuine interest in younger colleagues and not averse to offering them advice and relating mildly scurrilous anecdotes, especially about members of the broadcasting establishment in Wales. "News is what they don't want you to hear" was one of his favourite axioms.

His genial, rather shy personality marked a mischievous sense of humour which is to be seen at its best in his plays, especially *Y Cymro Cyffredin* ("The ordinary Welshman", 1960) and *Mi Glywaf Dyner Lais* ("I hear a tender voice", 1982). His choice of Welsh as the medium for his plays was explained in a no-nonsense manner in an essay he wrote for my book *Artists in Wales* (1971): "I think in dialogue, I talk to myself, and when I hear other people talking, they do so in Welsh."

Writing of the prospects for literature in the Welsh language, he referred to what he called the Ozymandias syndrome: "In the all-English desert of 21st-century Wales, some diligent researcher may stumble on this mysterious body of writing and will no doubt be impressed by its glorious past, if he manages to decipher it. We still have time, though, to try the other way." It comes as something of a surprise to learn that he chose to bring up his two sons without the language.

Tom Richards's masterpiece is the novel *Mae'r Oll yn Gysegredig* ("All, all is Sacred", 1966), set in the fictitious town of Llanathrod ("Libelville"), where a miracle is reported by the local paper. The story is taken up by the London dailies and is about to be made into a film, much to the consternation of the chapels and the town's bigwigs.

Out of this farcical little story, not unlike that of *Clochemerle*, the author pokes a good deal of delicious fun at the expense of small-town attitudes; it is one of the funniest novels ever published in Welsh. I can still hear him chuckling as he explained to me how he had based much of it on his own experience as a newsman of more than forty years.

Thomas Hugh Richards, journalist and playwright: born Towyn, Merioneth 28 September 1909: News Editor, BBC (Cardiff) 1952-63: representative, BBC West Wales 1963-69; married 1944 Aelwen Williams (two sons); died Swansea 19 June 1998.

The Independent (25 June 1998)

J. Eirian Davies

Poet and Nonconformist minister of a Bohemian bent

Clergyman and poet, J. Eirian Davies combined the best of the religious and literary traditions of Wales, often in a challenging and sometimes provocative way that won him the respect of his co-religionists and fellow writers.

For most of his life a minister of the Presbyterian Church in Wales (Calvinistic Methodist), he was to be found on the more radical wing of that somewhat conservative Connexion, winning a reputation as a fiery preacher who was noted for his outspokenly liberal views and commitment to the cause of Plaid Cymru. His poetry, too, while touching its cap to traditional forms such as the *englyn* and sonnet, was more typically free-wheeling and "open-field" than that of many of his contemporaries and he was not averse to writing for public performance and radio. No preacher-poet he.

Born at Nantgaredig in rural, Welsh-speaking Carmarthenshire, James Eirian Davies was educated at Queen Elizabeth Grammar School, Carmarthen, and the University College of Wales, Aberystwyth. He came to prominence as a poet while still an undergraduate, winning the Chair and Crown in the Students' Eisteddfod which has been the cradle of many a Welsh writer. His first volume, *Awen y Wawr* ("Dawn muse"), was published in 1947 by Keidrych Rhys at the now legendary Druid Press, which also brought out R.S. Thomas's first book, *The Stones of the Field* (1946).

His second volume, *Cân Galed* ("Hard song", 1974), contains his best work, in particular the apparently naive but, in fact, highly skilful use of rhyming couplets which he, like so many of our poets, learned from T.H. Parry-Williams and other poems in what is still called in Welsh prosody *vers libre* – to distinguish it from writing in the centuries-old strict metres.

The book also includes pieces he wrote for the Dial-a-Poem scheme, the first of its kind in these islands when it was launched in Cardiff in 1970, and another "*Rhaid imi brynu sgidiau*" ("I'll have to buy some shoes"), which was commissioned for an open-air reading organised by the Arts Council on the field of the National Eisteddfod in 1971. I remember Eirian, in the Garibaldi-red shirt he often wore, declaiming his poem to a small cluster of mildly astonished

52

bystanders with all the conviction and eloquence of which he was capable.

This willingness to experiment and to use his deeply resonant voice in the delivery of hard-hitting poems with a distinct social message was a hallmark of all Eirian Davies's work and it brought him into the avant-garde of Welsh literary life if not always into the favour of the diaconate. Another of his characteristics, doubtless a reflection of his genial and egalitarian nature, was to employ the second person singular pronoun *ti* (thou), which Welsh like French has kept, rather than the more formal *chwi* (you), when addressing friend and stranger alike.

His ministries were at Hirwaun in Glamorgan, Brynaman in Carmarthenshire and Mold in Flintshire – all urban places where he seemed most at home. It was while living in the last-named town that he served, from 1978 to 1982, as general factotum to his wife, Jennie, in her editorship of *Y Faner*, the Welsh national weekly magazine, contributing a racy column that became essential reading for anyone with an interest in Welsh affairs. This work came to an abrupt end with her death.

Some critics have taken the view that Eirian Davies was for too long in the shadow of his wife, a woman of formidable intellect and charismatic personality who was one of the most brilliant journalists ever produced in the Welsh language. She was also, during the late 1950s, a leading member of Plaid Cymru and the party's candidate in Carmarthenshire, increasing its vote in a constituency which was eventually won by Gwynfor Evans in 1966. Eirian certainly supported his wife in all her many activities, both journalistic and political, perhaps devoting time and energy to the role which might otherwise have gone into poetry. But it was his choice to put his shoulder to the wheel in these ways, at the expense of his own writing.

His last two collections, *Cyfrol o Gerddi* ("A volume of poems", 1985) and *Awen yr Hwyr* ("Evening muse", 1991), are more darkly contemplative than his finest work, though not in any dogmatic way, and were written out of the loss he suffered by his wife's death.

They had two sons. Siôn Eirian is a freelance playwright based in Cardiff and Guto Eirian a railway worker at Pontypridd. Both have been active with the Welsh Republican Movement, to which their father was briefly attracted during the 1950s, and, while perhaps having rejected much of what he stood for as a clergyman, are their father's sons in their left-wing outlook and their readiness, in Æ's phrase, "against the sceptred myth to hold the golden heresy of truth".

James Eirian Davies, clergyman and poet: born Nantgaredig, Carmarthenshire 28 May 1918; Minister of the Presbyterian Church of Wales at Hirwaun 1942-54, Brynaman 1955-61, Mold 1962-81; married 1949 Jennie Howells (died 1982; two sons); died Ffairfach, Carmarthenshire 5 July 1998.

The Independent (10 July 1998)

R. Tudur Jones

Theologian and Church historian

Among the intelligentsia of Wales the name of R. Tudur Jones belongs to the most distinguished Church historian and theologian of the 20th century.

He was a prolific writer on both religious and political subjects, whose work is characterised by meticulous, wide-ranging scholarship, immense intellectual gifts, forthright judgements and, particularly in the case of his writing in Welsh, a profound sense of the beauty of language.

His contributions to the religious and literary life of Wales were many and varied, ranging from his histories of the Welsh Independents to his column in *Y Cymro*, one of the Welsh weekly newspapers, written over a period of twenty years or more.

Robert Tudur Jones was born at Llanystumdwy, Caernarfonshire, the boyhood home of David Lloyd George, and brought up in the seaside town of Rhyl in Flintshire, where his father was employed as a railway-worker and his mother kept lodgers who provided the boy with an insight into human personality and a fund of anecdote on which he never tired of drawing. He was educated at the University College of North Wales, Bangor, at Mansfield and St Catherine's Colleges, Oxford, and at the University of Strasbourg, and was a Congregational minister at Aberystwyth before his appointment in 1950 as Professor of Church History and later Principal of Bala-Bangor Theological College, where he remained until it was merged with the Memorial College at Aberystwyth in 1988.

His DPhil thesis at Oxford was on the Welsh Puritan Vavasor Powell, one of those whose mission was the evangelising of Wales under the Act for the Propagation of the Gospel in Wales of 1650. This set Jones on his life's work, which was the study and exegesis of that Radical Nonconformity of which he was such a notable exemplar.

Apart from myriad articles in learned and denominational journals, his first major book was *Congregationalism in England 1662-1962* (1962), which established him as a Church historian. It was followed by the magisterial *Hanes Annibynwyr Cymru* (1966), a history of Independency in Wales, one of the major strands of the

Welsh religious tradition and still a potent force in contemporary Wales. It is required reading not only for the student of theological thought in Wales but for anyone with an interest in the history and society of post-Reformation Wales. He returned to this subject in *Yr Undeb: Hanes Undeb yr Annibynwyr Cymraeg 1872-1972* (1975), a history of the Union of Welsh Independents.

His sympathy with the radical theology of the Independents helped Tudur Jones to embrace the political philosophy and practice of Plaid Cymru. He stood twice as the party's candidate at general elections in Anglesey, in 1959 and 1969, and was for a while editor of one of its newspapers, *Y Ddraig Goch*. His exploration of Nationalism in modern Europe, *The Desire of Nations* (1974),was an influential book placing the principles of Plaid Cymru in a wider context and with reference to world events.

He was also a journalist with a light touch in both Welsh and English. Indeed in a recent televison interview, he told with some glee how the editor of a popular London daily newspaper, having spotted his articles in the *Liverpool Daily Post*, tried to cajole him into giving up his academic career in favour of a job as its Welsh columnist, which would have commanded a salary three times greater than what he was earning at the Theological College. But he turned the offer down, preferring to follow his own course as unpaid contributor to his church's journal *Y Tyst* and the leading monthly *Barn*.

A selection of his journalism, in which he gave full rein to his impish humour and imperious scorn for those of whom he disapproved, together with a number of his essays on cultural and historical themes, is to be found in the books *Darganfod Harmoni* ("Discovering harmony", 1982) and *Ffydd yn y Ffau* ("Faith in the den", 1993). One of his finest essays, in which he described how he'd thought he sensed the ghostly presence, in an Anglesey church at the time of the Dissolution of the Monasteries, of a posse of the King's Commissioners come to make an inventory of a nearby religious house, demonstrates a startling sensitivity to what such a visitation meant to those caught up by it. The essay appears, in English translation, in my recently published anthology of Welsh prose, *Illuminations*. A full bibliography of R. Tudur Jones's writings is included in the Festschrift, *Y Gair a'r Genedl* ("The Word and the nation"), which was published in his honour in 1986, the year in which he was awarded the degree of DLitt by the University of Wales.

The Protestantism and Puritanism of R. Tudur Jones was Evangelical in its precepts and application. He was a Calvinist and in the great schism that took place in the 19th century between the orthodox, Evangelical wing and the new Liberalism coming in from Germany, a controversy which still animates the religious life of Wales, he was firmly entrenched on the side of the fundamentalists.

He wrote extensively on Abraham Kuyper, the theologian who became Prime Minister of the Netherlands in 1900, and was generally influenced by Karl Barth and the school of Barthians associated with Princeton University.

His Evangelicism is to be seen at its most learned in the two volumes, *Ffydd ac Argyfwng Cenedl* ("A nation's faith and crisis", 1981-82), a history of religion in Victorian Wales, and at its most trenchant in *Grym y Gair a Fflam y Ffydd* ("The power of the Word and the flame of faith") a selection of his essays and lectures on theological subjects, which is to appear next week in time for the National Eisteddfod at which R. Tudur Jones was a regular visitor.

Robert Tudur Jones, theologian and Church historian: born Llanystumdwy, Caernarfonshire 28 June 1921; Independent minister at Aberystwyth 1948-50, Professor of Church History, Bala-Bangor Theological College 1950-66, Principal 1966-88; married 1948 Gwenllian Edwards (two sons, two daughters and one son deceased); died Bangor, Gwynedd 23 July 1998.

The Independent (27 July 1998)

Horace Charles Jones

Rhymester with a very high opinion of himself

There is a living tradition in Wales, and in Ireland and Scotland, of the *bardd gwlad* – the country poet who is called upon to write verses in celebration of local events such as births, marriages and deaths. His function is to praise, to honour, to make the community feel good about itself, often in verse that is witty and sometimes memorable. Many of his poems are carved on tombstones or committed to memory for generations after the events they celebrate have been virtually forgotten.

The tradition is inextricably bound up with the Welsh language and the status of the poet in Welsh-speaking Wales, particularly the rural areas where many can still turn their hand to the writing of verses in *cynghanedd* – the ancient prosody which Gerard Manley Hopkins called "consonantal chiming". Rarely have there been poets of this kind writing in English and they are rarer still in the industrial areas.

Horace Charles Jones turned all this on its head. He wrote in order to offend, to degrade, to make fun, and to castigate those among whom he lived and who, for one reason or another, had upset him. And he was very easily upset, taking umbrage at the slightest hint of criticism and reserving his most vicious spleen for those who did not share his own high opinion of himself as a poet.

I fell out with him in 1963 when I lived in Merthyr Tydfil, the town where he spent most of his life. I had it in mind, as a fledgling publisher, to bring out a small booklet of my poems, together with a selection by Harri Webb, another Merthyr poet, perhaps two dozen in all. When Horace heard about this he called on me to insist that I include him in the project. I was prepared to consider it until I found that he wanted me to print a hundred of his poems, on an all-or-nothing basis. He would not be persuaded and left in high dudgeon, never to speak to me again. When the booklet eventually appeared, he burned a copy in Merthyr's High Street.

What had made him think he was a great poet was being taken up by Keidrych Rhys, the editor of the prestigious magazine *Wales*, to whom I had introduced him, and who – in what seemed a temporary lapse of judgement – wrote a fulsome foreword to his first and only hardback collection of verse, *The Challenger* (1966). With this accolade, he would never again doubt that he was as good as Dylan Thomas. The book was published with the help of a grant from the Merthyr Borough Council. Immediately after publication Horace, who always savaged those who tried to help him, took the council to task in the local newspaper for wasting rate-payers' money.

At the time both Harri Webb and I, and Peter Gruffydd, who was to join us as a third contributor to *Triad*, were active members of Plaid Cymru, and now Horace's animus was extended to the party and all its works. He began denouncing Welsh Nationalism and became an inveterate writer of vitriolic letters to the newspapers. Between 1976 and 1985, when Plaid Cymru was in control of the Merthyr Borough Council, he voted with his feet and left Wales for England, returning only when the Labour Party, which he detested only a little less warmly, was returned to power in the town.

He also took against the Welsh Arts Council, perhaps because I had joined its staff in 1967, although I do not recall the Literature Committee ever receiving an application from him for financial support. More likely, his suspicion of all Welsh institutions and the grim satisfaction he gained from attacking them fuelled his sense of his own importance. The chapels, the Church in Wales, BBC Wales and the University of Wales were also among his targets, mainly because he thought they had failed to recognise his talent.

All geniuses are neglected, his argument seemed to run; I am neglected, therefore I am a genius. As for solicitors, magistrates, civil servants, headmasters, bank managers and policemen, he had nothing but bile for them, printing his lampoons at dead of night and circulating them anonymously next day. I once saw him put the witch's hex on someone with whom he disagreed.

Horace had a talent for self-publicity that was encouraged by some sections of the local press. He was usually to be found standing against a lamp-post in Merthyr's High Street where, for a few hours every day, he would harangue anyone who had the slightest connection with the town's public life, from councillors to lollipop ladies. Most ignored him, but some were entertained by his lashing tongue, and a few would egg him on to say ever more outrageous things.

He had a huge repertoire of aphorisms, some of which are memorable: "The best place to bury the hatchet is in your enemy's head" is one that has remained with me; "A nation can be great only when it's hungry" is another. About 200 such one-liners were published as *A*

Dose of Salts in 1957. Scottish readers who remember the late Oliver Brown or are familiar with the flyting tradition will recognise the genre.

Horace Jones was brought up at Abermorlais, a poor district of Merthyr. When he was thirteen, his father was killed in an accident in a coal-mine and the boy left school soon afterwards to work underground. He received little formal education and it showed, particularly in his lack of self-criticism and his steadfast refusal to read any modern literature. He once told me that he had been given the name Horace but, thinking it not literary enough, had taken to calling himself Charles after the author of *Great Expectations*. It was clear to me that he had never heard of the Latin poet until then.

He was often in trouble with the law and with the townspeople of Merthyr. He used to recount with glee how in 1955 he had been escorted from the field of the National Eisteddfod because someone had spotted a mildly satirical remark about that august festival in one of his pamphlets: "An eisteddfod is a cultural circus where everything is Welsh except the money". He was also fined for refusing to fill in a form prior to the Census of 1971 because it was, he told the court, "an insidious attempt on my rights as a free man".

He carried a homemade knuckle-duster as a precaution against being beaten up by the rougher elements of the pubs and cafés he frequented, although I can't help thinking that in such an easy-going place as Merthyr it was hardly necessary; it was, rather, part of his paranoia, which he cultivated assiduously.

The theme of personal liberty and the threat of interference by the state recurred in many of his poems, as in "The Jingle" (1971). He was capable of writing a vivid line but too often went in for the worst kind of word-play and usually ruined the meaning with bizarre syntax. Only one or two of his poems are wholly coherent and none has found a place in any anthology, although municipal patronage ensured that for a while his books were used in Merthyr's schools. Perhaps his most passable poem is "My River", which was inscribed near a path known as Poet's Walk on the bank of the River Taff that runs through the town.

It must be said that, for the most part, what Horace wrote was the worst kind of doggerel, without the genius of a McGonagall or even the charm of an unlettered versifier or the truly comic talent of a Pam Ayres or Spike Milligan. To have suggested as much while he was alive and kicking would have been to incur his displeasure and a campaign of vilification that few were prepared to risk.

If there was a whiff of brimstone about Horace – someone has said, "Had Satan been a spiv, he would have looked like Jones" – there was also something sad about this venomous man who, with little talent except for controversy, believed himself to be a poet, and was encouraged in that belief by people who were really making fun of him. If he had been an innocent rhymester, like the 19th-century Cockle Poet of Anglesey who believed that Queen Victoria wanted to marry him, it might have been possible to take him seriously. But Horace was fired only by the hatred he felt even for those who relished him at his barmiest.

He may have been one of the last "characters" of the old Merthyr, that raffish, ramshackle town that was the cradle of the Industrial Revolution. But if so, he also marked its demise and, with his passing, will be missed only from that lamp-post in the High Street.

Horace Charles Jones, writer: born Merthyr Tydfil, Glamorgan 6 February 1906; married 1928 Delia Griffin (one daughter); died Merthyr Tydfil 12 September 1999.

The Independent (18 September 1998)

T. Arfon Williams

Civil servant and poet in the traditional metres

If Welsh poetry is a closed book to most English readers, with but a few honourable exceptions, it is not only because the poet in Wales has had a function different from that of his counterpart in England but also because for the last thousand years Welsh poetry has been written in a prosody so complex that John Cowper Powys was once prompted to remark that the people among whom he had made his home were "the most conservative, the most introverted, the most mysterious nation that has ever existed outside China".

Making some allowance for hyperbole – Powys learned to read Welsh during his years at Blaenau Ffestiniog and allowed things Welsh to colour his own writing – his remark is fairly typical of the bewilderment many cultivated English people feel when first confronted by a literature which seems to be hermetically sealed as much by the language in which it is written as by the metrical forms on which it depends.

But it is not as if writing in traditional Welsh forms is something antiquarian or arcane. Although there is primitive *cynghanedd* – what Gerard Manley Hopkins, who had studied the language, called "consonantal chiming" – in the earliest Welsh poetry dating from the sixth century, and although it was the stock-in-trade of the great medieval masters such as Dafydd ap Gwilym, a good deal of verse is written by contemporary poets according to the age-old rules.

That such writing has enjoyed a renaissance during the last twenty years is largely due to Cymdeithas Cerdd Dafod, the society for poets and others interested in this important aspect of Welsh culture, and in particular to Alan Llwyd, the brilliant poet, editor and its indefatigable secretary since its inception in 1976.

Among the many poets encouraged by Alan Llwyd, and one who became a leading member of the society, and latterly its treasurer, was T. Arfon Williams. It says something about the vigour and appeal of the tradition that such a man could have had an interest in the writing of poetry at all. He was, for a start, born at Treherbert, in the Rhondda, a valley which in the 1930s retained only a vestige of the rich literary heritage associated with the heyday of the coal industry and the Nonconformist culture which had produced so many writers.

It was the Welsh language which "saved him for the nation": he was brought up to speak it by parents, both teachers, who were devoted to the culture into which they had been born and who, unusually for that time and place, passed it on to Arfon and his sister Gwerfyl.

Nor did he come to poetry by the usual routes. He was, in fact, a dentist; he trained at King's College and King's College Hospital in London, where he was a house surgeon, and was later appointed Licentiate in Dental Surgery by the Royal College of Surgeons. His first job was with a general practice at Penmaenmawr in Caernarfonshire, and it was in the surgery that he met Einir, the woman who was to become his wife.

After spending four years as Dental Officer in his native Rhondda and another two in Swansea, in 1970 he was promoted to a similar post with an all-Wales remit at the Welsh Office and spent the rest of his working life as a civil servant, retiring in 1993. He was elected Chairman of the South Wales Branch of the British Paedodontic Society in 1969 and among the delights of his latter years was his honorary Presidency of Cymdeithas Deintyddol Cymru, the society for Welsh-speaking dentists.

He lived for many years in Whitchurch, a suburb of Cardiff, where he was a neighbour of mine. A generous host, he took a keen pleasure in discussion of literary matters. His last home was at Caeathro, a village in Welsh-speaking Gwynedd where his wife's family had its roots.

Arfon discovered an interest in Welsh poetic forms in 1974. He began attending an evening class in Cardiff and competing anonymously in the weekly newspaper *Y Cymro*, where his talent was recognised by the adjudicator Alan Llwyd. He quickly won a reputation in the pages of *Barddas*, the monthly magazine, as a master of the *englyn*, the four-lined epigrammatic poem which has been popular among Welsh poets since about the ninth century. He had mastered the rules of Welsh prosody by dint of wide reading and with the help of other poets whose company he sought, no mean feat, for the rules are devilishly complicated.

There are at least six kinds of *englyn*, and as many variations of *cynghanedd* within the lines, but the basic rules can be roughly summarised as follows. The first two lines have ten and six syllables respectively, and the other two have seven each. There is usually a dash after the seventh syllable of the first line and that syllable announces the rhyme at the end of the other three. All four lines have assonance and are accented according to fixed rules so stringent that they make the *haiku* look as sophisticated as the limerick.

There have been many attempts to write *englynion* in English, and other languages, sometimes by poets as eminent as W.H. Auden and Robert Graves, but they are usually only forlorn attempts to capture the special effects of the form, rather than true imitations. Few have taken the advice of Wallis Evans to heart:

> An *englyn*'s just like angling – cast a line
>   For fine bits of writing.
>   Alliterate your lett'ring,
>   See that your consonants sing.

Arfon was so accomplished an exponent that he not only wrote immaculate *englynion* in Welsh, often memorably, but could also turn them out in "the thin language" (as English is known in Welsh) when he wanted to illustrate what the form requires. Furthermore, he made a point of demonstrating the superiority of his craft by casting his verse as a single sentence and, putting aside all jokiness, addressed serious themes.

Many of his tenderest verses were dressed to his wife, Einir, "*gem o wraig ddigymar*" ("an incomparable jewel of a wife"), who was the muse in whom he found so much of his inspiration.

Here is an example of Arfon's work in English illustrating the entry on the *englyn* which appears in *The New Companion to the Literature of Wales* (1998):

> A bee in your flower bed – I alight
>   on the lips full-parted
>   of your fox-glove, beloved,
>   and am freely, fully fed.

The *englyn*, although miniaturist in length, can carry a powerful emotional charge and its very brevity and intricacy lend it a unique intensity. Arfon exploited its potential to the full, writing on a variety of subjects (including the erotic) in a style which has been compared to the effect of oil on moving water, capable of more than one interpretation and reflecting whatever the reader brings to it. He also wrote chains of *englynion* addressing philosophical and social questions not usually found in this form, and even brought touches of *cynghanedd* into poems in the free metres. Unlike many of his fellow practitioners, he eschewed the obscure and the over-literary.

He published three collections: *Englynion Arfon* (1978), *Annus Mirabilis* (1984) and *Cerddi Arfon* (1996); and edited a symposium on the Welsh poetic craft, *Ynglyn â Chrefft Englyna* ("About the craft of writing englynion", 1981), in which he contributed an essay exploring the creative process. For him the phenomenon of *cynghanedd* was the most precious part of the Welsh literary heritage and the *sine qua non* of what made a poet. He accepted its strict rules gladly, finding in them not the fetters of which lesser poets complain but a useful mould into which he could pour his words to marvellous effect. His best work – several hundred verses in all – is assured of a place in the standard anthology of 20th-century Welsh poetry when that book comes to be compiled.

His monograph on *Cerdd Dafod* (Welsh prosody), illustrated by many of his English *englynion* and commissioned by the University of Wales Press, had been virtually completed in the months before his death.

Arfon Williams was sustained during his last long illness by his devoted family and a Christian faith which never deserted him. A staunch Congregationalist, he was elected President of the Union of Welsh Independents for the year 2000, and would have brought to that august office not only dignity and erudition but a delightful wit and genial personality which, in life, won him many friends. He will be commemorated in the time-honoured way – by his peers in the *englyn* form to which he devoted his rare talents.

Thomas Arfon Williams, dentist, civil servant and poet: born Treherbert, Glamorgan 17 May 1935; married 1963 Einir Wynn Jones (two sons, one daughter); died Bangor, Gwynedd 16 October 1998.

The Independent (28 October 1998)

A.O.H. Jarman

Professor of Welsh and Arthurian scholar

In the international field of Arthurian studies, A.O.H Jarman had a reputation as a meticulous scholar and tireless researcher. For twenty-two years he was Professor of Welsh at University College, Cardiff, where he specialised in the study of the earliest Welsh and Latin sources and made a distinguished contribution to their interpretation.

The central figure of his research was Arthur – not the hero of medieval romance or the clanking knight of Malory and Tennyson (and certainly not the swashbuckling star of Hollywood's *Camelot*), but the British warlord about whom little is known for certain and around whom so many tales have accumulated in several literatures.

This Arthur, "the Arthur of the Welsh", was a *dux bellorum* or military leader who, in the late fifth and early sixth century, fought to sustain Roman *civitas* in southern Britain and whose most famous victory, about the year 519, was against Saxon invaders at Mount Badon in which, according to the *Annales Cambriae* (two manuscripts written in the 12th/13th centuries and now kept in the British Library and the Public Record Office), he bore the Cross of Christ for three days and nights. His death at Camlann (perhaps the fort now called Birdoswald on Hadrian's Wall) in about 537 is also recorded in this, the most authentic of the early references to Arthur.

Alfred Owen Hughes Jarman (to give his full name is somehow to trespass on the privacy of this very reserved man) was born in Bangor, Caernarfonshire, in 1911. His father, who kept a corner shop, was a monoglot English-speaker from Montgomeryshire and the boy might have been brought up without the Welsh language had his mother not seen to it that he attended the Sunday School at Twrgwyn, a bastion of the Calvinistic Methodist cause in the city.

At the University College of North Wales he took degrees in both Welsh and English, and then, in 1936, was awarded an MA for a thesis on that part of *The Black Book of Carmarthen* which deals with the legend of Myrddin, the wizard known in English as Merlin. He began his career as a tutor with the college's Extra-Mural Department and the Workers' Education Association, but moved to Cardiff in 1946 to take up a lectureship in the Welsh Department at the University College, there.

Unlike most of his colleagues at Bangor, Fred Jarman soon became active in politics on behalf of Plaid Cymru, in those days a small group of intellectuals, students, writers and ministers of religion. In the bitter schism which rent the Welsh intelligentsia in the late 1930s after the symbolic act of arson at Penyberth, near Pwllheli, where an RAF bombing school was being built, he was to be found in the Nationalist rather than the Socialist camp, especially after Saunders Lewis, a lecturer in Welsh at Swansea and an eminent writer, was gaoled for his part in the affair and, while serving a prison sentence, was dismissed from his post.

A.O.H Jarman was one of those who mounted an unsuccessful campaign to have Lewis reinstated. He also helped in the equally ineffective attempt to elect Lewis, the Plaid Cymru candidate, to the University of Wales seat at Westminster. For five years during the Second World War he was editor of the party's monthly newspaper, *Y Ddraig Goch*, and played a leading part in the formulation of the party's policies. He took the view that Wales, like Ireland, should remain neutral during the conflict of 1939-45 and, when called up for military service, refused to serve. His hope was that, if a thousand young Welshmen had agreed to do the same, Wales would have been given a new political status after the war.

The tribunal refused to accept this political argument and, as a consequence, he and a few others served a brief term in prison. His commitment to the work of Plaid Cymru, and his allegiance to the seminal but controversial figure of Saunders Lewis, never faltered and he remained a staunch member of the party for the rest of his life.

Two years after coming to the Chair in Welsh at Cardiff, he began publishing the fruits of his research. In his book *The Legend of Merlin* (1960) and in many articles in scholarly journals such as *Studia Celtica* he traced the development of the Merlin story from its Celtic and Welsh roots to its French versions. His later research is to be found in his article "The Legend of Myrddin and the Welsh Tradition of Prophecy" which appeared in the magisterial book he edited with Rachel Bromwich and Brinley F. Roberts, *The Arthur of the Welsh* (1991).

He also contributed to the compendium *Arthurian Literature in the*

Middle Ages (1959), edited by R.S. Loomis, and published a complete edition of *The Black Book of Carmarthen* (1982). From 1963 to 1986 he was editor of *Llên Cymru*, a journal published by the University of Wales Press on behalf of the Board of Celtic Studies. He was also an authority on Geoffrey of Monmouth, the author of the *Historia Regum Britanniae*, and on *Y Gododdin*, a sixth-century poem in Old Welsh which, because it describes the defeat in battle of a British war-band from what is today lowland Scotland, has been wryly called "the oldest Scottish poem".

The Merlin to whom A.O.H Jarman devoted many years of study was a legendary poet and prophet who, after the battle of Arfderydd in 573, lost his reason and fled to the wood of Celyddon, where he lived as a wild man and received the gift of prophecy. The scholar reconstructed the tale, not only from Galfridian sources, mainly the *Vita Merlini*, but also from the writings of the 12th-century Giraldus Cambrensis, showing how Merlin had become one of the central characters of the continental Arthurian legend.

With his wife Eldra, who is descended from a famous family of Welsh gypsies who were talented musicians, A.O.H. Jarman wrote an authoritative account of the Romanies in Wales, *Y Sipsiwn Cymreig* (1979), of which an English version, *The Welsh Gypsies: children of Abram Wood*, appeared in 1991. She brought a vivacity to their marriage which nicely complemented the somewhat taciturn, but not humourless, scholar in him. I well remember his droll comments about those who claimed to have discovered Arthur's grave, his caustic dismissal of the efforts of "amateur" Arthurian enthusiasts like Nikolai Tolstoy, and his laughter when I told him that there was a roadside café just outside Glastonbury which served Excaliburgers.

During his time as Professor of Welsh at Cardiff, Fred Jarman (as he was known to friends and some of his colleagues) served *inter alia* as Dean of the Faculty of Arts and, in the wider academic world, on the board of the University of Wales Press and the Board of Celtic Studies, on the Court of the University of Wales and various committees of the National Library of Wales. Among his initiatives in his own department was the establishment of a Linguistics Research Unit, which nurtured the talents of a generation of young scholars, particularly those engaged in the study of Welsh dialects and, most notably, its first Director, Ceinwen Thomas, Glyn E. Jones, who succeeded him to the Chair of Welsh, and David Thorne, now Professor of Welsh at Lampeter.

A.O.H. Jarman received many honours in his chosen field. He was the Sir John Rhys Fellow at Oxford University and Fellow of Jesus College in 1975-76, O'Donnell Lecturer in the University of Wales in 1984, Sir John Rhys Memorial Lecturer in the British Academy in 1985, President of the British Branch of the International Arthurian Society from 1980 to 1983, and thereafter its honorary President.

Alfred Owen Hughes Jarman, Arthurian scholar: born Bangor, Caernarfonshire 8 October 1911; Professor of Welsh, University College, Cardiff 1957-79; married 1943 Eldra Roberts (two daughters); died Cardiff 26 October 1998.

The Independent (29 October 1998)

R. Gerallt Jones

Poet and prolific prose-writer

One of the most prolific Welsh authors of the post-war period, R. Gerallt Jones excelled both as poet and prose-writer, and more unusually, in both Welsh, his first language, and English, the language of his early schooling. He also took a passionate interest in the affairs of the Third World, especially those of the Indian subcontinent, and of Jamaica, where he spent two years as the first Principal of Mandeville Teachers' College.

He was born, a poor Anglican vicar's son, at Nefyn on the Llŷn in north-west Wales, the rugged peninsula that points towards Ireland. At the age of ten, still a monoglot Welsh-speaker, he was sent by his Anglophile, High Church, High Tory father as a boarder to a school near Shrewsbury and thence to Denstone College, a minor public school for boys, in Staffordshire.

Although his schooldays were happy – his exceptional intelligence and prowess at cricket ensured that he was not ragged on account of his very un-English background – the experience made him think of Wales, and the wild scenery of Llŷn in particular, as an ideal country. "Wales for me," he wrote, "was a hearth, a home, a wonderful world, hidden, separate from the world of school, a proud possession of my own, a secret room that my English friends knew nothing about."

It was to the sea-girt peninsula that he was to return so often in his writing, sometimes to the rather daunting figure of his father who, of illegitimate birth and Methodist upbringing, had decided that his only child would not be tainted by what he considered to be the hypocrisy of the Welsh Nonconformist chapel.

At the University College of North Wales, Bangor, where he first encountered the harsher realities of Welsh life, Gerallt took a degree in English and went on to write an MA thesis on the work of Robert Graves. Also at Bangor, in association with Bedwyr Lewis Jones, a lifelong friend and co-religionist who later became Professor of Welsh at the College, he launched and edited the magazine *Yr Arloeswr* ("The pioneer"). Brief though its lifespan was – it ran to only eight numbers between 1957 and 1960 – the magazine published the work of Gwyn Thomas and Bobi Jones, who were to join him in a triumvirate of poets now acknowledged as the most important of their generation.

This interest in literary journalism remained with him for the rest of his life: he was a regular contributor to Welsh periodicals and from 1987 to 1992, again with Bedwyr Lewis Jones, he edited the Welsh Academy's influential magazine *Taliesin*.

The versatility of R. Gerallt Jones as a writer was quite remarkable. He published five volumes of verse in Welsh; *Ymysg y Drain* ("Among the nettles", 1959), *Cwlwm* ("Knot", 1962), *Cysgodion* ("Shadows", 1972), *Dyfal Gerddwyr y Maes* ("The relentless walkers of the field", 1981) and *Cerddi 1955-89* ("Poems 1955-89", 1989); and one in English, *Jamaican Landscape* (1969), the fruit of his two years in the Caribbean. A deeply meditative poet, he was able to give the numinous concrete form by the use of striking imagery and the rich idiom of his native district. His command of English, together with his belief that Welsh poetry deserved and needed a wider audience, led him to translate a good deal of it, notably in the substantial anthology *Poetry of Wales 1930-70* (1974).

In his prose writing, he tackled contemporary social problems with a special sympathy for the marginalised and dispossessed. His first novel, *Y Foel Fawr* ("The great hill", 1960), is about a Welshman who campaigns for the rights of black people in South Africa; its sequel, *Nadolig Gwyn* ("A white Christmas", 1962), set in Bangor, is more concerned with politics and social justice at home. In *Triptych* (1977), one of two novels with which he won the Prose Medal at the National Eisteddfod, he dealt with the spiritual disintegration of 20th-century culture as a background to the slow death from cancer of a physical education teacher, while the other, *Cafflogion* (1979), described a commune in Llŷn after an unnamed catastrophe in a dark, dystopian future. His novel *Gwyntyll y Corwynt* ("Fanning the whirlwind", 1978) is about terrorism in Ireland.

But perhaps his most celebrated book is *Gwared y Gwirion* ("The loss of innocence", 1966), a collection of seven short stories exploring the innocence of childhood and the burgeoning of conscience in a boy growing up in Llŷn during the Second World War. In 1982 the stories were adapted for television by their author as *Joni Jones*, one of the most enchanting films made since the advent of S4C, the Welsh-language television channel, and filmed by the American Stephen Bayly. One episode, "The Evacuees", was the first Welsh-language production to be screened at the London Film Festival.

In his literary criticism Gerallt displayed a fundamentally liberal outlook, examining Wales and its culture in a wider context which took in the problems of the Third World, about which he made several television programmes. He published three collections of essays on literary subjects: *Yn Frawd i'r Eos Druan* ("Brother to the poor nightingale", 1961), *Ansawdd y Seiliau* ("The quality of the foundations", 1972) and *Seicoleg Cardota* ("The psychology of begging", 1989). Particularly concerned about the effects of television on literature, and how to use the medium creatively, he grappled with some of the threats to a literate society in much the same way as cultural analysts like Richard Hoggart have done in England.

He also wrote monographs in Welsh on T.S. Eliot and T.H. Parry-Williams; his full biography of the latter is due to be published by the University of Wales Press later this year. Among his miscellaneous prose are *Jamaican Interlude* (1977), an account of his time at Mandeville College, and several books in both Welsh and English about Ynys Enlli, the island off the furthermost tip of Llŷn known in English as Bardsey, to which he was a frequent visitor. As a literary critic, he was always ready to put his gifts at the service of his English-speaking countrymen, publishing numerous reviews and articles in such magazines as *Poetry Wales* and *Planet*, in which he wrote engagingly about what was being produced in the Welsh language.

The professional career of R. Gerallt Jones reflected his restless energy and preference to be always "fully stretched". He began as a teacher of English at the Sir Thomas Jones School at Amlwch in Anglesey in 1957 but, four years later, was appointed lecturer in the Education Department at the University College of Wales, Aberystwyth. After his sojourn in Jamaica, he returned to Wales in 1967 to take up the wardenship of Llandovery College, a public school in Carmarthenshire and one of the few in the whole of Wales, and there he remained until 1979.

After a year spent as a freelance writer, he was appointed Senior Tutor in the Department of Extra-Mural Studies at Aberystwyth. From 1989 until his retirement in 1995 he was Warden of Gregynog Hall, the University of Wales residential study-centre near Newtown in Powys. It was in the last-named post, amid the old mansion's mock-Tudor architecture and splendid park, with access to a fine library and an ever-changing company of visiting students and academic staff, that his genial personality, wide interests and independent views (he was active on behalf of no political party) were given fullest play. His dark, Venedotian features, broad grin and generous disposition made him a popular Warden, although he sometimes gave the impression the minutiae of administration held little appeal for him.

Although he once described himself as a reluctant committee man, the list of public bodies of which Gerallt was a member is a long one. Principal among them was the Church in Wales, in which he had been brought up and to which he remained loyal throughout his adult life, despite his profound understanding of Nonconformist Wales and the pressures which had led to Disestablishment in 1920. He served as a lay reader in the Church in Wales, editor of its quarterly journal *Impact*, and a member of its Governing Body. But there was nothing narrow or exclusive about his allegiance to the Communion. In fact, he was interested in all religions, and I well recall how during a trip to the Caucasus in the 1970s, he could not be kept from the icons and rites of the Georgian Orthodox Church.

Among other bodies on which he served were the Broadcasting Council for Wales, the Welsh Academy (of which he was chairman), the Welsh Arts Council, the Court of the University College of Wales, Aberystwyth, the Welsh National Film and Video Archive, and the Board of Governors of S4C. To all these appointments he brought balanced judgement, a dryly witty manner, and a broad spectrum of interests which, though deeply rooted in Wales and the Welsh language, looked out at England, Europe, and the wider world with a mixture of fascination, amusement, sympathy, and sometimes consternation.

Robert Gerallt Hamlet Jones, writer and educationist: born Nefyn, Caernarfonshire 11 September 1934; Principal, Mandeville College, Jamaica 1965-67; Warden, Llandovery College 1967-79; Senior Lecturer, Department of Extra-Mural University College of Wales, Aberystwyth 1979-89; Warden, Gregynog Hall 1989-95; married 1962 Susan Lloyd Griffith (two sons, one daughter); died Dol-y-bont, Ceredigion 9 January 1999.

The Independent (13 January 1999)

Meredith Edwards

Character actor with Ealing Studios

Meredith Edwards was one of those Welsh character actors who, during the post-war years, found parts in the comedy films largely associated with Ealing Studios. In *A Run For Your Money* (1949), an affectionate but stereotypical view of the Welsh in which a group of rugby-loving miners spend an international day in London with uproarious results, he starred alongside the wild-eyed, dissolute harpist Hugh Griffith and the handsome dimwit Donald Houston who is fleeced by a West End tart played by Moira Lister – the sort of woman, as one collier puts it, who paints her toenails.

Now the Welsh are notoriously difficult to please when it comes to seeing themselves on film and many found *A Run For Your Money*, which Ealing intended to be the Welsh equivalent of *Whisky Galore*, too simplistic and, at worst, patronising. The film does have some nice comic touches, however, as when a voice over the loudspeaker at Paddington asks Mr Thomas Jones and Mr David Jones to come to the stationmaster's office, and a horde of leek-bedecked fans answer to these archetypal Welsh names.

It was characteristic of Meredith Edwards that, offered a chance to work in Hollywood on the strength of his memorable performance, he turned it down and chose to stay at home. He was never to regret his decision, for he was rarely out of work thereafter. Although he had no formal training – his first job after leaving Ruabon Grammar School was that of laboratory assistant at the Courtaulds factory in Flint – he had become a professional actor in 1938 when he joined the Welsh National Theatre Company which the quixotic Lord Howard de Walden was trying to found at Plas Newydd, the former home of the Misses Butler and Ponsonby, "the Ladies of Llangollen". This touring group, although it made little headway as a national company, taught him the rudiments of his craft and inspired in him the ideal of a permanent home for the theatrical profession in Wales, for which he was to campaign long and hard, but to no avail.

His acting career proper began at the Liverpool Playhouse, where he played in *Julius Caesar*, but it was interrupted in the war when, as a conscientious objector on Christian pacifist grounds, he was set to

work as a fireman in Liverpool, Chester and London, and later draft-
ed into the Non-Combatant Corps, where he entertained the troops
with amateur theatricals sponsored by ENSA.

He spent most of the war years in Palestine. His stage career was
resumed after the war at the Old Vic, where he played Glendower in
Henry IV, and less predictably, John of Gaunt in *Richard II*; of his
Churchillian rendering of the "happy breed" speech in the latter play
the London *Evening News* commented, "After hearing Meredith
Edwards's impassioned delivery of John O'Gaunt's speech, every
schoolboy who has got it from memory will go back and get it by
heart."

Meredith Edwards was born, a collier's son, in 1917 in the hill-top
village of Rhosllannerchrugog, near Wrexham, in industrial north-
east Wales. The district has a robust Welsh-speaking culture and a tradition of Radical politics of which he was immensely proud. He
spoke Welsh fluently, delighting in the local peculiarities of Rhos
speech, including its retention of the familiar *ti* (thou) with which its
inhabitants habitually address friend and stranger alike, and he wrote
it with panache in his autobiography, *Ar Lwyfan Awr* ("On an hour's
stage", 1977).

The language was at the heart of his patriotism and he worked tire-
lessly on its behalf, contributing generously to such causes as the
Welsh Schools Movement, in particular the Welsh School in London
(now at Willesden Green) in the days when the LCC was refusing to
fund it. He was also a political Nationalist and left-wing member of
Plaid Cymru, serving as a member of the Flintshire County Council
and standing as the party's candidate in the West Denbigh constituency at the General Election of 1966. During the referendum on
the National Assembly in 1997 he played a prominent part in the Yes
campaign.

In demand as a specifically Welsh character actor throughout the
1950s, he made about fifty films in all, notably *The Blue Lamp*
(1950), which led to the television series *Dixon of Dock Green*, *Where
No Vultures Fly* (1951), *Girdle of Gold* (1952), *The Cruel Sea* (1953),
The Long Arm (1956), and *Dunkirk* (1958). In the last, he insisted on
delivering the dying words of his character, a Welsh Tommy lying
wounded in an orchard, in Welsh. "Who the hell's going to understand?" asked the exasperated producer, Leslie Norman. "I have the
feeling that when someone is dying," Edwards replied in his eirenic

way, "they go back to their childhood, and if I went back to mine, it would be a Welsh-speaking one". So he expires in Welsh, while John Mills, with stiff upper lip, tells his men they will have to leave him and push on.

Returning permanently to Wales in the early 1960s, although still making forays to London for work with *Z Cars*, *Coronation Street* and *Softly Softly*, in which he made regular appearances, usually as the affable Welshman with homely features and a mischievous grin, Meredith Edwards settled in the village of Cilcain, in Flintshire, so that his children could be educated in Welsh. One of the best theatres in Wales, Theatr Clwyd, was situated nearby and he returned to the stage with great success, particularly in Chekhov's *The Three Sisters*.

Among his finest cameo parts was as the stern clergyman in *Only Two Can Play* (1962), based on the Kingsley Amis novel *That Uncertain Feeling* (1955), who presses the hapless Peter Sellers, a candidate for a librarian's job, about his knowledge of Welsh literature. He was much in demand on Welsh television, initially with Granada (where Siân Phillips was his co-presenter) and especially after the advent of S4C, the Welsh-language fourth channel, in 1982.

He appeared in Welsh versions of plays by Molière and Pinter, and was one of the German generals plotting against Hitler in Saunders Lewis's *Brâd* ("Treason"). His last film was *Bride of War* (1997), a tragic love-story set in occupied Poland and directed by his son Peter, now Head of Drama at HTV; both his other children, Ioan and Lisa, also work in television.

In addition he worked with Amnesty International, CND Cymru, Cymdeithas yr Iaith Gymraeg (The Welsh Language Society) and Equity, the actors' union, of which he was a Life President. In 1996, as part of the celebrations marking the centenary of cinema, he was chosen to unveil the plaque at Rhyd-y-main, where Emlyn Williams's film *The Last Days of Dolwyn* had been made in 1949, an acknowledgement of his contribution to the theatre, cinema and television of Wales over more than half a century.

Gwilym Meredith Edwards, actor: born Rhosllannerchrugog, Denbighshire 10 June 1917; married 1942 Daisy Clark (two sons, one daughter); died Abergele, Denbighshire 8 February 1999.

The Independent (15 February 1999)

Emyr Wyn Jones

Heart specialist and historian

In addition to having a long and distinguished career as a heart specialist at hospitals in Liverpool and his prominent roles on committees responsible for the administration of the health service in Wales, Emyr Wyn Jones was also a writer and book collector who served on numerous public bodies involved in the cultural life of Wales.

Having taken first class honours in Medicine and Surgery at Liverpool University in 1928, at the age of twenty-one, he became a Doctor of Medicine in 1930, a Member of the Royal College of Physicians in 1933 and a Fellow in 1949. During his training at the London teaching hospitals he carried off a number of prestigious prizes.

His association with the Liverpool Royal Infirmary began in 1928 but he did not join its full-time staff until 1938. From 1945 until his retirement in 1972 be was in charge of the Cardiology Department, but also played a leading role in the hospital's administration and, from 1953, taught medicine at Liverpool University, latterly as Director of Cardiac Studies. He ended his career as Senior Physician at the Liverpool Royal infirmary and the Regional Cardiac Centre.

In Wales, he served on numerous committees, including those of the Welsh Hospitals Board (1952-74), and as consultant to the North Wales Hospitals, which included those at Bangor, Rhyl and Wrexham (1934-74), he became perhaps the best-known representative of the medical profession in the region. The administrative systems which he was instrumental in setting up in North Wales provided a firm basis for the implementation of the provisions ushered in by the National Health Service in 1948. He was also a keen advocate of the wider use of Welsh in medical circles and, although never active on behalf of any political party, took a stern view of those who denied the claim of Welsh nationality which, in his view, was inextricably bound up with the language.

Emyr Wyn Jones was born at Waunfawr in Caernarfonshire in 1907, the son of a Calvinistic Methodist minister, and received his secondary education at the County School in the county town. His older brother, who had begun to win a reputation as a brilliant pathologist, died at the age of twenty-three, after which it was taken for granted that he would follow the same career. From his parents he inherited the rich Welsh culture of the Llŷn peninsula, in which he found great relief from the rigours of his professional life and to which he often returned in his writings; his last home was at Rhiw, near Aberdaron, almost at the extreme tip of the peninsula.

The *violon d'Ingres* which gave him greatest pleasure was the writing of local history, in both Welsh and English, and the exploration of the folk-culture associated with medicine. His book *Bosworth Field* (1984) was published in time for the quincentenary of the battle fought at Market Bosworth in Leicestershire on 22 August 1485. In it he traced the progress of Henry Tudor from his landing-point at Dale in Pembrokeshire through mid-Wales and into England via Shrewsbury, with particular reference to the Welshmen, under Rhys ap Thomas of Dinefwr, who flocked to Henry's banner, brought about the death of Richard III and helped establish a new English dynasty.

The author was especially concerned to elucidate the many references in Welsh poetry to Henry as "the Son of Prophecy" who would restore to the Welsh the sovereignty of the Isle of Britain, a task which he carried out with typical lucidity and a delightfully light touch. He also published a study of John Rowlands of Denbigh, better known as H.M. Stanley, the journalist who found Dr Livingstone at Ujiji in 1871.

His books *Ar Ffiniau Meddygaeth* ("On the fringes of medicine", 1971), *Ysgubau'r Meddyg* ("The doctor's sheaves", 1973), *Cynddyn Ddorau* ("Reluctant doors", 1978), *Ymgiprys am y Goron* ("Competing for the Crown", 1991), *Lloffa yn Llŷn* ("Rummaging in Llŷn", 1994) and *Y Bysedd Cochion a'r Wladfa Cyntaf* ("Foxgloves and the first settlement", 1997) are written in the same elegant style but from a much more personal point of view. They take in not only his experiences as a practising physician and his knowledge of doctors both famous and obscure, but the myths and legends which have accrued to the practice of medicine over the centuries, his keen interest in folklore, both Welsh and Gaelic, in alternative medicine, in hill-walking, and in music.

In the pursuit of the last-named interest, he was particularly well placed in that he and his first wife, Enid, whom he married in 1936, lived, from 1942 – when their Liverpool home was damaged by German bombs – at Llansannan in Denbighshire, a village in the

Hiraethog hills renowned for its tradition of folk-singing to the accompaniment of the harp. Their home, Llety'r Eos ("The nightingale's lodge"), became a meeting-place for poets and musicians, where the ancient traditions of the *noson lawen* ("merry evening") were maintained with gracious hospitality and a good deal of fun. There, too, he built up a splendid collection of rare books, including the early productions of the Gregynog Press, which was one of the best private libraries in Wales.

Enid Wyn Jones was the sister of the poet Alun Llywelyn-Williams, whose poem "*Taith i Lety'r Eos*" evokes the cultured atmosphere of the house. She died in 1967 while asleep on board an aeroplane which was bringing her and her husband back from an international YWCA conference in Australia. As part of the grieving process for her, Emyr Wyn Jones edited a memorial volume and a collection of her essays, *Cyfaredd Cof* ("The enchantment of memory"). His second wife, Megan, was the widow of Thomas Jones Pierce, formerly Professor of Welsh History at the University College of Wales, Aberystwyth; they married in 1973. She brought to their marriage a vivacity and keen interest in all things Welsh which chimed nicely with his own.

Although a man of temperate judgement and a somewhat reserved personality, who preferred scholarly pursuits to the public arenas in which he spent his professional life, Emyr Wyn Jones gave his services to the National Eisteddfod and the Gorsedd of Bards which is closely associated with it, the National Library, the National Museum, the University of Wales, the Welsh National School of Medicine, the Welsh League of Youth, the Honourable Society of Cymmrodorion, and the Denbighshire Historical Society; he was High Sheriff of his native county in 1947.

During the post-war period he was particularly concerned to see the end of National Service, offering practical advice to those expecting to appear before tribunals because they had refused conscription on grounds of conscience. He also maintained his links with the Welsh life of Liverpool, as President of both the University's Welsh Society and its Medical Students' Society. For his services to Welsh culture he was awarded the honorary degree of LLB by the University of Wales.

A fascinating insight into his views on modern surgery, especially heart transplants and his response to the ethical problems of saving life and the inevitability of death, was given in Welsh during a television interview broadcast in 1971 and published in the symposium *Dan Sylw*. While not disapproving of the experimental work of Dr Christiaan Barnard, he deplored the publicity surrounding heart transplants and spoke movingly of the relationship between doctor and patient when death is known to be imminent. It was his Quaker faith, with its emphasis on pacifism, the value of silence in the face of the great mysteries, and George Fox's dictum that there is a part of God in all men and women, which sustained him at such moments and, indeed, throughout the greater part of his life.

Emyr Wyn Jones, surgeon and writer: born Waunfawr, Caernarfonshire 23 May 1907; Head of the Cardiology Department, Liverpool Royal Infirmary 1945-72; married 1936 Enid Llywelyn-Williams (died 1967; one son, one daughter), 1973 Megan Jones Pierce (one stepson, one stepdaughter); died Bangor, Gwynedd 14 January 1999.

The Independent (19 February 1999)

Ioan Bowen Rees

Chief Executive of Gwynedd County Council and political thinker

Ioan Bowen Rees, one of his country's leading political thinkers, died two days before the people of Wales voted in the election of their National Assembly. As County Secretary and Chief Executive of Gwynedd County Council from 1974 to 1991, he made a major contribution to the administration of local government and, an influential writer, argued doggedly for the creation of a democratically elected body such as Wales now has.

A left-wing member of Plaid Cymru by the time he came down from Queen's College, Oxford, where he had read Modern History, even as a young man he was regularly consulted by Gwynfor Evans, the party's president, and subsequently by Dafydd Wigley, its long-serving MP for Caernarfon. He was also a member of the working party which advised Ron Davies, the former Secretary of State for Wales, in preparation for the Bill which paved the way for the National Assembly. He had never made a secret of his Nationalist convictions, having stood twice as the Plaid Cymru candidate in Conwy at the general elections of 1955 and 1959 and in Merthyr Tydfil in 1964.

Born in Dolgellau, Ioan Bowen Rees was educated at the town's grammar school, where his father was English master, and then at Bootham School in York. At Oxford, where he joined the Dafydd ap Gwilym Society, he resolved to brush up the Welsh language of which a wholly English education had nearly deprived him. He wrote with a vigour and authority which placed him among the political heavyweights of his generation. He had a profound interest in the writings of his compatriot Raymond Williams, who helped him to see himself as a Welsh European.

The country which inspired Ioan most was Switzerland, in particular its cantonal form of government. He was a regular visitor to the Grisons, where he found not only a small language, Romansch, whose fortunes resembled those of Welsh, but also "a community of communities" whose model he sought to apply to Wales. For his seminal work *Government by Community* (1971), a study of Swiss democracy and an argument for saving local government in Britain from an overweening Whitehall, he was awarded the Haldane Medal by the Royal Institute of

Public Administration; the book has an introduction by Max Beloff who described it as "essential reading for public servants".

Ioan Bowen Rees began his career in 1956 as assistant solicitor with Lancashire County Council. Returning to Wales two years later he worked as Prosecuting Solicitor for Cardiff City Council before moving to Pembrokeshire, where he became Deputy Clerk and, in 1973, County Secretary of the newly formed Dyfed County Council. In his professional capacity he played a prominent role in the public life of Wales: he advised the Association of County Councils and served as Chairman of the Society of Local Authority Chief Executives.

He devoted his energies to strengthening local democracy in all its forms, often daring to argue against what he saw as the centralising policies of the Welsh Office. Much of what he set forth in his writing had for long been part of Plaid Cymru' s decentralised Socialism but it gained a wider currency, not least in some quarters of the Labour Party, and is now one of the several strands which make up the fabric of current political thinking in Wales.

Although he believed pessimism to be a healthier state of mind than an unfounded optimism, especially with regard to Welsh, he was a staunch friend of the language, which he spoke at home, and did much to establish it as the natural working medium of Gwynedd County Council, which serves a region that is still largely Welsh-speaking and on which Plaid Cymru has a majority of seats. But, no desiccated bureaucrat, he always saw things in human terms: "We bring up our children to speak Welsh, not for the sake of the language, but for the sake of our children."

At the heart of his concern for local democracy in Wales was his antipathy towards the numerous quangos which ruled Wales under the Thatcher government and of which the new Assembly is expected to make a bonfire. "There is always a danger of a small nation under the thumb of a large state becoming a nation of boot lickers," he wrote. "The rise of the quango in Wales today is a threat to our self-respect." But he never failed to see Wales on a wider canvas: "The battle for Wales is a battle for all small nations, all small communities, all individuals in the age of genocide."

He published a number of pamphlets, notably *The Welsh Political Tradition* (1961) and *Beyond National Parks* (1995). His views found their first full expression in his contribution to *Celtic Nationalism* (1968), which he co-authored with Gwynfor Evans, Hugh

MacDiarmid and Owen Dudley Edwards. More recently, his collection of essays *Cymuned a Chenedl* ("Community and Nation", 1993), represents his mature thinking about the nature of modern democracy and local autonomy, not only in the British but also in the European context. In this comparative work the Swiss cantons were again the source of his inspiration, but the federalism of Proudhon came to the fore, together with a staunch belief in a Europe of the Regions.

Ioan made his home at Llanllechid, near Bethesda in Gwynedd, a former slate-quarrying district where he enjoyed the close communal ties and democratic spirit more commonly associated with the industrial valleys of south Wales. There he was elected president of the local rugby club and indulged his passion for climbing; a few days before his death he had been on the summit of Moel Wnion (alt. 580 metres).

He published four collections of Welsh essays about the mountains of Snowdonia, the Alps, the Himalayas and the Andes, and compiled an anthology, *The Mountains of Wales*, which was published in 1987 in a fine edition by the prestigious Gregynog Press and subsequently, in 1992, by the University of Wales Press. He was a founding member of the Welsh Mountaineering Club.

During retirement he explored two aspects of family history which gave him immense pleasure. His grandfather had been a missionary in Ndebeland, now Zimbabwe, where he was placed under the protection of King Lobengula during the Bantu uprisings of the 1890s. Having visited one of the schools established by his grandfather and made contact with the tribe which had shielded him, he was writing an account of this episode at the time of his death. Another ancestor was the cartographer John Evans of Waunfawr who, in 1793, set out to search for the Mandans, the reputed descendants of Prince Madog, who according to legend had landed on American shores some 600 years earlier.

One of his sons, Gruff Rhys, is lead singer in the Welsh pop group Super Furry Animals.

Ioan Bowen Rees, solicitor, writer and local government officer: born Dolgellau, Merioneth 13 January 1929; Secretary and Chief Executive, Gwynedd County Council 1974-91; married 1959 Margaret Wynn Meredith (two sons, one daughter); died Bangor, Gwynedd 4 May 1999.

The Independent (7 May 1999)

Robert Thomas

Sculptor whose work was much in demand

With only a few exceptions, the public statuary of Wales is not very distinguished. It consists, for the most part, of grandiose monuments commemorating famous soldiers like General Picton at Carmarthen or local worthies such as John Batchelor "the Friend of Freedom", whose likeness stands on a plinth in the Hayes, in the very heart of Cardiff, where not one in a thousand passers-by could say who he was.

The work of Robert Thomas represents a more private, more intimate, almost domestic style of sculpture and a more indigenous tradition that seeks to honour Welsh men and women by the making of portrait busts which take their place in quiet corners of our national buildings, where they are appreciated on account of who their subjects are as much as for their intrinsic artistic merit. He made some fifty casts in all, several of which – for example, the larger-than-life monument to a hortatory Aneurin Bevan in one of the capital's main thoroughfares – have become icons of contemporary Wales.

Robert Thomas's first major commission, in 1965, was to make a portrait bust of James Griffiths, the first Secretary of State for Wales, which is housed at Parc Howard in Llanelli. It was followed by a bust of Lord Edmund Davies, the Welsh judge who presided at the trial of those accused of the Great Train Robbery of 1963 and at the Aberfan Disaster Inquiry of 1967, and another of the entertainer Ryan Davies, now kept at the headquarters of BBC Wales in Llandaf.

From the world of opera Robert Thomas made busts of Sir Geraint Evans and Dame Gwyneth Jones. His head of the Welsh writer Gwyn Thomas, stolen from the foyer of the Sherman Theatre, Cardiff in 1988, and never recovered, had to be recast and is now displayed in the New Theatre, where it was unveiled by Anthony Hopkins in 1994.

Perhaps his best-known work, at least in the popular view, was his life-size bronze of Diana, Princess of Wales, the only sculpture for which she posed and with which she was said to have been delighted. Made in 1987, it is displayed at St David's Hall in Cardiff where, after her death, it became the daily focus for many hundreds of mourners.

A more robust work is his magnificent cast of Captain Cat, from Dylan Thomas's *Under Milk Wood*, which was unveiled in Swansea Marina on St David's Day 1990. His last commission was a full-length figure of Isambard Kingdom Brunel, the Victorian engineer. At present in foundry, it is to be unveiled next July at Neyland in Pembrokeshire, where Brunel designed many of his big ships, and at the terminal of the Great Western Railway line which was built under his supervision.

Robert Thomas was born in Cwm-parc, a mining village in a side-valley of the Rhondda Fawr, in August 1926, during "the Angry Summer" of the General Strike which crippled South Wales and made it a hotbed of militant Socialism. His father was a miner, as was almost the entire male population, and the time and place left their mark on him.

In 1944 he left Pentre Grammar School while still in the Sixth Form to become a Bevin Boy, and worked underground as an electrician for the rest of the war. Ever after he was left-wing in his political sympathies, staunchly humanist, and was attracted as a sculptor to subjects whom he revered for their humanitarian ideals. One of his most admired works is the miner's family group which now stands in Tonypandy, near the scene of the famous riots of 1910; while not quite Socialist Realist, it leaves no doubt as to where the artist's sympathies lie.

After the war he won a scholarship to Cardiff College of Art. But he always claimed that it was the daily train journey up and down the Rhondda in the company of his fellow-artists Charlie Burton and Ernest Zobole, during which they argued fiercely about the nature and function of art, which taught him most.

Although not a formal member of the Rhondda Group, which consisted mainly of painters, Robert Thomas remained in contact with them and shared many of their preoccupations. In 1949 he was the first student of sculpture to leave Cardiff for the Royal College of Art in London. After graduating, he and his wife Mary, a textile designer, taught part-time at Ealing Technical College in west London, returning to Wales in 1971.

A modest man, Bob Thomas never sought the limelight and held no exhibitions of his work. When not in his studio, he took great pleasure in playing the piano and writing verse, some of which was published. Jovial in company and good-natured, especially in his relations with other artists, he served as Vice-President of the Royal Society of British Sculptors (1979-84) and as President of the Society of Portrait Sculptors (1972-77).

Robert John Roydon Thomas, sculptor: born Cwm-parc, Glamorgan 1 August 1926; teacher, Ealing Technical College 1953-71; married 1952 Mary Gardiner (two sons, one daughter); died Cardiff 11 May 1999.

The Independent (21 May 1999)

J.E. Caerwyn Williams

First Director of the Centre for Advanced Welsh and Celtic Studies

J.E. Caerwyn Williams, formerly Professor of Irish at the University College of Wales, Aberystwyth, and after his retirement in 1979 the first Director of the University of Wales Centre for Advanced Welsh and Celtic Studies, was one of the most distinguished luminaries in the world of Celtic scholarship.

For more than sixty years he wrote prolifically on the civilisation of the Celts, both ancient and modern, those of the Goidelic branch as well as those of the Brittonic, and particularly on the native litera-tures of Ireland and Wales. His learning was wide, profound and grounded in meticulous research and a close acquaintance with the notoriously difficult texts written in early medieval times in the Celtic languages.

As a former pupil of Sir Ifor Williams, he wrote on the Cynfeirdd – mainly Aneirin and Taliesin – poets of "the Old North" of Britain (now southern Scotland, and much of Cumbria, Lancashire and Yorkshire), where in the sixth century a form of Old Welsh was spo-ken before those regions were overrun by Germanic invaders still known in Welsh tradition as "the children of Horsa and Hengist".

In another area of his academic research, namely the Gogynfeirdd, or Poets of the Princes, he wrote so extensively and brilliantly that all subsequent scholarship has been indebted to him. These court poets, who flourished in Wales between the first half of the 12th century and the latter half of the 14th, were professional craftsmen who expressed their erudition in archaic diction and extremely intricate metrical forms. Their function was to celebrate the military prowess of their lord and, in times of peace, his generosity as a patron of the bardic order; at the end, they sang his elegy.

Caerwyn Williams wrote two major studies of these poets: *Beirdd y Tywysogion* (1973) and *The Poets of the Welsh Princes* (1978). Their complete works have now been published in seven volumes under the editorship of R. Geraint Gruffydd, who succeeded Caerwyn Williams as Director of the Centre for Advanced Welsh and Celtic Studies in 1985.

John Ellis Williams was born in 1912 in Gwauncaegurwen, a Welsh-speaking mining village in the Upper Amman Valley on the boundary between industrial Glamorgan and rural Carmarthenshire, although his father's people had their roots in the slate-quarrying districts of north-west Wales. He adopted the name Caerwyn, it seems, on entering the University College of North Wales, Bangor, to avoid confusion with another student or two named John Ellis Williams. He took a degree in Latin in 1933 and in Welsh in 1934, both in the first division. From Bangor he went to University College and Trinity College, Dublin, and then to the United Theological College at Aberystwyth, where he read Greek and Church History, graduating BD in 1944. By this time his interest in Welsh and Irish literature, as well as in theology and philosophy, was well developed and it was to become the focus of his life's work.

He joined the staff of the Welsh Department at Bangor in 1945; eight years later he was appointed Professor, remaining in that post until 1965, when he moved to Aberystwyth as the first Professor of Irish in the University of Wales.

In 1947 he published a volume of the stories and essays of Pádraic O Conaire (1882-1928) in Welsh translation and a selection of stories translated from the Irish, *Yr Ebol Glas* ("The green foal"), in 1954. Both are mere apprentice work in comparison with his later achievement in writing three studies of Irish literature: *Traddodiad Llenyddol Iwerddon* ("The literary tradition of Ireland", 1958), *Y Storiwr Gwyddelig a'i Chwedlau* ("The Irish storyteller and his tales", 1972) and *The Court Poet in Medieval Ireland* (1972); and in co-editing with Patrick Ford the symposium *The Irish Literary Tradition* (1992). For his contribution to Irish and Celtic scholarship he was awarded the honorary degree of DLittCelt by the National University of Ireland in 1967 and in 1978 he was elected Fellow of the British Academy.

Caerwyn Williams did not confine his interests to medieval literature, however. He wrote a great deal on the early modern period and on the work of major 20th-century poets such as T.H. Parry-Williams and Waldo Williams and the playwrights Saunders Lewis and John Gwilym Jones. In his many essays, articles and reviews he displayed a thorough knowledge of literary criticism and theory, keeping abreast of modern trends and drawing on his wide reading in several languages.

His interest in Celtic philology extended to Breton: he published two volumes of stories translated from it into Welsh, its sister-language. A full list of his myriad publications on philological and literary subjects is found in *Bardos*, a Festschrift presented to him shortly after his retirement from the Chair of Irish at Aberystwyth.

In addition, he was a meticulous and sensitive editor, perhaps one of the most tireless and prodigious ever to serve the Celtic languages and their periodical literatures. He edited the series *Ysgrifau Beirniadol* ("Critical essays"), of which twenty-five substantial volumes have appeared since it was launched in 1965, and to which almost every Welsh scholar of note has contributed.

In the same year he was appointed editor of *Y Traethodydd* ('The essayist'), the most venerable of Welsh literary journals, for it has been published by the Presbyterian Church of Wales since 1845. In 1966 he became the first editor of *Studia Celtica*, the prestigious journal of the Board of Celtic Studies, and in 1970 the Consultative Editor of *Geiriadur Prifysgol Cymru: a dictionary of the Welsh language*, a work on historical principles which is indispensable to all students of the language's long and rich history.

J.E. Caerwyn Williams was widely regarded as the greatest Celtic scholar of modern times. Even after retirement he astonished former colleagues by the range and volume of his selfless commitment to the world of Celtic scholarship. Anecdotes about this immense industry and erudition – his preferred bedtime reading was said to be German commentaries on the Old Testament, which he read in its original languages – only added to the great affection and esteem in which this modest but genial man was held by colleagues and students alike. Nor were his talents confined to the study: he lectured frequently in Wales, Ireland, England and America, sat on many committees, notably the Council for Name Studies in Great Britain and Ireland, and from 1966 to 1975 enjoyed a stint as President of Yr Academi Gymreig, the national association of writers in Wales.

Many will recall the sheer delight with which, at the Academy's Taliesin Congress in 1969, he welcomed delegates from the other Celtic countries to Wales. They included not only his friend Máirtín Ó Cadhain but also Hugh MacDiarmid, Sorley MacLean and the Breton poet Maodez Glanndour. The occasion lent credence to his cherished view that the Celts, though geographically dispersed and disparate in their political circumstances, still belonged to the same family of peoples and might yet make something of their common culture – an ideal of which he was the living embodiment.

John Ellis Caerwyn Williams, Celtic scholar: born Gwauncaegurwen, Glamorgan 17 January 1912; Professor of Welsh, University College of North Wales, Bangor 1953-65; Professor of Irish, University College of Wales, Aberystwyth, 1965-79; FBA 1978; Director, University of Wales Centre for Advanced Welsh and Celtic Studies 1979-85; married 1996 Gwen Watkins; died Aberystwyth, Ceredigion 10 June 1999.

The Independent (14 June 1999)

Raymond Edwards

First Principal of the Welsh College of Music and Drama

The fluctuating fortunes of professional theatre in post-war Wales have produced none so staunch and articulate in his views as Raymond Edwards, from 1959 the first Principal of the Welsh College of Music and Drama. For more than thirty years he was at the centre of things, whether as administrator, producer, adjudicator or member of the myriad committees on which Wales's cultural life depends. He was a pillar of common sense and a passionate advocate of all that was best in the Welsh tradition, but always ready to assimilate whatever the world had to offer.

The traditional amateur base of Welsh theatre began to give way to a new professionalism during the 1960s, but the magnet for many actors remained Hollywood and the London stage: Richard Burton, Rachel Roberts, Emlyn Williams, Meredith Edwards and Hugh Griffith were among those who made their names in America and Elstree. Foremost among those pressing for a professional home-based theatre with adequate resources and a programme of works by native talent was Raymond Edwards, who became Head of the Drama Department at the Cardiff College of Music and Drama in 1951 and was appointed Principal when it won national status eight years later.

In the long-running battle for a Welsh National Theatre, which has still not been resolved, he took the side of those in favour, but refused to be caught up in the bitter internecine rows between the camps led by the great Welsh-language dramatist Saunders Lewis and Professor Gwyn Jones, who as Chairman of the Drama Panel of the Welsh Committee of the Arts Council, was resolutely against the creation of such an institution. Even as late as 1977, when Raymond Edwards became an influential member of the Welsh Arts Council, it was an issue close to his heart. Michael Bogdanov has recently revived the idea.

Although a gifted actor and producer of plays for the stage, Raymond Edwards put his prodigious talents into the development of the college which will be his permanent memorial. When he joined its staff in 1959 it was housed in rather cramped quarters amid the mock-medieval splendours of Cardiff Castle, but so single-minded was his commitment that in a land short of surnames he was soon known as

"Raymond y Castell", to distinguish him from several others with the same name.

Under his direction the college grew from small beginnings and not only parried all attempts to have it incorporated into the Cardiff Institute of Higher Education but moved into splendid purpose-built premises in nearby Cathays Park, thanks mainly to the Principal's diplomacy and driving force. He was an inspired teacher, popular with colleagues and students alike. Among his most famous former students are Anthony Hopkins, Victor Spinetti, Peter Gill, Anthony O'Donnell, Iris Williams, Jane Freeman and Victoria Wicks.

Edwards was born, a collier's son, in 1919 in Rhosllannerchrugog, a large Welsh-speaking industrial village in Denbighshire famous for its male-voice choirs, which in his day had an amateur opera company, an orchestra, a drama company and the communal ties more commonly associated with the mining valleys of south Wales. He found the place grim and unprepossessing. "It was not the kind of village which attracts sightseers," he wrote in *Artists in Wales* (1973), "and if any came to Rhos, it was because they had gone off course on the main Ruabon-Wrexham road".

Nevertheless, he was proud of his people's heritage, an amalgam of radical politics, Nonconformist religion and a respect for education typical of working-class Wales. Above all, the people of Rhos were great talkers and public speakers. Raymond Edwards, who had a deeply resonant voice, was fond of saying that he had inherited his father's way of speaking and that what came naturally to the miner – breathing deeply, with nostrils dilated and chest distended – was something that as an actor he had never had to learn. His voice served him well as a broadcaster in both Welsh and English, as an adjudicator of competitions sponsored by the British Theatre Association and as an after-dinner speaker much in demand.

After training as a teacher at Bangor Normal College, and lecturing at Wrexham Technical College, he took his first private lessons in stage technique at the Liverpool Repertory School. From the start, and unusually for a Welshman, he was determined to acquire skills as an actor by dint of discipline, economy and the control of emotion. Thus he learned how to avoid "the huffing and puffing" of the Welsh pulpit and to cultivate a nonchalance which I once found highly effective in his master-class of Saunders Lewis's verse-play *Siwan*, a tale of adultery and political intrigue set in medieval Wales. "Above all," he wrote, "I was taught to be on guard against becoming a conjuror's apprentice, against acquiring a set of tricks which I could pass off as art and which I could at some future date teach to others in the same way."

So it was as a teacher at the College of Music and Drama in Cardiff he encouraged his students to aim for technical confidence combined with an unruffled, straightforward acting style that had only a hint of personal involvement. It is said that Anthony Hopkins learned something of his chillingly malevolent part in the 1990 film *Silence of the Lambs* from his old teacher.

Outside the College of Music and Drama, Raymond Edwards enjoyed wearing many hats. He was a director of Harlech Television; President of the Drama Association of Wales; Chairman of the Welsh National Theatre Company (1971-76); a board member of the Welsh National Opera Company (1971-77); an examiner in Drama to the Universities of Wales, Bristol and Birmingham (1975-81); a member of the Court of University College, Cardiff, and the Council of the National Museum of Wales; and a magistrate of the City of Cardiff.

For this public work he was awarded the honorary degree of LLD by the University of Wales and, for forging links with the State University of New York, a Doctorate in Fine Arts from that institution. He was a Fellow of the Royal Society of Arts, of Trinity College, Carmarthen, of the London College of Music, and of the Guildhall School of Music and Drama

The last ten years of his life were beset by poor health, which he faced with stoicism and humour, and by major operations which confined him to a wheelchair. But his genial spirit and interest in the affairs of others, particularly those younger people making their names in a Wales where theatre and television had been transformed since his retirement in 1984, remained undiminished. He was pleased to learn, shortly before his death, that the Old College is to be renamed the Raymond Edwards Building and the Mews, part of the new complex opened this year, after Sir Anthony Hopkins.

Thomas Raymond Edwards, drama teacher: born Rhosllannerchrugog, Denbighshire 15 April 1919; Principal, Welsh College of Music and Drama 1959-84; OBE 1977; married 1952 June Griffiths (one daughter); died Cardiff 18 June 1999.

The Independent (24 June 1999)

Alex Gordon

Architect of many public buildings in Wales

Alex Gordon was one of the most distinguished Welsh architects of the post-war period. In a country then with only a few modern buildings of distinction, he began his career in 1948 after training at the Welsh School of Architecture in Cardiff and soon became known for the progressive style of his work. He was not particularly interested in developing a native version of contemporary architecture, nor in emulating the achievements of Scandinavian architects, and yet his buildings have a distinctive character which chimes nicely with the sites they occupy, so that they take their place unobtrusively in the urban landscape of Wales.

One of Alex Gordon's most typical and visually satisfying creations is the Music Building at the University College, Cardiff, put up in 1971 on the northern perimeter of Cathays Park, still one of the finest civic centres in Britain. It is in striking contrast to its red-brick neighbours, and acts as a foil to the Portland Stone grandeur of the Victorian and Edwardian buildings of the park. But the large sculpture by Barbara Hepworth which stands outside attracts far more attention.

The same blend of materials and concern for meticulous detail can be seen in the Students' Union and the nearby Sherman Theatre, which Alex Gordon also designed. Completed in 1973, the union faces W.D. Caröe's splendid Great Court across Park Place and consists of a series of tiered balconies which take in, at the rear, the railway line which runs under the building. The theatre, in dark brown brick, seems to have no windows, but inside it is surprisingly roomy and airy.

Less pleasing perhaps, except to the taste of the ultra-modernist, is the headquarters of what was once the Wales Gas Board (and now British Gas) in Churchill Way in central Cardiff, which Alex Gordon erected on an extremely cramped site in 1968. This office tower is an eight-storey glass box raised on stilts over a more traditional base at street level. Yet it offended no one and became something of a cherished landmark in a district which has few other points of reference, being largely taken up by terraces of solicitors' and estate agents' offices. Similarly, his twelve-storey Post Office Telephone Exchange in Swansea, though it dwarfs the castle, forms an imposing feature which is an attractive addition to the architecture of a city centre virtually destroyed by the Luftwaffe in 1941.

The only unpopular building designed by Alex Gordon is the five-storey rectangle situated behind the main block of what was once the Welsh Office in Cardiff. Overhanging massively at its tip and set on a steeply sloping plinth, it was described in the *Architects' Journal* as "a symbol of closed inaccessible government" which conveyed an impression of "bureaucracy under siege". The entire complex became part of the National Assembly earlier this year and can thus expect a quite different role from now on as an annexe of the new "open government" of Wales.

It seems that when Alex Gordon came to design the Princess of Wales Hospital in Bridgend in 1981, he tried to make institutional architecture less formidable, choosing to build a series of pavilions under pitched roofs. The same attempt to soften the more brutal effects of modern architecural styles is to be seen in Transport House, the offices of the Transport and General Workers' Union at the junction of Cathedral Road and Cowbridge Road in Cardiff.

The most impressive of all Alex Gordon's buildings is perhaps the Crown Court in St Helen's Road, opposite the Guildhall in Swansea. Formal, symmetrical and neoclassical, it has deep eaves supported on slender pillars, a broad, canted window bay over the cavernous entrance and a flight of wide steps. It is described in John Newman's *The Buildings of Wales: Glamorgan* (1995) as "an essay in mannerist wit" in which the faceted shapes are used to confound expectations: the angles of the building are chamfered back and the oriel windows of the courtrooms at first-floor level are blind where they project but glazed where they recede. This is a building meant to inspire respect for the law but it also manages to intrigue the informed eye.

On a more intimate, almost domestic, scale is Alex Gordon's Methodist chapel in Cyncoed, a leafy suburb of north Cardiff, again a box of glass and buff-coloured brick but none the less touching in its simplicity and elegance. This is the building which I always think is most like the man who designed it – modest, well- mannered and yet sure of itself and quietly assertive in its marrying of the devotional and the functional. His staff houses at Atlantic College at St Donat's in the Vale of Glamorgan, built with flat roofs and black brick and weatherboarding, and his St David's Lutheran Church in Fairwater, on the north-western side of Cardiff, also have this quality.

Born in Ayr in 1917, Alex Gordon was brought up in Swansea and educated at the town's Grammar school, where he worked with Dylan Thomas on the school magazine. In 1935 he was articled to the Swansea Borough Architect and studied part-time to pass the RIBA Intermediate Examination as an external candidate. While still a student he won the Lord Mayor's competition for the design of Cardiff's street decorations in the year of the Coronation.

After war service with the Royal Engineers, during which he served in Northern Ireland and Palestine, he studied at the Welsh School of Architecture in Cardiff and, in 1948, became a partner of T. Alwyn Lloyd, one of only two practitioners who, before the war, had made important contributions to the development of thinking about the function of architecture in Wales.

Lloyd's small-scale buildings reflected his deep feeling for place, in both historical and environmental terms, as in the Garden Villages for which he was responsible in various parts of Wales. Something of Lloyd's feel for interior design and his attention to detail was passed on to his junior partner. Initially the practice worked on housing schemes for local authorities and the Forestry Commission, but Gordon's appointment as consultant architect to the Wales Gas Board in 1949 was to provide a secure base for work in the future.

After Lloyd's death in 1960, Alex Gordon set up his own firm, Alex Gordon and Partners, of which he was head until his retirement in 1982 and then consultant until 1988. Before the onset of the Parkinson's disease and blindness which afflicted him in his last years, he was active on behalf of professional bodies both at home and abroad. He was a member of the Design Council, the British Council, the Arts Council, the Royal Fine Art Commission and the University Grants Committee, and President of the Royal Institute of British Architects from 1971 to 1973. He was a corresponding member of the Society of Mexican Architects and the Federation of Danish Architects, and served as President of the Comité de Liaison des Architectes du Marché Commun, and as a member of many consultative bodies. He was an honorary member of the Bund Deutscher Architecten and a Fellow of the American Institute of Architects. The University of Wales awarded him an honorary LLD in 1972.

One of the projects which gave Alex Gordon particular satisfaction was the completion by his old firm in 1993 of the final phase of the west wing of the National Museum of Wales, which now houses a magnificent gallery of modern art. He was passionately interested in painting and sculpture and took great pleasure in knowing that buildings of this calibre were at last possible in Wales. His private collection of modern art, which included works by Ben Nicholson, John Piper and Marc Chagall, was given to the Glynn Vivian Gallery in Swansea.

Alex Gordon was unmarried and lived for many years at Llanblethian in the Vale of Glamorgan.

Alexander John Gordon, architect: born Ayr 25 February 1917; senior partner; Alex Gordon and Partners 1960-82; FRIBA 1962, PRIBA 1971-73; OBE 1967, CBE 1974; Kt 1988; died Saint Hilary, Vale of Glamorgan 23 July 1999.

The Independent (28 July 1999)

Ernest Zobole

Painter of his native Rhondda Valley

Ernest Zobole was a painter who, despite his untypical surname, was firmly rooted in industrial South Wales, more specifically the Rhondda Valley, formerly one of the great coal-bearing districts of Britain and still visually spectacular in its juxtaposition of densely populated townships and, on the hills between, stretches of wild moorland which not even afforestation has spoiled.

He painted the bustling streets of Rhondda Fawr (to distinguish it from the Rhondda Fach, the lesser valley which joins it at Porth), the bridges over the Stygian-black river, the railway with its level-crossings, the buses and lorries, the terraces and the people for whom they are the main conduits of life up and down the narrow Valley ending at Pontypridd. This "marvellous place" was not so much documented or commented upon in his paintings as internalised by an artist who considered himself part of the landscape.

Unlike many Welsh artists who soon leave their native patch for the metropolis, whether Cardiff or London, Erni Zobole spent most of his life in the Valley, hardly ever moving more than a few miles from Ystrad, the village where he was born in 1927, the year after the General Strike in which the militant miners of Rhondda played a leading part. Both his parents were Italians who had emigrated to Wales in 1910. His father worked above ground at the local pit and his mother kept a small shop in the village; for years, one of the boy's early paintings was proudly displayed above the counter.

The Zoboles were thus among the numerous Italians – generically known as Bracchis after the pioneers of the trade, though more likely to be Bernis, Severinis, Fulgonis, Sidolis, Marenghis or Castagnettis – who became part of the social fabric of South Wales at a critical time in its history. Among other distinguished Welsh painters of Italian extraction are Andrew Vicari and David Carpanini, while the actor Victor Spinetti comes from the same background.

These families became well integrated and popular among the convivial Welsh who patronised their cafés, chip-shops and ice-cream parlours. It was as if something in the Italian character chimed with that of their hosts; not for nothing have the Welsh been called

"Mediterraneans in the rain". When, in July 1940, the *Arandora Star*, a boat in which hundreds of "enemy aliens" were being deported back to Italy, was sunk by a German torpedo off the north-west coast of Ireland, with the loss of 486 lives, many from South Wales, sympathy was widespread and the outcry heartfelt.

The young Erni, who was brought up bilingual in English and Italian, attended the Grammar School at Porth and, after serving with the British army in Palestine and Egypt, married his childhood sweetheart and then spent five years training at Cardiff College of Art. He was an early admirer of Chagall, particularly his Surreal sense of perspective in which, for example, houses are seen from several viewpoints in the same picture and figures, out of scale, often appear larger than the buildings over which they float.

Many of his canvases have a dreamlike, lyrical, phantasmagorical quality, with the frequent use of a translucent blue to suggest an aesthetic space contained within the actual confines of the Valley, while at the same time taking in panoramas which, strictly speaking, must have been beyond the artist's field of vision.

"There is a real space," he told Tony Curtis in a rare interview published in *Welsh Painters Talking* in 1997, "and the space in a painting." In many of his canvases it is as if he is trying to make contact with everything – the moon, the hills, the wet road, the street-lamps, the houses, the figure hurrying through the rain – and to be everywhere at the same time, not missing anything. There is, too, a hint at a personal iconography which, given the painter's reluctance to explain his work, whether on film or for publication, awaits its interpreter.

The daily train-journey to and from Cardiff which in the post-war years took two hours, proved a splendid opportunity for Erni Zobole to discuss art with his companions – Charles Burton, Glyn Morgan, Nigel Flower, David Mainwaring and Robert Thomas, all Rhondda men who got on at stations down the line. The six students would spread their work over the seats to give the impression that their compartment was full and so have it for their own boisterous arguments. The Rhondda Group was never a school and published no manifesto, but these painters were to help create an awareness of industrial landscapes as a fit subject for Welsh art.

The work they produced over the next decade, although social in its concerns, reflected their growing interest in abstraction which tended to over-ride the descriptive element the subject being retained only when it served as a point of entry into a satisfying pictorial form and as an additional means of communication with the viewer. Erni Zobole, in particular, was determined "to overthrow the tyranny of perspective" and to explore "other worlds". As a consequence, the Welsh began to see the mining valleys, as the poet Idris Davies put it, "more beautiful than we ever saw them with our eyes".

The main influence on Erni Zobole at this time was Heinz Koppel, a German expatriate with a studio at Dowlais in the nearby valley of the Taff. It was Koppel's devotion to his painting and the Germanic harshness and barbaric intensity of his work, something akin to Mexican art, which convinced him that he wanted to be a professional painter. He was encouraged in this ambition by David Tinker, Eric Malthouse and Arthur Giardelli, with whom he formed the 56 Group with a view to promoting contemporary Welsh art by means of exhibitions both at home and abroad.

But alas in those days, as now, there were few opportunities in Wales for young men intent on earning a living with their brush and, like so many, he took up teaching. His first post as an art teacher was at Llangefni in Anglesey, where he stayed from 1953 to 1957. It proved a barren time for the painter: he found the island flat, featureless, desolate, "all wind and chapel", and the largely unpopulated mountains of Snowdonia, so often painted since the time of Richard Wilson, held little appeal for him; his lack of Welsh, moreover, made it difficult for him to participate in the life of the community.

Above all, he was homesick for the teeming valleys of South Wales, still a vibrant working-class society despite the rundown of the mines, to which he now returned to take up an appointment at a Church in Wales school in Aberdare; two years later he moved even closer to home, to the County Secondary School at Treorchy in the Rhondda. "When I did return," he said, "it was like getting back into a warm bed."

In 1963 he began teaching at Newport College of Art, where he remained until his retirement. Although the college was going through a period of rapid change in which the emphasis on traditional skills was fast giving way to the claims of photography and film, he held fast to his conviction that creativity found its highest expression in painting. He was deeply suspicious, too, that courses now had to be sanctioned by civil servants who did not know much about art, if the college was to attract government funding.

It was a relief when in 1984, on taking early retirement, it became possible for him to spend the rest of his painting life in the former Victorian vicarage which was his last home, just under the Penrhys housing estate, notorious as one of the most socially deprived places in South Wales, but from which – on days without cloud or rain – there are breathtaking views down the Valley.

A modest, private man, not easily deflected from his daily stint at the easel and wryly amused by what his neighbours thought of his occupation, he worked slowly and painstakingly, claiming that he was not particularly interested in aesthetic theory and giving the impression that he was loth to talk much about his own work. "Of course it is possible to have all sorts of theories and ideas," he was quoted as saying in the catalogue to the 1963 exhibition which he shared with Brenda Chamberlain, "but what it comes to in the end is to use paint rather than words – to do your talking or thinking with your medium. The only thing with which you should concern yourself when working is the craft of making a picture. Things have to fit into a picture to remake a world."

Ernest Zobole, painter and teacher: born Ystrad Rhondda, Glamorgan 25 April 1927; Lecturer, Newport College of Art, 1963-84; married 1950 Christine Baker (died 1997; one son, one daughter); died Llwynypia, Rhondda Cynon Taff 27 November 1999.

The Independent (7 December 1999)

Gwyn Jones

Editor, writer and Viking scholar

Gwyn Jones, the writer and Viking scholar, sometimes gave the impression that, had he not been a Welshman, he might have been a character out of the Icelandic sagas to which he had devoted so much of his academic career – Eirik the Red, perhaps, who may have discovered Greenland, or the legendary Olav Tryggvason, or Snorri Sturluson, the chronicler of the Kings of Norway, or any other Norseman who had lived up to the Heroic ideal. For him, physical prowess, unremitting effort, honourable conduct, a dignified manner, a command of lofty language, and courage in adversity were the manly attributes he most admired, and he had them in abundance.

At the University College of Wales, Aberystwyth, in the 1950s, he struck awe in the hearts of his students by his exegesis of *Beowulf*, in which he seemed to exult as if he were personally involved in the blood-curdling narrative. In those days, Anglo-Saxon was an integral part of most English syllabuses, but at Aberystwyth it was the professor's own specialism and, as some of us were dismayed to discover, the paper had to be passed with flying colours in the first year as a precondition of entry to the Honours class; success at the second attempt was deemed to be not good enough, however much of Henry Sweet's *Reader* had been learned by rote. Gwyn Jones applied this rule with an iron grip and unflinching eye that redirected the aspirations of many an undergraduate, myself included. Even so, I can still recite "Othere told his lord Kind Alfred that he of all Norwegians dwelt the furthest north... " and conjugate a number of Old English verbs, though that Henry Higgins in Shaw's *Pygmalion* was partly based on Henry Sweet I was left to discover for myself years later.

His own prodigious energies went into the translation and study of Nordic literature in its early phases. For the American-Scandinavian Foundation he translated *Four Icelandic Sagas* (1935), the subject of his MA thesis, and *The Vatndalers' Saga* (1944); they were followed by *Egil's Saga* (1960), *Eirik the Red and Other Icelandic Sagas* (1961) and *The Norse Atlantic Saga* (1964). Two more of his major works were *A History of the Vikings* (1968) and *Kings, Beasts and Heroes*

(1972); the first of these is the standard history in English and the second a richly allusive study of *Beowulf*, the Welsh *Cullhwch ac Olwen*, and the Norse *King Hrolf's Saga*. It was in recognition of his eminence as a scholar of the Viking world that the President of Iceland, in 1963, presented Gwyn Jones with the Commander's Cross of the Order of the Falcon, an honour of which he was inordinately proud.

In a preface to the Folio Society edition of Gwyn Jones's *History of the Vikings*, published in 1995, Magnus Magnusson described him as "the most gallant of war-horses, the most generous of friends" and his book as "a formidable feat of eclectic scholarship" which did much to rehabilitate the Vikings as a subject for academic research, by highlighting the achievements of the Viking Age in terms of Scandinavian art and commerce – the Vikings as traders rather than raiders. Gwyn Jones was wont to take such huge compliments in his stride, quoting the advice given to him as a young man by Sigurdur Nordal, the doyen of Icelandic scholars: "It is very pleasant to be a little drunk, on a little pony, in a little rain."

Gwyn Jones was born in 1907 at New Tredegar in Monmouthshire and brought up in nearby Blackwood, the son of a collier and a midwife, and educated at Tredegar County School and the University College, Cardiff. After spending six years as an English teacher at schools in Wigan and Manchester, he returned to Wales in 1935 as a lecturer at his old college. In the same year he published his first novel, *Richard Savage*, an endlessly inventive evocation of life in Augustan England.

Three very different novels followed in quick succession: *Times Like These* (1936), *The Nine Days' Wonder* (1937) and *Garland of Bays* (1938). The first of these is a moving account of family life in South Wales during the General Strike of 1926, the second a tale of low life set near Manchester and the last an historical novel about the Elizabethan dramatist Robert Greene.

In 1939, prompted by the gathering strength of Welsh writing in English, Gwyn Jones founded *The Welsh Review*, editing it (with an interregnum during the Second World War) until 1946. The magazine provided a much-needed forum for the discussion of Welsh affairs in English and attracted, besides most of the younger Welsh writers of the day, such as Alun Lewis, contributions from T.S. Eliot, H.E. Bates, J.R.R Tolkien and A.L. Rowse.

In his many editorials and articles, Gwyn Jones did much to define Anglo-Welsh literature at a crucial point in its development, and was later to edit *The Oxford Book of Welsh Verse in English* (1977) and other influential anthologies. Even so, he steadfastly refused to have the work of Welsh writers taught in his own department; nor did he ever pay much attention to those who had made their reputations after what he considered to be the heyday of Anglo-Welsh writing in the 1930s and 1940s. He stuck doggedly to this view even after the emergence of a new generation of writers in the 1960s and 1970s; many found this disappointing in a man who was something of a hero.

He nevertheless continued to make distinguished contributions to the canon of Anglo-Welsh literature with his novels and collections of short stories; these included *The Buttercup Field* (1945), *The Flowers beneath the Scythe* (1952), *Shepherd's Hey* (1953) and *The Walk Home* (1962). His *Selected Short Stories* were published by Oxford University Press in 1974, a round-up of his miscellaneous writings on English, Welsh and Nordic subjects appeared as *Background to Dylan Thomas and Other Explorations* in 1992, and his *Collected Stories* were published in 1997. His lectures, *The First Forty Years* (1957), *Being and Belonging* (1977), and *Babel and the Dragon's Tongue* (1981), are among the most perceptive and seminal statements about Anglo-Welsh literature ever published.

The major achievement of Gwyn Jones's years at Aberystwyth (1940-64) was his collaboration with Thomas Jones, the college's Professor of Welsh, in the translation of *The Mabinogion*, the collection of tales which was the prose masterpiece of medieval Wales. This work, which was first published in a fine limited edition by the Golden Cockerel Press in 1948 and by Dent in Everyman's Library in the year following, not only managed to satisfy scholars in the Welsh departments of the university but also delighted a wider readership with its subtle rendering of the original and the unfailing elegance of its style. It was this translation, still regarded as definitive, which was largely responsible for re-awakening world-wide interest in these tales.

Gwyn Jones served as Chairman of the Welsh Committee of the Arts Council of Great Britain from 1957 to 1967. Many of the meetings of its Drama Panel were taken up with wrangling over whether Wales should have a National Theatre. The chairman was an implacable opponent of the idea and as a left-winger with little spoken Welsh of his own, found himself in disagreement with Saunders Lewis, the great Welsh-language dramatist, on this as on just about every other issue concerning the cultural life of Wales.

Years before, Gwyn Jones had been the anonymous author of a particularly piquant profile of the playwright which had appeared in *The Welsh Review*. In the end the Nationalist camp was defeated, largely as a result of Gwyn's intransigence. Saunders Lewis was later to write in the foreword to one of his plays that "the theatre arts in Wales would have greatly benefited if the Welsh Committee of the Arts Council had not existed" during the years of Gwyn Jones's chairmanship.

I myself had first-hand experience of Gwyn's strongly held views on two occasions. Although he had appointed me as the Arts Council's Literature Director in 1967, he made it clear that no money was to go directly into the pockets of writers: they would have to write without subsidy from the public purse, as he and his generation had done. When the minutes of the first meeting of the Literature Panel suggested a new policy of bursaries for writers, they were promptly referred back for reconsideration and the scheme had to wait until after his departure. Ever after, he steadfastly refrained from discussing Arts Council matters with me and kept his distance from all its activities.

Ten years later, Gwyn Jones was the first chairman of the editorial board responsible for overseeing the compilation of *The Oxford Companion to the Literature of Wales*, of which I was editor. The chairman's view was made clear from the outset: in this reference book there were to be no entries for living writers because, he said, they were only "minnows" in comparison with the illustrious dead; again we had to wait a while before a different counsel prevailed. Despite these contretemps, we kept in touch for the rest of his life and he sent me an affectionately inscribed copy of all his books, and a poem at Christmas.

After the death of Thomas Jones in 1972, and that of Gwyn Jones's first wife, Alice, in 1979, Gwyn married Mair, the widow of his former colleague, and they made their new home at Aberystwyth. She brought a vivacity to their marriage which complemented the unruffled Viking manner with which Gwyn usually faced both triumph and calamity alike, serving as his amanuensis during his last years when he was afflicted by failing eyesight and fading physical strength. His last act of generosity was to present his collection of rare books to the National Library of Wales.

Gwyn Jones, writer and scholar: born New Tredegar, Monmouthshire 24 May 1907; Professor of English Language and Literature, University College of Wales, Aberystwyth, 1940-64, Fellow 1987; Chairman, Welsh Committee of the Arts Council of Great Britain 1957-67; Professor of English Language and Literature, University College, Cardiff, 1964-75, Fellow 1980; CBE 1965; married 1928 Alice Rees (died 1979), 1979 Mair Jones (two stepdaughters); died Aberystwyth, Cardiganshire 6 December 1999.

The Independent (10 December 1999)

Tudor David

Editor, journalist and leading figure among the London Welsh

As journalist, editor, impresario and publisher, Tudor David played a prominent part in the life of the London Welsh for more than thirty years, never missing an opportunity to promote the interests of Wales not only among expatriates but wherever he found a sympathetic ear in the wider world. Most of his working life was spent in London and, conscious of the incongruity of his position, he often turned a sardonic eye on the activities of what he once called "the long-distance patriots" of whom he was such a distinguished example. Nor did he mind having his leg pulled by the more zealous among his compatriots back home.

He was born in 1921 in Barry, the port and seaside resort near Cardiff, and educated at Barry Grammar School, then one of the best in Wales. Unusually for the time and place, his first language was Welsh, which he wrote in later life with some panache. He left Wales for Manchester University where he took a degree in Geography, and never lived in his homeland again, but kept up his Welsh by frequent visits, particularly to the National Eisteddfod every summer.

One of his contacts with Welsh life in London was through the Honourable Society of Cymmrodorion, perhaps the most pinstriped of all the expatriate societies, in whose affairs he played a modest part. But, mild-mannered though he was, he preferred the company of journos and politicos, particularly the less abstemious of his compatriots on visits to London.

After service with the RAF from 1942 to 1947, in which he achieved the rank of Squadron Leader, he became an extramural lecturer for Newcastle University and then a youth employment officer in Scunthorpe.

His first publication, *Scunthorpe and its Families* (1954), announced his interest in local history, which he subsequently applied to Wales and the Isle of Dogs, where he lived for many years. A lifelong member of the Labour Party, he also wrote *Defence and Disarmament* (1959), a contribution to the current debate about the deployment and use of nuclear arms.

It was in the field of education that he was to make his most permanent mark. Appointed assistant editor of Longman's magazine

Education in 1955, he moved to *The Teacher*, the journal of the NUT, ten years later, then returned to *Education* as managing editor, where he remained for another seventeen years. As a journalist he had a nicely mischievous streak: it was once said of him that, as a regular but anonymous obituarist for *The Daily Telegraph*, he could always be counted on to make the ears of even the dead start to burn.

As an editor he was a stickler for deadlines and accuracy, and always kept an eye on circulation, mixing news, record and commentary to widen his journal's appeal. He also gave more than usual space to the discussion of specifically Welsh issues and even published articles in Welsh by leading educationists, mostly on subjects like bilingualism and the growth of Welsh-medium schools. He wrote three pamphlets on aspects of education, namely *Church and School* (1963), *Perspectives in Geographical Education* (1973) and *Education: the wasted years 1973-86* (1988).

On becoming editor in 1959 of *Y Ddinas*, the venerable journal of the London Welsh Association, whose title he changed to *The London Welshman*, Tudor David turned it into a lively monthly, broadening its scope to include not only accounts of the county societies, chapels and social events of which London Welsh life had always largely consisted, but also articles about the cultural and political life of Wales itself. Suddenly, during the 1960s when there was an upsurge in national feeling and new institutions such as the Welsh Office were being created, it became required reading for all activists.

Many of us disapproved of the London Welsh Association, believing the best place for patriotic Welsh people was at home, there being so much to do in Wales, and some were faintly jealous of what seemed to be the hectic social life centred in the Association's headquarters in the Gray's Inn Road, but we were willing to make an exception of Tudor David, who brought tone and dignity into what might otherwise have been mere hedonistic junketing and jingoistic flag-waving.

One of his magazine's most attractive features was the space it gave to writers, especially those poets who were to contribute to "the second flowering of Anglo-Welsh poetry" after the launch of *Poetry Wales* in 1965. Some, such as John Tripp, Sally Roberts, Tom Earley and Bryn Griffiths, were domiciled in London, where they had come together in a loose group known as the Guild of Welsh Writers. Out of the excitement of those days, encouraged by Tudor in his magazine, grew the first moves to establish a national society of English-language writers in Wales, which eventually resulted in the creation, in Cardiff, of their own section of the Welsh Academy in 1968.

Most of those writers subsequently returned to Wales, but by now Tudor was unable or unwilling to leave London, inured as he was to what Dylan Thomas had once called "the capital punishment". After he left the editorial chair in 1973 *The London Welshman* reverted to being what the Nationalist poet Harri Webb, an associate of Tudor's, dismissed with typical acerbity as "the parish magazine of Tregaron-on-Thames".

Having never lost touch with the reality of his home country, Tudor David maintained his interest in literary journalism by transferring his allegiance to *Planet: the Welsh Internationalist*, a bi-monthly founded in Aberystwyth by his friend Ned Thomas, the former editor of *Angliya*, the British government's Russian-language magazine; he served on its editorial board for several years.

In his retirement he ran *The Islander*, the community freesheet of the Isle of Dogs, published *The Journal of Oil and Gas Finance and Accounting* and, in his last two years, managed Langham Legal Publishing with his son, Martyn, a lawyer. His daughter Glenwyn Benson, is a former editor of *Panorama* and now Head of Science at the BBC.

Tudor David, journalist: born Barry, Glamorgan 25 April 1921; Extramural Lecturer, Newcastle University 1947-49; Careers Officer, Lincolnshire Education Authority 1950-55; Assistant Editor, Education 1955-65, Managing Editor 1969-86; Editor, The London Welshman 1959-73; Editor, The Teacher 1965-69; publisher, Langham Legal Publishing 1998-2000; OBE 1984; married 1944 Nancy Ramsay (died 1984; one son, one daughter), 1987 Margaret Dix; died London 21 February 2000.

The Independent (26 February 2000)

R.M. Lockley

Naturalist and writer about islands

The prolific author R.M. Lockley was one of the founding fathers of the conservation movement but none of his books dealing with environmental issues met with as much success as his most influential work, *The Private Life of the Rabbit* (1965), on which Richard Adams drew when writing *Watership Down* (1972).

The book was the result of an intensive four-year scientific study of rabbit behaviour, carried out at Orielton, a large estate near Milford Haven in Pembrokeshire, which he undertook for British Nature Conservancy during the 1950s. Like all his books, it sparkles with his enthusiasm for wildlife and his lyrical sense of wonder at the natural world, but without anthropomorphism or the slightest sentimentality. Talking rabbits, badgers and otters he left to his friend Adams. His years at Orielton were crucial to his development as a naturalist and he repaid his debt to the old house, the seat of the Owen family from Norman to Victorian times, in a fine tribute, *Orielton*, published in 1977. The estate was bought for use as an educational centre by the Field Studies Council.

But if R.M. Lockley had a keen and informed eye for the presence of the past, it was his passion for islands that was the *idée fixe* of his long life and distinguished career and it was as the author of books about islands, some forty in all, that he made his reputation as a writer.

Ronald Mathias Lockley was born in Cardiff in 1903 and brought up in the northern suburb of Whitchurch, where his mother supported herself and her six children by running a boarding school. His father, a railway manager, was often away from home and the delicate boy grew up to be solitary, studious and resourceful.

His discovery of flora and fauna began while recovering from appendicitis in the summer of 1914: he made a detailed inventory of the garden's wildlife. While still at Cardiff High School, and having read Thoreau's *Walden*, he spent his weekends and summer holidays living rough in the woods and wetlands adjoining the old Glamorgan canal which ran near his home, building bivouacs and cooking his own food as best he could.

These early experiences were described in his book *The Way to an*

Island (1941), reprinted as *Myself When Young: the making of a naturalist* in 1979. The area is now managed by the City Council as a nature reserve and a hide for the observation of the wild birds attracted to this riparian spot has been named after Lockley. The British Trust for Conservation Volunteers has an office at nearby Forest Farm.

After leaving school, R.M. Lockley worked with his sister on a poultry farm near St Mellons, on the eastern outskirts of Cardiff, but by then his passion for islands had taken firm hold. In 1926, with his first wife Doris, he took a twenty-one-year lease of Skokholm, an island of about 240 acres some four miles off the western tip of Pembrokeshire, which was inhabited only by rabbits and seabirds; the annual rent was £26.

His intention was to be self-sufficient, and he resolved to raise chinchillas, since they had no natural enemies on the island. He soon abandoned this idea, however, because he found the rabbits too difficult to handle. Life on Skokholm was nothing if not Spartan and his work was cut out just staying alive. There was no fresh water and he relied for fuel and building materials on timber washed up on the beach. The renovated barn in which he lived and the shelter he put up at Martins Haven, known rather grandly as Lockley Lodge, which he used when the weather prevented him from crossing to Skokholm, are still there, testimony to the resilience and ingenuity of the island's most famous resident.

Unperturbed by his failure to breed chinchillas, he began to study the migratory birds of Skokholm – puffins, razor-bills and Manx shearwaters – setting up Britain's first observatory on the island in 1933. He described his research in several books, including *Dream Island* (1930), *Island Days* (1934) and *I Know an Island* (1938), and published what is still an authoritative study of the species, *Shearwaters* (1942).

R.M. Lockley's years in Pembrokeshire brought him to the notice of a wider circle of conservationists and naturalists, among them Peter Scott and Julian Huxley, founder of the World Wildlife Fund. During the Second World War, when Skokholm was taken over by the Army, he returned to farming on the mainland, at Dinas Cross. A less rigorous way of life now allowed him to devote his prodigious energies to organising the conservationist lobby in the county.

After the war he played a leading role in the affairs of the

Pembrokeshire Coast National Park, was one of the founders of the Wildlife Trust for West Wales, edited *Nature in Wales*, and served as a member of the Council of the Royal Society for the Protection of Birds. It was he who was instrumental in mapping out the coastal footpath which attracts thousands of visitors to Pembrokeshire every year.

As chairman of the West Wales Field Society, he led a campaign against the building of the oil refinery at Milford Haven on the grounds that it threatened the special status of the county's coast and its rich wildlife, but the Society's objections cut no ice and the complex was not only built but, a few years later, substantially extended.

His belief that successive British governments were not sufficiently aware of the threat to the landscape from industrial development led, in part, to his decision to emigrate to New Zealand in 1970. He settled, with his third wife, Jean, at Te Puke on North Island, not far from the Bay of Bounty.

There he continued to write, mostly about islands and birds, but also novels, and to travel among the islands of Polynesia and in the Antarctic. Among his last books were a volume of autobiography *The House above the Sea* (1980), *Voyage through the Antarctic* (with Richard Adams, 1982) and *Flight of the Storm Petrel* (1983).

Towards the end of his life we corresponded from time to time. Since I happen to live in the very road where his mother kept her school and often walk through the woods which he described so lovingly in *The Way to an Island*, I was able to keep him up to date about the area. Now that the mines further up the valley have closed, the river Taff between Whitchurch and Radyr is turning green once more and becoming the haunt of eel, kingfisher, otter cormorant, moorhen, badger and hawk. This news seemed to give him immense pleasure and, in his letters, he was a boy again.

Ronald Mathias Lockley, naturalist, writer and conservationist: born Cardiff 8 November 1903; married first Doris Shetland (one daughter; marriage dissolved), second Jean Stocker (two sons; marriage dissolved), third Jean St Lawrence (deceased); died Auckland 12 April 2000.

The Independent (13 April 2000)

David Tinker

Abstract painter and founder-member of the 56 Group

David Tinker was a founder member of the 56 Group, a loose asso-ciation of artists whose work ushered in a new phase of painting in Wales at a moment when the realistic depiction of the urban scene was beginning to appear old hat to a new generation more open to the theories and practices of the international art world.

The emerging "Welsh school" of painters in the period after the Second World War had up to then been dominated by men like Will Roberts and Josef Herman, the Polish refugee who painted miners in a naturalistic style, and by others inspired by the landscape of indus-trial South Wales, often sentimentally. The only living Welsh abstract painter of international repute was Ceri Richards.

With Eric Malthouse and Michael Edmonds, like him teachers of art, David Tinker brought together a small band of younger men which took its name from the year of its formation. They were joined by other painters, including some of those who had contributed to the previous phase of painting in Wales, but more significantly by Arthur Giardelli and Robert Hunter, who shared their views. This move was in the heroic tradition of European painting and unique in the history of art in Wales.

Although they were few in number, had no common aesthetics or manifesto, and rarely met, these painters set out to make opportuni-ties for the exhibition of their work, which was influenced by Abstract Expressionism, a trend then fashionable among the avant-garde of London, Paris and New York. Unfortunately, they had but little influence on the art establishment in Wales at first, and their inaugural exhibition had to be held in Worcester.

Shortly after the group's inception, however, its members were encouraged by the opening in Cardiff of the Howard Roberts Gallery, which soon began to show their work, albeit to a largely indifferent, or at best suspicious, public. The art historian Eric Rowan has suggested that the reason why they caused little stir was that their challenge to the art establishment was orderly and polite, although some of their work was so provocative that it was van-dalised.

Their first major exhibition of painting and sculpture, consisting of the work of a dozen artists, was held at the National Museum of Wales early in 1960 and opened by Lady Megan Lloyd George. David had one-man exhibitions at the Prospect Gallery in 1956, at the Howard Roberts in 1961, and at the Woodstock in the same year.

Such was the group's success, at least among the *cognoscenti*, that the burgeoning National School of Welsh Painting, which had taken many years to emerge, was rapidly sidelined in the rush to catch up with metropolitan trends. Many, though not all, Welsh painters abandoned their painterly skills and began imitating the styles of the international avant-garde. As a consequence, the very notion of an art related to the particular experience of life in Wales became highly unfashionable and was even denigrated by English incomers as "provincialism". During the 1960s, as the art critic Peter Lord has argued, a new cultural imperialism, masquerading as "internationalism", was encouraged by the art colleges, the Arts Council, the galleries, and the National Museum of Wales in particular.

Like most of the 56 Group's members, David Tinker was an incomer to Wales, an Englishman who had been teaching at the Cardiff College of Art since 1949. Born of Irish stock in the London suburb of Charlton and brought up in Gillingham, Kent, he had been educated at schools in Portsmouth, Canterbury and Rochester. His school days were unhappy: a shy boy, he had been bullied by teachers and, like Poil de Carrotte, mocked by fellow-pupils on account of his mop of bright orange-red hair; in later life he sported a beard of the same colour. "School was loathsome to me," he wrote in an essay for my symposium *Artists in Wales* in 1973. "The unhappiest hours of my life were spent under the tyranny of pompous men."

But from his mother, a professional embroideress, and his father who had trained as an artificer in the Navy, he learned how to make things from everyday objects and to decorate them with paints. During a bout of ill-health he was given a set of drawing materials and, while recuperating, began cycling into the Weald of Kent, drawing churches, lych-gates and oast-houses. His art course at Winchester and then Bath was interrupted by service with the Royal Navy Voluntary Reserve, after which he attended the Slade School of Fine Art in London, where he came under the melancholy influence of Euston Road Romanticism.

In Cardiff, as well as teaching, he worked as a stage designer for plays put on under the auspices of the Welsh Committee of the Arts Council and in which the young Siân Phillips took leading roles. In this capacity he came into contact with Saunders Lewis, the distinguished Welsh dramatist, who was to help further his career by writing a glowingly appreciative article about him in *The Anglo-Welsh Review* in 1963. Tinker went on to design sets for the Welsh National Opera Company and was awarded a bursary to tour the main theatre centres of Europe.

By then he had moved to Aberystwyth, where he became Head of the Art Department at the University College of Wales, and in 1973 Director of a new Department of Visual Art. He remained in this post until his retirement in 1988, when he returned to Cardiff, making a home with his new partner, a former student of his, the filmmaker Tracy Spottiswoode, whom he married last month.

In Aberystwyth he designed and executed concrete murals and metal sculptures for the Llandinam and Zoology buildings, large works which recall his earlier stage designs and show him at his boldest. Not for nothing did he admire the frescoes of Piero della Francesca.

He yearned, as an artist, to break out of the small and precious circle in which painters are sometimes trapped by making large-scale works which would be seen by many people, and by selling his sculptures at low cost wherever he was able. "The product of the artist," he wrote, "should be available to all, and that means everyone, not only the mass of people who have never met it before and really don't want to bother with it, but also the people who are interested but cannot afford the present prices."

It was not to be. Such commissions and sales outlets were rare in the Wales of the 1960s and his more typical work consisted of smaller canvases on abstract themes, often treated in the manner of Paul Klee. He had found a new direction to his work in 1956, at the time of the uprising against the Soviet regime in Hungary. "It dawned on me," he wrote in the catalogue to an exhibition of Welsh drawings organised by the Arts Council in 1963, "that here was something which deeply moved me, which I wanted to do something about, but which I could not do using the exterior pictorial facts, so I turned to an abstract means, totally divorced from the events, to express what I felt."

The delicately poetic character of his work after 1964 had to do not so much with exterior reality as with the interior, intuitive responses which he strove to depict in paint. The creative process, for him, began in delight at using the medium spontaneously, and lusciously, only afterwards organising the disparate parts of his picture into a coherent whole, though without too much intellectual analysis. Constantly striving for a unique form of self-expression, his work seemed to be always in a state of flux and moving towards some new discovery about himself.

David Tinker has a secure place in the history of art in Wales during the 20th century, if only for the part he played in founding the 56 Group Wales, as it is now called, and the innovatory individualism of his own work. Although in no wise political and not much interested in his physical environment, he was committed to working in Wales: "I want things to happen here by original thought and enthusiasm," he once remarked, "not by imitation. I want a living culture which faces the present situation in the arts and creates the conditions needed for their flowering."

He put his shoulder to the wheel as champion of innumerable artistic enterprises in Wales, most recently as a leading member of the General Arts Lobby, for which he gave evidence to the National Assembly as part of an attempt to review the policies of the Arts Council. He was also a keen advocate of a Modern Art Gallery for Wales and would have been appalled by the announcement, on the day of his death, that the Centre for the Visual Arts in Cardiff, opened only last year, has foundered and seems likely to close.

David Trevor Tinker, painter and sculptor: born London 4 December 1924; married 1946 Mary Edwards (deceased; two sons, one daughter), 2000 Tracy Spottiswoode; died Cardiff 25 August 2000.

The Independent (31 August 2000)

R.S. Thomas

Poet of 'the untenanted Cross'

If, in the world's eyes, Dylan Thomas is the most famous writer ever to have come out of Wales, his namesake R.S. Thomas is, in the view of many, the better poet. In Wales, where the bard is still held in high esteem, opinion may be divided, but in England and America there is little doubt among contemporary critics that the later Thomas is by far superior. The work of the two Thomases is, of course, very different, so that comparisons are difficult and perhaps unrewarding, but it is a measure of how taste in English poetry has changed since Dylan Thomas's premature death in 1953 that, instead of the logopoeic fireworks of "the windy boy and a bit", the austere and sometimes chilling verse of the Anglican clergyman is now generally preferred.

It is a curious fact that the reputation of R.S. Thomas was largely based, at least in England, on the poems he wrote about the hill country of mid-Wales during the 1940s, despite the fact that by the time he achieved wider recognition – he was awarded the Queen's Gold Medal for Poetry in 1964 – he had virtually given up writing about Iago Prytherch, the archetypal countryman to whom some of his best-known poems are addressed. By then he had turned to more numinous subjects such as the nature of God and religious belief in a scientific and technological age. Nevertheless, even after the appearance of his *Collected Poems 1945-1990* in 1993, his 80th year, metropolitan critics tended to overlook the work of the previous two decades and to concentrate on the earlier poems about "peasant Wales".

If there is still some uncertainty as to R.S. Thomas's stature as a poet, the reason may lie in the circumstances of the poet's upbringing and in his view of the country and people to which he wanted so much to belong. Ronald Thomas (the Stuart was added later in deference to his mother, a possessive and snobbish woman who was incapable of showing him real affection) was born in 1913 in a suburb of north Cardiff. His father was in the Merchant Navy and often away from home and the parents moved from place to place before settling in Holyhead, the ferry-port to Ireland, when their only child was five.

After reading Classics at the University College of North Wales, Bangor, he received his theological training at St Michael's College, Llandaf, in Cardiff, a city he heartily disliked. Ordained deacon in 1936 and priest in the year following, he held two curacies in the Marches, first at Chirk, where he met and married the English painter Mildred (Elsi) Eldridge, and then at Hamner in Flintshire. According to his autobiography *Neb* ("Nobody", 1995), written in Welsh and entirely in the third person, it was while gazing westward that he first found himself attracted to the hills of Wales, to which was linked in his mind the notion that he might be Welsh.

It was at Manafon in Montgomeryshire, where he became rector in 1942, that Thomas began seriously to learn Welsh, taking it to be the *sine qua non* of Welsh nationality, though it was not the language of most of his parishioners, and to write the poems which appeared in his first three booklets, *The Stones of the Field* (1946), *An Acre of Land* (1952) and *The Minister* (1955), and collected in his first substantial volume, *Song at the Year's Turning* (1955), for which John Betjeman wrote a preface. Here Iago Prytherch makes his first appearance, whether named or not, a complex persona who is, by turns, the poet's confidant, spokesman, protagonist and *alter ego*.

Here, too, are the poems such as "The Welsh Hill Country" in which R.S Thomas laments the passing of the harsh upland way of life as the attraction of the towns, depopulation and the influx of English settlers take their toll. Although these, and other poems like "Welsh History", helped fuel the revival of Welsh Nationalist feeling in the 1960s, they were also seen, by no less a literary critic than Dafydd Elis Thomas (the Plaid Cymru peer Lord Elis-Thomas, now Presiding Officer of the National Assembly), as "despair-laden", as in "Welsh Landscape", where the Welsh are castigated as "an impotent people, sick with inbreeding, worrying the carcass of an old song".

Although his cold manner and patrician way of speaking raised a few hackles in Manafon – one parishioner is recorded as saying, "He did toss the hay too high in the cratch for the likes of we" – Thomas took his priestly duties seriously, regularly visiting the old and infirm in their remote farmsteads and trying hard to understand what kept them "yoked to the soil". But for the Welsh people in general, especially those town dwellers who acquiesced in the English scheme of things, he had less sympathy, and often said so.

It may be that in his Nationalist poems R.S. Thomas was engaged in what he called "the winnowing of the people", and such a tactic may have been salutary in the Wales of the 1950s, but it stuck in the craw of those who were working hard to rebuild confidence in the country's cultural and political life in the post-war period. That R.S. Thomas, both by upbringing and by his status as a priest in the Church in Wales, only recently disestablished and still, in the view of many, the Church of England, was alienated from much of Welsh rural life, especially in its overwhelmingly Nonconformist manifestations, was clear from the start. He felt the exclusion keenly, once remarking that an anglicised childhood such as his "prevents one from ever feeling a hundred per cent at home in Welsh Wales".

The quintessential land for which he yearned existed only in his imagination, as he explained in his lecture "Abercuawg", the name of a spot on the Dyfi estuary near Machynlleth mentioned in some ninth-century verses which also inspired that other Thomas, Edward, in his response to "the magic of Wales". Against the ideal of a Christian, rural, civilised, Welsh-speaking Wales, its language and landscape unsullied, its people staunchly committed to upholding the national heritage, the poet measured the reality and found it wanting.

Partly to draw closer to Welsh-speaking Wales – he was fond of drawing the distinction between "Wales", where English is spoken, and "Cymru", the Welsh-speaking heartlands in the north and west of the country, although the distinction is no longer entirely valid – he moved in 1954 to take the living of Eglwys-fach in northern Cardiganshire. The parish, like others where be was to serve, was dominated by English incomers, most of whom R.S. Thomas treated with his famous *saeva indignatio*, but at least it provided him with wild, sparsely populated countryside, ample opportunity to watch wild birds, the red kite in particular; and time enough to write his poetry. He stayed in Cardiganshire until 1967 and to this period belong *Poetry for Supper* (1958), *Tares* (1961), *The Bread of Truth* (1965) and *Pietà* (1966).

His verse now began to take a new direction. While these books contain poems which are fiercely nationalist and, it must be said, sneeringly anti-English and unsparing in their condemnation of the Welsh who fawn on them, they also touch on religious themes such as the figure of Christ and, from an increasingly unorthodox viewpoint, meditate on the crisis of faith in the modern world. One of the recurring images of these poems is the "untenanted Cross", the *deus absconditus*, who in the poem "*Via Negativa*" is "that great absence / In our lives, the empty silence / Within, the place where we go / Seeking, not in hope to / Arrive or find". He lived with this perception and made it the material for some of his most profound poems, but drew no conclusions that were not bleakly disconcerting and over which literary critics of a theological bent continue to argue.

R.S. Thomas's nationalism was grounded, like that of Saunders Lewis, the right-wing Catholic convert who was the first leader of Plaid Cymru, in the Welsh language, which by about 1950 he was able to speak fluently and in which he wrote a good deal of prose, notably the essays translated by Jason Walford Davies and collected in the volume *Autobiographies* (1997). The language evidently meant a great deal to him, so much so that he was ready to dismiss as English those Welsh people (about four-fifths of the population) who did not have it. Even so, it has to be pointed out that one of the inconsistencies about R.S. Thomas was that he and his English wife failed to pass the language on to their only child, Gwydion, born in 1945, and made sure he would not acquire it from the village children by sending him to public school in England.

The precise nature of the poet's political beliefs is even more difficult to summarise. A lifelong pacifist and a member of the Campaign for Nuclear Disarmament, he found his natural home in Plaid Cymru, but he deplored what he considered the party's milk-and-water, punctiliously constitutional tactics and lent moral support to several ultra-Nationalist groups, condoned the burning of English holiday homes in Welsh-speaking areas, and habitually expressed himself in favour of a Welsh Republic. He would have regretted it, he once remarked, if the arson campaign of Meibion Glyndŵr had caused anyone's death, but it was better that one person should die than for the Welsh language to become extinct and it was high time that English tourists and settlers were put off coming to Wales. Even more darkly he wrote in a Welsh essay in 1946, "It is true the Welsh have a good reputation as a democratic people, but in my opinion they show all the weaknesses that belong to democracy." Only a few took him seriously, those literary critics who revered him as a poet preferring to believe that the real man was to be found in his poetry and not his political utterances. Even fewer can speak with authority in this connection for R.S. Thomas, a shy man who did not share the homelier mores of his compatriots and lacked the knack of compromise which would have made a politician of him, zealously guarded his own privacy to a point just short of being a recluse. Although anecdotes about his gruffness towards unwelcome callers are legion, a small band of acolytes can bear first-hand witness to his wry sense of humour and his enjoyment of convivial company.

His poems about Wales began to diminish in number after his move to St Hywyn's, Aberdaron, at the furthermost tip of the Llŷn peninsula and the embarkation point for the bird sanctuary of Ynys Enlli (Bardsey), in 1967. Here he found what he had been searching for: a parish where he could immerse himself in the rich culture of the village and the rugged beauty of its shoreline and hinterland; and, having found it, he no longer needed to write about it. Instead, he resumed the exploration of those religious and philosophical themes which he had read in the work of the Danish philosopher Kierkegaard and which were to become typical of his later writing.

Among the finest of the poems he wrote at this time is "Kneeling" in *Not That He Brought Flowers* (1968), in which, belatedly, he made an uneasy peace with his priestly vocation. He continued in this vein with the publication of the volumes *H'm* (1974), *Laboratories of the Spirit* (1975), *The Way of It* (1977) and *Frequencies* (1978), which contain many poems considered to be among the finest ever written on religious themes in English and comparable with the work of Herbert, Vaughan and Donne.

Having retired from the priesthood in 1978, the poet went to live in a cottage at Y Rhiw, near Pwllheli, where he entered his last prolific phase. There he wrote the poems in *Between Here and Now* (1981), inspired by Impressionist paintings in the Louvre; *Ingrowing Thoughts* (1985), which continued to ask the question "How far is it to God?"; *The Echoes Return Slow* (1988), largely autobiographical and mixing verse with densely woven prose; *Counterpoint* (1990), in which he grappled with his old enemy, the Machine; and *Mass for Hard Times* (1992), dedicated to Elsi, his first wife, who had died in the previous year.

The poignant poems in the last-named volume, and in *No Truce with the Furies* (1995), gave some critics the impression that R.S. Thomas, so long renowned for his obdurate rejection of every solace, might have grown in old age a little more tolerant of human frailty and more receptive to the claims of love, both human and divine; and in his second marriage, to a Canadian woman with whom he moved to live near Holyhead, he seemed to have discovered a new vivacity. Only towards the Welsh, the people for whom he was unable to find compassion, did he not relent.

The appearance of his *Collected Poems* in 1993, the compilation of which he left to his son and which in fact is no more than a selection from some thirty books published over more than half a century, confirmed R.S. Thomas's reputation as a major poet and one of the finest religious poets in the English language.

His last years were spent at various places deep in rural Gwynedd. In 1996, shortly after the publication of a biography by Justin Wintle, with whom he refused to co-operate because the author was English, the poet was nominated by the Welsh Academy, the national association of writers in Wales, for the Nobel Literature Prize. In 1999, although in failing health and having announced that he would write no more verse, he recorded 145 of his poems for Sain Records and accepted an honorary Professorship in the Welsh and English Departments at the University of Wales, Bangor, where an R.S. Thomas Study Centre has been established.

Ronald Thomas (Ronald Stuart Thomas), poet and priest: born Cardiff 29 March 1913; ordained deacon 1936, priest 1937; Rector of Manafon 1942-54; Vicar of Eglwys-fach 1954-67; Vicar of St Hywyn, Aberdaron with St Mary, Bodferin 1967-78; Rector of Rhiw with Llanfaelrhys 1972-78; married 1940 Mildred (Elsi) Eldridge (died 1991; one son), 1996 Betty Vernon; died Pentre-felin, Gwynedd 25 September 2000.

The Independent (27 September 2000)

Alun Talfan Davies

Barrister and prominent figure in the public life of Wales

One of the most distinguished barristers and judges ever to practise and sit in the courts of Wales, Alun Talfan Davies also played a prominent part in the country's public life as publisher, banker, expert on the constitution, television magnate, Liberal grandee and leading member of just about every institution on which the cultural life of the nation depends. There is hardly a sector in which he did not have an interest, hardly a committee to which he did not belong, hardly a pie in which he did not have a finger, so that he became one of the very pillars of the Establishment, to the service of which his many talents were devoted.

He was born at Gorseinon, near Swansea, in 1913, one of the four sons of the Reverend William Talfan Davies, a Calvinistic Methodist minister. His brother, Aneirin Talfan Davies, was for many years Head of Programmes with BBC Wales, and a prominent lay-member of the Church in Wales.

With Aneirin, in 1940, Alun founded Llyfrau'r Dryw, the publishing house later known as Christopher Davies Ltd. The firm also published the monthly magazine *Barn* ("Opinion") and, for a while, the literary quarterly *Poetry Wales*. It was Alun who kept the imprint's head above water with regular and substantial sums of his own money over many years and his son, Christopher, now runs it, though on a much reduced scale. This largesse was typical of Alun Talfan Davies's patriotic spirit and generosity to writers, whose company and friendship he sought and enjoyed throughout his life.

When, in 1975, Christopher Davies Ltd published a Festschrift in honour of Saunders Lewis, the greatest Welsh writer of the 20th century, it was at the Talfan home in Penarth, near Cardiff, that Lewis chose to receive it. Although a convert to Catholicism, he too had been brought up in a Presbyterian manse and the two patricians, albeit fundamentally opposed in their politics, recognised the patriot in each other. It was a good opportunity for the host on that piquant occasion to play the conciliatory role which he always preferred to confrontation and recrimination.

Alun Talfan, as he was generally known in Wales, was educated at Gowerton Grammar School, then studied Law at the University

College of Wales, Aberystwyth, and at Gonville and Caius College, Cambridge. He was called to the Bar at Gray's Inn in 1939 and went on to pursue a successful legal career in the public service. He was in turn Recorder of Merthyr Tydfil, Swansea, Cardiff and the Crown Court, and Judge of the Court of Appeal, Jersey and Guernsey.

He also served on a large number of boards charged with responsibility for legal matters, such as the Criminal Injuries Compensation Board (1976-85), and was Chairman of the Trustees of the Aberfan Fund (1967-90) which had the onerous task of dispensing the millions of pounds contributed by people from all over the world in response to the disaster in which 116 children and twenty-eight adults had lost their lives. The collapse of the waste-tip, which raced down a hillside into the valley as slurry, burying a whole generation of the village's children, was a disaster which affected him deeply, touching as it did a tender spot in his character which only those close to him had hitherto observed.

The cultural life of Wales claimed his allegiance on many fronts. Welsh-speaking and fully literate in the language, as befits a son of the manse, he not only wrote extensively for Welsh periodicals, including his own magazine *Barn*, but also served as President of the Court of the National Eisteddfod (1979-82) and as a member of the Council of the Welsh National Opera Company (1978-81).

But his keenest interest was in television. As Vice-Chairman of the HTV group, and Chairman of its Welsh Board (1967-83), he poured a good deal of oil on the choppy waters of broadcasting in Wales,bringing his gifts of quiet diplomacy and, when necessary, the big stick, to bear on the company's fortunes in its inaugural years.

The board of directors and senior executives knew him as one who demanded detailed briefs and was constantly on the lookout for new ideas, and they were often astonished at the zeal with which he pursued them and put them into practice. An inveterate optimist, he would greet its employees at times of crisis with the question, "What's the best news?", and this question became something of a catch-phrase among them.

A close associate of Sir Julian Hodge, the banker, Talfan Davies was also Deputy Chairman (1973-91) and then Chairman of the Bank of Wales (1991-95), Director of the Cardiff World Trade Centre, a member of the Welsh Centre for International Affairs (1985-89) and of the Court of the University of Wales and the councils of its constituent colleges at Aberystwyth and Swansea.

His political convictions had found their first expression while he was a member of the fledgling Plaid Cymru in the 1930s but he soon left the party in disenchantment with its social policies which, at the time, were heavily under the influence of the right-wing, ultra-Nationalist Saunders Lewis.

Talfan Davies contested the University of Wales seat as an Independent in a famous by-election in 1943 at which Lewis was defeated by the Labour candidate and, after throwing in his lot with the Liberal Party, stood as its candidate at Carmarthen in 1959 and 1964 and at Denbigh in 1966. For a while he was Chairman of the Liberal Party in Wales.

But his greatest contribution in the political arena was made between 1969 and 1973 while he was a member of the Royal Commission on the Constitution which published its findings (named after its second Chairman) as the Kilbrandon Report.

The principle of a modest measure of devolution set out in this document and in the discussion papers *Devolution and Democracy* (1974) and *Our Changing Democracy* (1975), in which the fine Talfanic hand was clearly discernible, was accepted by the Labour government and passed into law as the Wales Act of 1978, only to be defeated when, on 1 March (St David's Day) 1979, a majority of the Welsh people rejected it.

Although the report did much to clear the ground in political thinking about the governance of Wales, the defeat at referendum was a heavy blow to patriots like Talfan Davies who had for long been a keen advocate of administrative devolution for Wales and Scotland.

His spirits were not lifted again until the referendum of 1997, at which the electorate voted in favour of the Government's proposals for a National Assembly. Even so, he continued to hold the view, in line with Liberal Democrat thinking, that a greater degree of self-government than that represented today in Cardiff Bay was required if the experiment in democracy is to work.

The biography of Alun Talfan Davies, if ever it comes to be written, will not only touch on almost every aspect of life in Wales during the 20th century but will also reveal the multifarious ways in which he brought influence to bear, sometimes from behind the scenes, for he was a consummate power-broker, on individuals and institutions far removed from the immediate sphere of his professional career.

We shall have to wait for his voluminous papers to be lodged at the National Library of Wales before a start can be made on that Herculean task and it will be a brave researcher who tackles it.

Alun Talfan Davies, barrister and judge: born Gorseinon, Glamorgan 22 July 1913; called to the Bar, Gray's Inn 1939, Bencher, 1969; QC 1961; Recorder of Merthyr Tydfil 1963-68, of Swansea 1968-69, of Cardiff 1969-71, of the Crown Court 1972-86; Director, HTV Ltd 1967-83; Judge of the Court of Appeal, Jersey and Guernsey 1969-83; Deputy Chairman, Bank of Wales 1973-91, Chairman 1991-96; Kt 1976; married 1942 Eiluned Christopher Williams (one son, three daughters); died Penarth, Vale of Glamorgan 11 November 2000.

The Independent (13 November 2000)

Thomas Firbank

Author of I Bought a Mountain

Thomas Firbank's book about sheep-farming in the mountains of Snowdonia, *I Bought a Mountain,* became a best-seller as quickly as *How Green Was My Valley,* Richard Llewellyn's novel about the mining valleys of Glamorgan published a year before, in 1939. The two have remained the most consistently popular books ever written in English about Wales.

Although Richard Llewellyn and Thomas Firbank had something in common, in that they came as strangers to the communities they depicted, the difference between their styles could hardly have been more marked. Whereas Llewellyn wrote lyrically about a never-never land of singing miners and the lost innocence of youth, thus creating a myth that has plagued the Welsh ever since, because it deals largely in stereotypes and misty-eyed romance, in *I Bought a Mountain* Firbank wrote realistically, and sometimes in brutally critical fashion, about the harsh landscape and sturdy people of the mountain fastnesses of Eryri, as Snowdonia is known in Welsh. They had not been treated thus since George Borrow, perhaps the last of the the great English Romantic tourists, had described them, as the epitome of the sublime and picturesque, in his *Wild Wales* of 1862.

Thomas Firbank's book recounts his dogged and sometimes disastrous attempts to breed sheep on a farm of some 2,400 acres known as Dyffryn Mymbyr, on the southern slopes of the Glyders near Capel Curig, which he bought for £5,000 in 1931, and where he was joined four years later by his wife, Esmé, a former actress, after a whirlwind courtship lasting barely a week. Together they battled against the rigours of the weather in this bleak valley and, with the help of a few local men, like the inestimable shepherd John Davies, who were more used to the arduous life than they, faced the task of running the farm with a hard-bitten fortitude and a sunny sense of the comic that often stood them in good stead. Esmé was every bit as tough as Tom and did heavy work which was beyond the physical powers of most men.

Besides tending their 1,300 sheep, the Firbanks eked out a living by catering for visitors to the valley, most of whom were climbers. They kept pigs and poultry, opened a snack bar, put up guests in a gypsy caravan, constructed their own hydro-electric scheme and gradually mechanised their farm in an attempt to make themselves self-sufficient. This was "the good life" before it became modish and, despite its vagaries, they found it deeply satisfying.

Their account of life at Dyffryn Mymbyr immediately won the hearts of the book's readers, the Welsh taking to it because it was so finely observed, the English finding in it an idyll that appealed to the wartime sense of "a land of lost content" which, in the popular mind, would be regained once the conflict was over. It was, above all, its eulogy of what H.E. Bates, in a glowing review, called "real and permanent values", as the author had observed them among the farming community of Snowdonia, and his own search for an inner peace which had hitherto eluded him, that struck a chord. The book ends with an appeal to the British government to invest in agriculture and for young people to rediscover the joys of working the land.

Like Peter Mayle's *A Year in Provence* (1989), which it resembles in its clear-eyed approach to what was essentially a foreign country, *I Bought a Mountain* became one of those books which, largely by word of mouth and without the help of extensive advertising, seem to soar into the best-seller charts and remain there almost permanently, delighting generations of readers. It was reprinted seven times in the year of its publication, has never been out of print and is now in its 29th edition. Although he published other books, this is the one by which Firbank will be remembered, because it has been in the bookshops and tourist centres of Wales for sixty years.

Thomas Firbank was born in 1910 in Quebec city, where his father worked for the Canadian railways. The family was well-to-do, his grandfather, Joseph Firbank, a brother of the novelist Ronald Firbank, having been the contractor who built St. Pancras station in London. Soon after the child's birth, his father died and he was brought back to England, but retained his Canadian passport for the rest of his life. He was brought up by his maternal grandparents near Bala, with the result that his sympathy for Wales and its people was deeply ingrained in him and always to the fore in his writing.

Although he was to draw again on the ovine world of Dyffryn Mymbyr in his novel *Bride to the Mountain*, which appeared hard on the tail of his best-seller, by the time of its publication late in 1940, the author was serving with the Brigade of Guards at Caterham in

Surrey. During his absence his wife became involved with another man, who had been attracted to Snowdonia by Firbank's book. After the break-up of their marriage, in an extraordinary act of generosity, since he was not legally obliged to do so, Thomas Firbank gave the farm to his ex-wife who then ran it single-handedly, making ends meet by letting the farmhouse and moving into a cattle byre. In 1945, she married again and, as Esmé Kirby, became a formidable conservationist dedicated to the work of the Snowdonia National Park Society until, in 1988, when it refused to do the martinet's bidding, she was ousted and set up her own Snowdonia Trust so that she could get things done her way.

Tom Firbank's war was spent in North Africa and Italy, where he won the Military Cross and Bar in 1943, and after a spell at Staff College and his promotion to the rank of Captain, he took part in the Allied Airborne Armies' landings in the Nijmegen region of the Netherlands in September 1944. He was dropped by glider near the Dutch border and not far from the Riechswald Forest, the scene of some of the bitterest fighting of that famous operation. His war experiences, related with wry humour, an engaging scorn for heroics, and occasionally a disregard for higher ranks whenever the safety of the men under his command was in jeopardy, were the subject of *I Bought a Star* (1951), recently reissued by John Jones Ltd.

Ending the war in the rank of Lieutenant-Colonel, he was given the task of setting up a Parachute Regiment Infantry Training Centre near Dover and, two years later, responsibility for moving the Airborne Forces Depot from the north of England to the Isle of Wight. He left the Army in 1947 and went to live in a small house near Crawford on the edge of Dartmoor, about which he wrote in *Log Hut* (1953), but was also, according to his daughter Johanna, employed in intelligence at the time of the Burgess and Maclean affair.

He returned to Wales in 1953 to walk through the land to which he had always felt he belonged, and then to write, just like George Borrow, an account of his itinerary which was published as *A Country of Memorable Honour*. The book's title was taken from a conversation in *Henry V* in which the King tells Fluellen that he wears the leek on St David's Day "for a memorable honour", informing him that he too is Welsh and therefore his countryman. This patriotic strain runs like a leitmotiv through the book, making it one of the most attractive and readable guides to Wales published in the post-war period and a fair reflection of its cultural and political complexion at the time, as seen through the eyes of an informed observer.

Entering Wales by the Dee valley at Llangollen, Thomas Firbank walked through Snowdonia and then turned south via Dolgellau, Aberystwyth and Brecon to arrive in Cardiff a few weeks later. With many a digression on Welsh history and customs, most of which are notable for their percipience, he wrote not only about the places he passed, such as castles, mines and quarries, but also about the people he met on the way, including shepherds, innkeepers, landowners, ex-soldiers, farm wives, poets, clergymen, Welsh Nationalists – anyone who was prepared to tarry a while and talk to him, which in convivial Wales meant practically everyone.

Unlike Borrow, he was not taken in by humbug or wags and was as interested in industrial Wales as the rural parts. After an afternoon spent in the company of the eirenic Gwynfor Evans, president of Plaid Cymru, he was convinced that what the country needed most – besides the incorporation of Monmouthshire, in 1953 still not deemed by Whitehall to be one of the Welsh counties – was an officially designated capital and a measure of administrative devolution. One of the book's many charming cameos is the author's account of visiting a smithy at Cwm Dwr in Carmarthenshire where the blacksmith, who was also conductor of the village children's choir, had chalked up staves and words on the sooty walls to help them practise.

In the mid-1950s Firbank embarked on a third career as a businessman in the Far East. Based in Singapore and Hong Kong, he was employed by Perkin Diesels and was put in charge of representing the firm, which made agricultural machinery, in twenty-two countries. During the 1980s he served briefly as secretary of the British Chamber of Trade in Tokyo but, exasperated by British exporters' failure to take fuller advantage of the Japanese market, announced his resignation in a spirited letter to *The Times*.

He returned to Wales in 1994 to live with his daughter at Dolwyddelan, in the very heart of Snowdonia, a village redolent with the history he revered, for it is the site of a native Welsh castle that is the reputed birthplace of Llywelyn Fawr, Prince of Gwynedd in the 13th century, and it was there that Firbank was buried.

Thomas Joseph Firbank, writer, sheep-farmer, soldier and businessman:

Thomas Firbank

born Quebec 13 June 1910; married 1935 Esmé Cummins (marriage dissolved), 1943 Tessa Coudret (two daughters; marriage dissolved), 1975 Tsumemi Yogi; died Llanrwst, Conwy 1 December 2000.

The Independent (11 December 2000)

Glynne Jones

Conductor of the Pendyrus Male Voice Choir

The image of Wales as "the Land of Song" rests largely on the immense popularity and international renown of its male voice choirs, particularly those from the industrial valleys in the old county of Glamorgan. One of the most famous is the Pendyrus Male Voice Choir founded by unemployed miners at Tylorstown in the Rhondda Fach in 1924.

Glynne Jones, conductor of the Pendyrus for nearly forty years, spent his life trying to raise the standards of amateur music-making in Wales. For him, this meant not only extending the choral repertoire beyond the hoary favourites of the Victorian era but introducing the work of composers such as Dvořák, Bartók, Britten and William Mathias.

The full-throated sound of the ninety-eight-member Pendyrus, which still rehearses in a schoolroom in Tylorstown, became synonymous with Glynne Jones's inspirational flair as a conductor. Even in a land where the male voice choir has become something of a stereotype, the Pendyrus is widely regarded as a typical feature of a vigorous popular culture, rather like the brass bands of Yorkshire.

Innovative, eclectic and sometimes iconoclastic in his musical tastes, Glynne rebelled as a boy against the sterile exercises then in vogue among music teachers and soon taught himself to play a secondhand Crane's piano which his grandmother, who kept a sweetshop, bought for him at the age of eight. "If Every Good Boy Deserved Food," he wrote in my symposium *Artists in Wales* in 1973, "I was prepared to be naughty and hungry just to feel the ivories."

Born and brought up in Dowlais, the old iron-town high on a hill above Merthyr Tydfil, the son of a foundry worker, he had his first chance to play the harmonium and pipe-organ at Moriah, the Baptist chapel where his family encouraged him to compete in eisteddfodau and the annual singing festival. The greatest influence on him was his Uncle John, a packman who wrote music and taught him staff notation.

Although he had hoped to become a composer, he realised while a student at the University College, Cardiff, where Alun Hoddinott – the most distinguished of living professional Welsh composers – was a contemporary, that the adrenalin flowed most freely when he was conducting and that, anyway, he was "a creative non-starter".

His first job was teaching music at the County Grammar School in Merthyr Tydfil where he won a reputation as a flamboyant character who entertained both staff and pupils with his puckish wit. He had a most theatrical face, could roll his eyes to excellent effect and when he laughed, as a mutual friend observed, it was like the roar of a low-flying bomber. From 1955 to 1965 he led the Merthyr Philharmonic Orchestra, a mixed ensemble, and the Silurian Singers of Rhymney, just over the hill from Dowlais, never ceasing to introduce them to new music which they performed *allegro con brio*, his hallmark as a conductor. He once told me that the richly reverberating texture of their singing had something to do with the strenuous nature of their work in mine and furnace.

The Silurian Singers, composed mostly of steel-workers and colliers, won the prize for choral singing at the National Eisteddfod on three successive occasions, an all-time record, and a Gold Cup at the Cheltenham Festival of 1963. The choir's aim, Glynne said, was simply to encourage music-making among working-class people, to ensure the highest possible standards and to push back the boundaries of what they sang. Pendyrus became an icon of Welsh culture and its conductor a local hero.

In the late 1950s Glynne Jones became a man-about-town, relishing the less abstemious side of Merthyr's social life, often in the company of the poet Harri Webb, with whom he would lead convivial ceremonies of their own devising at the Church Tavern in the otherwise quiet village of Vaynor.

In 1965, after ten years at the County School, he took up the post of music adviser to Monmouthshire Education Authority, but continued to live in Dowlais. Like Joseph Parry, who became the first Professor of Music at the University College of Wales, Aberystwyth, the Welsh-speaker took great pleasure in describing himself as "*bach-gen bach o Ddowlais, erioed, erioed*" – "a small boy from Dowlais, always and for ever".

Among his achievements in Monmouthshire were the promotion of the County Youth Orchestra, the creation of the Gwent Music Trust and the organisation of youth festivals. In the 1960s he took the view that the National Eisteddfod was in danger of ossifying in its provision of music for younger people and caused some consternation among the old guard by recommending that rock and pop music should be introduced. To his surprise, the festival accepted his suggestion and it now has a pavilion where Welsh bands regularly perform. "It is puzzling that in Wales, the home of sweeping radicalism," he wrote, "we should be so conservative in our music. It is a form of hyper-mania with me to drag performers and audiences by their heels into the contemporary scene."

The Pendyrus Male Voice Choir which grew out of the ashes of the Silurians was even more successful. Its first concert under Glynne's baton was a performance of David Wynne's oratorio *Owain ab Urien* at the Queen Elizabeth Hall in 1962 and in 1971 it sang to great acclaim during British Week in San Francisco. In 1979 it became the first choir from western Europe to tour the Soviet Union.

Glynne Jones's greatest assets, apart from his musical expertise and love of discipline, were his ebullient personality and ability to inspire loyalty and affection in members of his choir. A bachelor, he also did good by stealth, making generous financial contributions to enable local men and women to embark on musical careers. For his services to Welsh choral music he was made a Fellow of the Welsh College of Music and Drama in 1994 and appointed MBE in the New Year's Honours List of 1996.

His last public appearance was on 15 December when he attended a "Glory of Christmas" evening given by the Welsh Concert Orchestra at St David's Hall in Cardiff and in which the Pendyrus had star billing. Although he did not conduct on this occasion, his radiant pride in his choir's performance was plain to see and he talked excitedly about its plans for the next year. He died shortly afterwards in the house in Dowlais where he had been born and which he shared with his ninety-two-year-old mother.

Glyndwr (Glynne) Jones, conductor: born Dowlais, Glamorgan 7 November 1927, founder and conductor of the Pendyrus Male Voice Choir 1962-2000; MBE 1996; died Dowlais 24 December 2000.

The Independent (1 January 2001)

John Stuart Williams

Teacher and poet of left-wing convictions

John Stuart Williams was among those Welsh poets writing in English who came to prominence in the early 1960s at roughly the same time as I launched the magazine *Poetry Wales*. He was already in his forties and, having published only a pamphlet of verse under Howard Sergeant's Outposts imprint, seemed to have fallen silent. In the very existence of the magazine, however, he found a spur for his own writing and soon became a regular contributor.

Up to then he had been known in literary circles as a critic who had written perceptively on Alun Lewis, the young Aberdare poet who died in Burma in 1944 and with whom he felt a special affinity, and on other writers who shared his upbringing in the industrial valleys of south-east Wales. Few were aware that he was also a composer who had studied under Grace Williams at the University College, Cardiff, or that he had been obliged to give up the piano because of arthritis.

John Stuart Williams was born in 1920 at Mountain Ash in the Cynon Valley, a mining village he preferred to call by its Welsh name, Aberpennar, and from the harsh conditions prevailing there during his boyhood he learned the Socialism to which he remained true for the rest of his life. He and his wife Sheelagh, whom he married in 1948, were staunch members of the Labour Party and for many years active on its behalf in Rhiwbina, a leafy suburb known as "the Hampstead of Cardiff". Both were prominent members of CND Cymru which played a part in declaring Wales a nuclear-free country and Sheelagh was among the Cardiff women who set up the protest camp at Greenham Common in 1981.

After attending Mountain Ash County School, where he excelled as a sprinter and rugby player, John took a First in English at Cardiff and was later awarded an MA for research into the history of criticism. He once told me he had read every number of *The Edinburgh Review* which had appeared between 1802 and 1929; and there was something of that Whig journal's scathing wit and high-mindedness in much of what he wrote about Anglo-Welsh literature.

He began his career as an English teacher at Whitchurch Grammar School in north Cardiff, where he had a reputation for robust pedagogical methods which did not rule out a box about the ears for recalcitrant pupils. Rhodri Morgan, now First Minister at the National Assembly, remembers him as something of a martinet, and the novelist and screenwriter Andrew Davies has famously described a bruising encounter between boy and master from which both emerged with enhanced knowledge of themselves. Davies was among the many writers who paid affectionate tribute to John at a celebratory evening organised by the Welsh Academy in Cardiff on the occasion of his eightieth birthday last summer.

As critic and editor, John Stuart Williams made a significant contribution to the emergence of a distinct Welsh literature in English at a crucial point in the cultural and political life of Wales. Unlike many academics who have been in a position to do so, he also found a place for it in the curriculum as Head of the Department of English and Drama at Cardiff College of Education, the post he held from 1956 until his retirement.

His anthology *Dragons and Daffodils* (1960), in the compilation of which he collaborated with Richard Milner, was a brave attempt to demonstrate that Cardiff had produced writers of note. It included Dannie Abse, Glyn Jones and Terry Hawkes, now Professor of English at the university, but was snootily dismissed in *The Listener* by R.S. Thomas, a native of the city who had refused to appear in it, for its "provincialism" and lack of awareness of a "Welsh national dimension".

John's second attempt at anthologising Welsh writing in English was more successful: *The Lilting House* (1969), of which he and I were co-editors, was the first authoritative attempt to present selections from the work of 20th-century Anglo-Welsh poets. Although we did not always see eye to eye, in poetry any more than in politics, we worked happily together, each finding himself able to endorse the choices made by the other in almost every case. We used to rib each other that if only Plaid Cymru and the Labour Party in Wales could co-operate in the winning of self-government as easily as we had done in the compilation of our anthology, our country would be the better for it.

Of his own verse, in addition to the Outposts pamphlet *Last Fall* (1962), John published three substantial collections: *Green Rain* (1967), *Dic Penderyn and Other Poems* (1970) which won a Welsh Arts Council prize, and *Banna Strand* (1975). Many of his poems refer to the ancient world and to Greek myth in particular, or else to the civilisation of the Mediterranean lands, in which the sun and the fecundity of the earth are the dominant images. In this he stands apart from Welsh writers of his time and place, who have been more preoccupied with the ravaged landscapes of South Wales and the social travail of the last hundred years or so.

Nevertheless, he could write movingly about the industrial valleys, as in his "poem for voices", "Dic Penderyn", broadcast by BBC Wales in 1968, which is about the workers' rising in Merthyr Tydfil of 1831, for his part in which the twenty-three-year-old miner Richard Lewis, known as Dic Penderyn, was made a scapegoat and hanged in Cardiff jail. It is said that Dic's last words from the scaffold were: "*O Arglwydd, dyma gamwedd!*" ("O Lord, this is a great wrong!").

The Merthyr Rising is to the history of the Welsh proletariat what the Peterloo Massacre (1819) is to that of England. Some two dozen rioters were killed by the muskets of the Argyll and Sutherland Highlanders and the Red Flag – a sheet soaked in calf's blood with a loaf of bread impaled on its staff – was raised for the first time in Britain as a symbol of workers' solidarity and revolution. Years later another man confessed to the crime of which Lewis had been found guilty and so Dic became the first martyr of the Welsh working class.

Even so, John Stuart Williams refrained from propaganda: always his own man and never one to settle for comfortable answers, he flew in the face of historical evidence and refused to draw any political conclusion from the injustice of Dic's death, for like the hapless martyr, who had been "caught in the cross-fire of circumstance", he found it hard to hate.

John Stuart Williams, critic and poet: born Mountain Ash, Glamorgan 13 August 1920; Head of Department of English and Drama, Cardiff College of Education, 1956-80; married 1948 Sheelagh Lee (two sons); died Cardiff 26 January 2001.

The Independent (30 January 2001)

R. George Thomas

Scholar and expert on Edward Thomas

After the poet Edward Thomas was killed during the opening barrage of the Battle of Arras on the morning of 9 April 1917, a small diary was found in his pocket, the creases in it suggesting that he had either been carrying it the previous day, when he had been knocked over by the blast of a shell, or on the morning of his death.

R. George Thomas, whose main academic interest was the study of Edward Thomas's work, was able to print the diary in full as an appendix to his magisterial edition of *The Collected Poems of Edward Thomas* which appeared in 1978. The document is of extraordinary significance for an understanding of the poet not only in the last three months of his life but, in particular, for his sensuous response to the natural world and for the germs of ideas, poems, essays and books which he was contemplating but was never to write.

The book was edited to a high scholarly standard which threw light on the provenance and drafting of all Edward Thomas's poems, its editor having worked from manuscript sources in libraries in both England and the United States, and with the full co-operation of the poet's daughters, grandson and nephews. He undertook the work at the request of Helen Thomas, the poet's widow.

Among the material he examined were the typescripts, notebooks, working drafts and printed versions left by the poet at the time of his death, a vast collection to which no other scholar had hitherto had access. He was thus able to assemble the poems in chronological order and in the final state in which they had left the poet's hand. The text of each poem was accompanied by all the variant readings and then placed within the context of the poet's prose writings, including his notebooks and letters.

R. George Thomas had the advantage of this meticulous scholarship when he came to write *Edward Thomas: a portrait* (1985) and to edit the poet's correspondence with Gordon Bottomley, the second volume of which appeared in 1996. He had already published a very useful summary of the poet's Welsh affinities in a monograph, *Edward Thomas*, in the *Writers of Wales* series in 1972. But these later works represented the sum of his researches and put all other biographers and critics in his debt.

Born in the mining village of Pontlotyn in Glamorgan in 1914, the son of a grocer who had once been a jockey, Richard George Thomas was educated at the University College of South Wales and Monmouthshire, Cardiff, where he read English. During the Second World War he served in Iceland, where he was able to take time off to attend the classes of Professor Sigurdur Nordal at the National University in Reykjavik. It was there he pursued an interest in the Old Icelandic sagas which he shared with his Professor, Gwyn Jones, already working in the field at Cardiff, and whom he helped in the preparation of the latter's translation of *The Vatndalers' Saga* (1944). He was also the translator of Nordal's *Hrafnkels Saga Freysgoda: a study* (1958).

Promoted to the rank of Major while with the Iceland Force, George later saw action against the Japanese in India and Burma and was about to be moved to Singapore when the atom bomb was dropped on Hiroshima. "It was," he once told me, "as if the world had come to an end and started at the same time."

He returned to Wales in 1946 to teach medieval and 18th-century literature and remained there for the rest of his academic career, latterly as Professor of English Language and Literature at Cardiff with a personal chair. College affairs held little fascination for him and he cast a cold eye on the rumbustious machinations which eventually led to the departure of Principal C.W.L. Bevan.

Although he spoke Welsh and was a member of the Welsh Academy, the national association of writers in Wales, he played almost no part in the country's literary life, preferring the groves of academe, and was rarely seen by colleagues outside his room and the university library.

He had, nevertheless, a keen admiration for the Socialist poet Idris Davies, whom he had known as a boy, and recalled him affectionately in a memorial volume, *I Was Born in Rhymney*, published in 1990 on the occasion of the National Eisteddfod's visit to their native Rhymney. He also wrote extensively on R.S. Thomas and was one of the first critics to grapple with the complex metaphysics of that poet's work.

A genial but rather shy man, George took his pleasure as a gardener at his home in Llanishen, a northern suburb of Cardiff, and as a staunch member of the Cardiff University and Bach Choirs, where he sang with his wife Jess, whom he had met while they were undergraduates.

Richard George Thomas, literary critic and editor: born Pontlotyn, Glamorgan 13 August 1914; Professor of English Language and Literature, University College, Cardiff 1967-80 (Emeritus); married 1943 Jess Moseley (two sons); died Cardiff 23 February 2001.

The Independent (28 February 2001)

Dafydd Rowlands

Poet, essayist and Arch-Druid of Wales

In the hoary rituals of the Assembly of Bards of the Isle of Britain, which take place every August during the ceremonies of the National Eisteddfod of Wales, not all those who parade in their white robes are writers – some are solicitors, rugby players or television personalities whose connection with literature is often tenuous. But the office of Arch-Druid is usually reserved for a poet who has won either the Chair, Crown, or Prose Medal, still regarded as the highest accolades to which a Welsh writer can aspire.

That was certainly the case when Dafydd Rowlands was elected Arch-Druid in 1996, for he was generally acknowledged to be one of the most accomplished writers in the Welsh language, having already published several volumes of verse and prose. He brought to the stage a patriarchal presence which was helped by a black beard of biblical dimensions, a fine bass voice and a sense of ceremony, not without humour, which stood him in good stead throughout his three-year tenure.

He first came to prominence as a writer in 1969 when he won the Crown, which is awarded for verse in the free metres as distinct from the strict or traditional metres, for which a Chair is the prize. In a sequence of ten poems he conducted a Socratic dialogue with his son that was meant not only to teach the boy about his family history but also to explore the writer's own identity as a Welshman and human being. His horizons were wide: some of the poems are about Vietnam, Israel, Prague and Biafra.

They are to be found in his first collection, *Meini* ("Stones", 1972). Three years later Dafydd repeated the feat by winning the Crown again with a longish poem entitled "*Dadeni*" ("Renaissance / Rebirth"), in which he sang the praises of the young militants who were being jailed for their part in the campaigns of Cymdeithas yr Iaith Gymraeg (The Welsh Language Society). What readers found attractive in his second collection, *Yr Wythfed Dydd* ("The eighth day", 1975), was that, although there was no doubt as to which side he was on in the often bruising confrontation between an embattled Welsh-language community and an indifferent, sometimes hostile bureaucracy, there was no hint of propaganda in his work. He handled his theme in the context of universal human rights, examining the role of language as a medium for the transmission of the highest cultural values.

The same concern for family, neighbourhood, nation, and civic responsibility informs his only collection of essays, *Ysgrifau yr Hanner Bardd* ("Essays of the half poet"), with which he won the Prose Medal in 1972. Taking as his guide a comment by the English writer A.C. Benson, "The essayist is really a lesser kind of poet", he revived public interest in this literary form and saved it from the rather formulaic doldrums into which, in Welsh, it was in danger of falling. One of his essays, which appears as "The Little Llandeilo Boots" in the anthology *Illuminations* (1998), is a small gem in which a gripping narrative and a strong emotional current combine to produce prose of great subtlety and power. The essays became a set text in the examinations of the Welsh Joint Education Committee.

His only other prose work was *Mae Theomemphus yn Hen* ("Theomemphus is old", 1977), which he called a novel/poem. The title refers to the eponymous hero of a dramatic work by William Williams of Pantycelyn, the Methodist hymn-writer, which deals with the spiritual pilgrimage of the true Christian, but Dafydd's poem is mainly about a man's love/hate relationship with his absent father, and in its profound and uncompromising self-examination and its use of "stream of consciousness" it achieves a synthesis which is rare in modern Welsh prose.

Dafydd Rowlands was born in 1931 in the steel and tinplate village of Pontardawe in the Swansea Valley and lived there all his life. The district produced one of the most famous Welsh poets of the 20th century, Gwenallt Jones (1899-1968), and although the two never met (curiously in a country as small as Wales), Dafydd compiled an illustrated account of Gwenallt Jones's life and work which is a loving evocation of the community in which they had both grown up.

He was highly equipped as a literary critic. After leaving the Independent (Congregationalist) ministry, he became a teacher at the Garw Valley Grammar School and then, in 1968, a lecturer in Welsh at Trinity College, Carmarthen, where his genial personality endeared him to staff and students alike. His gifts as a public speaker and reader of poetry soon brought him to the attention of television producers and, from about 1983, when he left the college, he began a third career as a script-writer and TV presenter.

Dafydd Rowlands

Among the many memorable programmes he made were documentaries on Gwenallt Jones, the hymn-writer Ann Griffiths and the Daughters of Rebecca, rioters disguised as women who attacked the hated toll-gates of west Wales during the 1840s. He also wrote scripts for *Pobol y Cwm*, the nightly soap-opera which provides many Welsh writers with a lucrative source of income, and for *Licyris Olsorts*, the Welsh-language counterpart of *Last of the Summer Wine*.

His *violon d'Ingres* was cricket. He was a keen supporter of the Glamorgan County XI, rarely missing a home match and often travelling to see away games, and it was this passion which led to the composition and publication of his last book of poems. At the beginning of 1992, feeling a lack of discipline, he had the idea of writing a poem a day for the next twelve months, in the hope that by the end of the year he would have 365. This number was significant for a devoted cricket fan because it was how many runs Gary Sobers had scored in the Test match against Pakistan in Kingston, Jamaica, in 1957-58 – a world record at the time. The poet resolved to call his next book *Sobers a Fi* ("Sobers and me"). By the following Christmas he had his 365 poems, but – always a stringent critic of his own work – decided that about 300 of them were not good enough for publication, and anyway, by then Brian Lara had improved on the record set by Sobers. He abandoned the idea, only to meet Sobers shortly afterwards during the cricketer's visit to Swansea. On learning of the plan, and his failure to implement it, the batsman urged Dafydd to publish the book none the less, so he did, keeping the original title, in 1995, and dedicating it to Ramesh Chandra Shah – poet, scholar and, like himself, a cricket fan.

Dafydd Heslin Rowlands, born Pontardawe, Glamorgan 25 December 1931; Arch-Druid of Wales 1996-99; married 1959 Margaret Morris (three sons); died Swansea 26 April 2001.

The Independent (30 April 2001)

Brian Morris

Poet, scholar and Labour peer

It was typical of Brian Morris that when, in 1990, he was made a life peer and took his seat in the House of Lords on the Labour benches, he chose to be known as Baron Morris of Castle Morris, of St Dogmaels in the County of Dyfed.

Even his closest friends had to enquire where the place was and would share his mirth on learning that Castle Morris is a hamlet in the north of Pembrokeshire, so small that it does not always appear on maps of the county, and that St Dogmaels is a good twenty-five miles distant. Few believed him when he claimed to have some family connection with the place, or with the ruins of its castle, or could accept that he took the grandiloquent title at all seriously, for he was an inveterate puller of legs. It was, we thought, his way of cocking a snook at the club he was about to join.

Yet he threw himself with characteristic enthusiasm into the life of the House of Lords and proved a conscientious and hard-working peer. Appointed the Opposition's Deputy Chief Whip in 1992, he became its principal spokesman on education two years later and served in that post until 1997. He often spoke in the House thereafter, mainly on education and cultural issues, especially galleries and museums, in which he had a keen interest, but was not given any further special responsibility after the Labour Party's victory at the general election of 1997, an oversight which he accepted with wry amusement.

At Westminster he was perhaps out of his natural habitat, which up to 1990 had been the academic world – first as a lecturer in English at Reading University, then Senior Lecturer at York and, succeeding William Empson, Professor of English Literature at Sheffield, where he was appointed Deputy Dean and Public Orator in 1971.

At the time of his elevation to the Lords he was Principal of St David's University College, Lampeter, one of the constituent colleges, and the smallest, of the federal University of Wales, and had been there since 1980. Few had guessed that he was a Labour man or that he held political opinions of any kind.

A year later he left Lampeter and went to live at a home he had kept at Foolow in Hope Valley, Derbyshire, severing his physical connection with Wales but staying in touch with friends whose counsel he valued and following the country's affairs as best he could – a "long-distance patriot", as he liked to describe himself.

He once told me that if he had been able to speak Welsh he might have made his entire career in Wales but, with only a little of the language at his command, he felt excluded from some sectors of the country's public life. He blamed the time and place of his birth and upbringing: he had been born in Cardiff in 1930 and educated at the High School in the city and at Worcester College, Oxford, where he read English.

Brian Morris's contribution to the life of Wales was mainly made through his membership of countless committees, the work of which he relished but which he sometimes viewed with a sardonic eye, especially when they proved ineffective on account of their ultra-democratic nature. He was always one for action and had little patience with the niceties of administrative procedure.

Among the bodies on which he served were the Welsh Arts Council, the Welsh Committee of the British Council, the Welsh Historic Gardens Trust, the National Library of Wales, and the Campaign for the Protection of Rural Wales.

I knew him as a writer and scholar. He published four collections of verse: *Tide Race* (1976), *Stones in the Brook* (1978), *Dear Tokens* (1987) and *The Waters of Comfort* (1998). His *Collected Poems* appeared earlier this year. Many of these poems deal with exile, the mountains of Snowdonia, and the rivers of west Wales, while the third book is concerned with love – sexual, divine and domestic – and with music. Some contain lines that stick in the mind because they are so acerbic, as when he says of the Welsh, "We are a gentle people, given to charity and abstinence".

On the strength of these books he was elected to membership of the Welsh Academy, the national association of writers in Wales, served on the Council of the Poetry Society, and was in frequent demand as a broadcaster on literary and arts topics.

A staunch Churchman, even before his appointment to Lampeter, a traditionally Anglican institution, he assembled an eloquent collection of essays in defence of the historic liturgy of the Established Church in *Ritual Murder* (1980), in which he and his contributors mounted a stout defence of the Book of Common Prayer and the

Authorised Version of the Bible against those who were seeking to replace them with revised versions at the General Synod of 1980. Stripped of its liturgy, he believed, the Church would lose one of its chief strengths, and in a spirited chapter on "Liturgy and Literature" he demonstrated vividly what the loss would be in both poetry and theology.

It was as editor and textual critic of English theatre in the Elizabethan, Jacobean and Caroline periods that Brian first made his mark. From 1964 to 1986 he was general editor of the *New Mermaid Dramatists* series and from 1974 to 1982 of the *New Arden Shakespeare*. He also edited the plays of John Ford, author of *Tis Pity She's a Whore*, and the poems of the royalist John Cleveland. These editions were widely admired for their meticulous editing and illuminating apparatus.

More surprisingly, perhaps, he contributed a 1993 monograph to the *Writers of Wales* series on the Welsh Republican poet Harri Webb, whose squibs and irreverent doggerel seemed to strike a chord with him. Harri, slow to praise anyone who was in any way part of the British Establishment, always referred to Brian as "a good chap". On the sole occasion on which the two met, however, they found they had little to say to each other, much to the biographer's chagrin, and the conversation turned on what each thought the expression "mosed in the chine", as it occurs in Shakespeare, might mean.

Although he was mildly patriotic, Brian was in no way a Nationalist, not even playing any significant part in the Labour Party's attempts to bring a measure of devolution to Wales in the 1990s. He may have been a great admirer of R.S. Thomas, with whom he had an Anglican background in common, but was percipient enough to take the poet's ultra-Nationalist pronouncements *cum grano salis*.

At the last Brian found Lampeter too small and uncongenial to contain him. I recall how dismayed he was when the French writer Eugène Ionesco, visiting west Wales, referred to the place as "*le village universitaire*": it was precisely its smallness and geographical remoteness that constricted Brian and made him yearn for a wider stage.

Back in England, he once again took on that gruelling round of committees which he had given up in 1980. He served on the Museums and Galleries Commission, the Council of the Prince of

Wales's Institute of Architecture, the Council for National Parks and the Board of the British Library, and as a Trustee of the National Portrait Gallery.

I got to know him better while on a tour of the Soviet Union as it was beginning to break up in the late 1980s. There was no food in the restaurants of Moscow, Tbilisi or Azerbaijan and the taxis were not working anywhere; as we signed in at one hotel, a large rat ran across the reception desk, and our bedroom doors had no locks or running water. What I remember about that trip is that he was such excellent company and how he entertained our hosts, across the language barrier, with his anecdotes and puckish humour.

As a friend I found him loyal and generous. Nothing seemed to get him down, not even the onset of leukaemia: he had adopted his life's motto, he said, as a National Service squaddie just after the Second World War when he had learned to box the hard way, his bantam weight being no match for burlier men. "Knickers up and keep boxing!" he would say, with a grin that was like the Cheshire Cat's, and somehow it always cheered me up.

Brian Robert Morris, writer and English scholar: born Cardiff 4 December 1930; Fellow, Shakespeare Institute, Birmingham University 1956-58; Assistant Lecturer, Reading University 1958-60, Lecturer 1960-65; Lecturer, York University 1965-67, Senior Lecturer 1967-71; Professor of English Literature, Sheffield University 1971-80; Principal, St David's University College, Lampeter 1980-91; Chairman, Museums and Galleries Commission 1945-90; created 1990 Baron Morris of Castle Morris; Opposition Deputy Chief Whip, House of Lords 1992-97; Vice-Chairman, Trustees, National Portrait Gallery 1993-2001; President, Brontë Society 1996-2001; married 1955 Sandra James (one son, one daughter); died Derby 30 April 2001.

The Independent (2 May 2001)

Dafydd Parri

Writer of popular children's books

The history of children's literature in the Welsh language, beginning in the 18th century, was for long dominated by a desire to save the child's soul by means of exhortation and admonishment. Biblical stories and translations of *The Pilgrim's Progress* were the standard fare. It was not until the late 19th century that pioneers such as O.M. Edwards, a Balliol man and Chief Inspector of Schools in Wales, began to show children and their parents that reading, as well as having a didactic purpose, could be fun.

Dafydd Parri, one of a new crop of children's writers to emerge in the 1970s, was in this tradition. Between 1975 and 1980 he produced more than three dozen novels for younger readers, often at the rate of six a year, which are among the most popular books ever written in Welsh. Twenty-five were published in the *Llewod* ("Lions") series by the enterprising publisher Y Lolfa, based at Talybont in Cardiganshire, which was enabled to install new machinery on the strength of his rocketing sales.

The title of the series is made up of the first letter in the names of the five main characters – Llinos, Einion, Wyn, Orig and Delyth – who became as famous in Welsh-speaking homes as the Famous Five. The books tell gripping yarns about a gang of youngsters who are always getting up to mischief and having adventures of the kind that are to be found in the stories of Enid Blyton, though without the "Oh mother, you are a brick" dialogue. They abound with ghost-trains, helicopters, pop-singers, caravan holidays, diamond thieves, smugglers, snowstorms, spies, kidnappers, tigers escaped from the zoo and mad scientists intent on destroying the world. There is not the slightest hint of a moral and the plots zip along in the best Dick Barton style.

The books, published as attractive paperbacks, were an immediate success, selling thousands of copies. They were so popular that a book club was launched to cater for their readers' enthusiasm and absorption in the tales, and discos were held at which young readers dressed up as the Lions. There was even a Lions joke-book and a painting competition, the winners of which were taken on a boat trip to Bremen.

The Welsh Books Council encouraged the craze, in the belief that the novels won new readers and spread the word that books in the Welsh language were not only of good quality but, in the idiom of the day, trendy. The books were in such demand that they were bartered in playgrounds and had to be rebound in plastic covers by school librarians to save them from wear and tear.

Dafydd Parri had long years of experience with children, including five of his own, before he became an author. Born at Rowen in the Conwy Valley, he was educated and trained as a teacher at the Normal College, Bangor and taught at various schools in Flintshire before taking up a post as a teacher of History and Geography at Ysgol Dyffryn Conwy in Llanrwst in Denbighshire. He was among a dedicated band of teachers and educationists who worked hard for the introduction of Welsh-medium education in north-east Wales. Among the material he produced in Welsh for the fast-growing syllabus of the bilingual schools were geography textbooks.

But his real delight was in writing stories for children. To watch him talking to young fans, who knew his characters and the intricacies of his plots better than anything they had learnt in the classroom, was to realise with what empathy, skill and sense of fun his books were written.

A staunch defender of the Welsh language's interests, he was to be found in the vanguard of every militant movement. He was especially concerned about the decline of the Welsh-speaking heartlands as a consequence of immigration by English-speakers, though in his books the children live in a robustly Welsh-speaking culture untouched by anglicisation and speak their language with pride and precision.

Dafydd had a keen business sense which he put to the service of literature in Wales. With his wife, Arianwen, he established in Llanrwst one of the first and best shops specialising in the books and records of Wales, which is now run by their daughter, Gwawr. One of their sons, the fine poet Myrddin ap Dafydd, chose to join his father in the production of Welsh books and now runs his own printing and publishing business, known as Gwasg Carreg Gwalch, in the town. Another son, Iolo, is a BBC Cymru correspondent currently reporting on the war in Afghanistan.

The runaway success of the *Llewod* series could hardly be repeated, but Dafydd Parri went on to write another about the adventures of a canny sheepdog known as Cailo, who might have been from the same litter as Lassie, so heroic were his exploits. He also wrote two volumes of short stories for adults, *Nos Lun a Storiau Eraill* ("Monday night and other stories", 1976) and *Bwrw Hiraeth* ("Rid of longing", 1981).

A quiet, genial and unassuming man, but steely in his commitment to the language in which he wrote and lived his life, Dafydd was content to be known as a popular children's writer and never sought the limelight or the approval of the literary establishment in Wales.

Dafydd Parri, teacher and writer: born Rowen, Caernarfonshire 29 July 1926; married 1953 Arianwen Walters (four sons, one daughter); died Llanrwst, Denbighshire, 29 November 2001.

The Independent (4 December 2001)

David Jenkins

Biographer and National Librarian

David Jenkins was for ten years Librarian at the National Library of Wales in Aberystwyth, a post he filled with distinction and a quiet pride that a son of working-class parents could rise to such illustrious heights. He was one of a long line of Librarians who made a substantial contribution to the cultural life of Wales both *ex officio* and as writers devoted to the Welsh tradition of scholarship and local history.

He never forgot that he had been born and bred, a collier's son, in the Rhondda Valley, at Blaenclydach, near Tonypandy, where in 1910, two years before his birth, the famous riots had taken place during a strike by miners employed by the Cambrian Combine. It was one of the major disturbances in the South Wales coalfield and ended only when Winston Churchill sent troops into the Valley, thus earning the abiding contempt of Rhondda people and a place in the mythology of militant Socialism.

For this reason David Jenkins, although a native Welsh-speaker, took a keen interest in the work of such English-language writers as Rhys Davies and Lewis Jones, also born in Blaenclydach, both of whom set some of their stories and novels against the events of 1910, and in that of Idris Davies whose long poem *The Angry Summer* caught the mood of the General Strike of 1926.

Most of David Jenkins's boyhood and adult life was spent, however, not in the Rhondda but in Penrhyn-coch in Cardiganshire, where he was sent at the age of seven to live with an aunt and uncle while recovering from a chest infection. He was educated at Ardwyn Grammar School in Aberystwyth and at the University College of Wales in the town, where he took a degree in Welsh Literature in 1936 and an MA two years later for a thesis on Huw Morys, the 17th-century poet and Royalist.

He joined the staff of the National Library in 1939 as an assistant in the Department of Manuscripts but was conscripted into the Army. He saw action during the Second World War as a major in north-western Europe, taking part in the liberation of Paris and the push into Germany and Poland, where he was among the first British soldiers to reach the concentration camps.

Returning to Aberystwyth and the National Library in 1945, he rose quickly in his chosen profession: appointed Assistant Keeper of Printed Books in 1949, Keeper in 1957 and Senior Keeper in 1962, he became Librarian in 1969, a post in which he remained until his retirement.

With the post came myriad responsibilities which he accepted with alacrity, his jovial nature helping him to win friends among his colleagues and to promote the interests of the National Library wherever he found an opportunity. He served on the committees of the Library Advisory Council and the British Library, the BBC Archives Advisory Committee and the College of Librarianship, Wales. Among the many bodies which benefited from his professional advice was the Welsh Books Council, of which he was Chairman, helping it to expand and assume the role of national body which it enjoys today.

But it was as a bibliophile that he found greatest satisfaction. He was editor of *The National Library of Wales Journal* and *The Journal of the Welsh Bibliographical Society*, and contributed prolifically to such learned periodicals as *The Bulletin of the Board of Celtic Studies*.

He also played a practical role in the legal affairs of his adopted town and county, serving as a Justice of the Peace and chairman of the local bench, and as a member of the Dyfed Magistrates Court Committee and the Dyfed-Powys Police Authority.

It is thought that, if his duties at the National Library had not been so onerous, he would have published more literary criticism ranging over the wide variety of his interests, particularly Welsh writing in English. Even so, in *Thomas Gwynn Jones: cofiant* (1973), he wrote one of the finest biographies ever published in Welsh: he had sat at the feet of Thomas Gwynn Jones during the poet's last years as Gregynog Professor of Welsh at Aberystwyth. He also edited the literary journalism and essays of Kate Roberts (*Erthyglau ac ysgrifau llenyddol*, 1978), generally regarded as the foremost Welsh prose-writer of the 20th century.

His most important essay is undoubtedly that on Dafydd ap Gwilym, the greatest of the medieval Welsh poets, whose youthful haunts he succeeded in identifying with places in the district of Penrhyn-coch. This seminal work, first published in *The Bulletin of the Board of Celtic Studies* in 1936, marked the beginning of modern research into what little is known of the poet's life and paved the way for the magisterial edition of his work which was edited by Thomas

Parry, one of his predecessors as National Librarian, and published in 1952.

In retirement he devoted himself to local history and toponymy, expanding his famous essay in *Bro Dafydd ap Gwilym* ("Dafydd ap Gwilym's district", 1992) and tracing the history of the Baptists of north Cardiganshire in *O Blas Gogerddan i Horeb* ("From Plas Gogerddan to Horeb", 1993). He was for many years a deacon at Horeb, the Baptist chapel at Penrhyn-coch, and one of his denomination's most liberal members. The literary society which he founded in the village is one of the most flourishing in the whole of Wales.

David Jenkins was a good example of the Welsh scholar who, fully equipped and of wide learning, chose to use his skills and knowledge in the service of his community, in the belief that the life of the cultivated mind should be firmly rooted in the experience of the people.

For the last twenty years of his life he had been working on a history of the National Library of Wales. *A Refuge in Peace and War: a history of the National Library of Wales to 1952* will be published in May.

David Jenkins, librarian: born Blaenclydach, Glamorgan 29 May 1912; Assistant Keeper, Department of Printed Books, National Library of Wales 1949-57, Keeper 1957-62, Senior Keeper 1962-69, Librarian 1969-79; Editor, Journal of the Welsh Bibliographical Society *1964-79; Editor,* National Library of Wales Journal *1968-79; General Commissioner of Income Tax 1968-87; Chairman, Welsh Books Council 1974-80; CBE 1977; married 1948 Menna Rhys Williams (one son, one daughter); died Aberystwyth 6 March 2002.*

The Independent (8 March 2002)

Robin Williams

Writer who brought new vigour to the essay

The essay in Welsh is a comparatively recent literary form, but in the 20th century it was practised by a number of gifted writers who developed its range until it became, belatedly perhaps, one of the most popular genres in Welsh literature.

The master was T.H. Parry-Williams (1887-1975), but in the hands of younger writers the essay lost many of its mannerisms, not least its whimsicality and precious style, and began to address contemporary themes which put it, with poetry, among the most socially aware genres in the Welsh language. No longer an exercise in *belles-lettres* in the manner of E.V. Lucas, whose baneful influence it eventually shook off, it found room for political comment, psychological analysis, metaphysical wit, satire and, mercifully, a sense of humour

Among the essayists who brought a new sophistication and vigour to the *ysgrif*, as the essay is known in Welsh, was Robin Williams, who published more than a dozen collections. The form, taken in new directions, attracted serious critical attention to what had been in danger of being overlooked by academic discourse on account of its sheer variety and its tendency to make something out of nothing, often for the purposes of a readership that delighted in mere polished prose.

Robin Williams was fortunate in having been born in Penycaerau, near Aberdaron, on the Llŷn peninsula of north-west Wales, and brought up at Llanystumdwy, the home village of David Lloyd George. This is a district known as Eifionydd and it is renowned for the rich culture of its people; the Welsh language is still spoken by a majority despite the incursion of English monoglots. Robin's father was a master carpenter and they shared a satisfaction in a job well done whether in wood or words. He was brought up on the Plas Gwynfryn estate, a place vividly evoked in *Maes Mihangel* (1974), a small masterpiece by his brother the late John Griffith Williams.

Many of the characters, places and incidents of the district are also immortalised in the essays of Robin Williams, who delighted in the local idiom and traditional ways that have survived for centuries in almost pristine forms. Like other writers, including the poet R.S. Thomas, he was staunch in his opposition to the anglicisation of the

Llŷn and did all he could to resist it.

Robin Williams was a Presbyterian minister with the Calvinistic Methodists, the most conservative of the Nonconformist sects in Wales. After graduating from the University College of North Wales, Bangor he trained for the Ministry at the Connexion's Theological Colleges in Aberystwyth and Bala and then served as pastor to congregations in Dinmael, Glanrafon and Penrhyndeudraeth, all within a few miles of his native patch.

There was nothing narrow or backward-looking in his writing, which roamed freely across areas not traditionally associated with men of the cloth. Among the subjects he treated were topics as various as the American West, the Letts diaries, Bulgaria, Muhammad Ali, furniture polish, A. E. Housman, the blessings of sun lotion, Edgar Allan Poe, the ruins of Rome, wandering in Ireland, English writers and their books, and whatever caught his fancy during his many trips abroad. The rich tapestry of his essays is informed by myriad allusions to his wide reading and travel.

One of my favourites is "*Cusan Sanctaidd*" ("An holy kiss"), an essay which takes its title from Corinthians and by which he agreed to be represented in *Illuminations*, an anthology in English translation which I compiled in 1998. It is an impressionistic account of three weeks spent in the company of a young Turk during the filming of a television programme about the Seven Churches of Asia mentioned in the Book of Revelation. He brought to the subject his immense theological knowledge and keen interest in popularising the Bible in a new technological age.

The Turk's name was Dinsher Hazirol and they struck up a friendship which, despite their ignorance of each other's language and the constant presence of a police minder, flourished with the help of a sense of humour which they found they had in common. On first meeting the two had shaken hands formally but after a few days in some pretty remote places and some hair-raising adventures, they had become firm friends. Dinsher's way of showing his brotherly affection for the Welshman was to put an arm round his shoulder and say, "Ah! Robin Hood!"

The essay ends at the airport as the Welsh film crew take leave of their Turkish colleagues:

After I had given him a small gift as a token of my thanks for everything,

Dinsher suddenly came up to me, embraced my shoulders tightly, and kissed me first on the one cheek and then on the other. It was a strangely unexpected experience but one which showed that the young Turk had accepted me as a friend. He had demonstrated it with the strong embrace of the East, and not with the limp, arm's-length handshake of the West. What was painful, however, was the realisation that it wasn't so much a greeting that had taken place between Dinsher Hazirol and myself on the morning of our departure, as a farewell. And a farewell for ever. But for long as I live, I shall never forget that holy kiss on the airfield of Izmir.

The same emotional tug and a sense of our common humanity run through many of Robin's essays, though perhaps not so touchingly as in this instance.

Robin Williams first came to prominence as one of the three vocalists who formed the close-harmony group known as Triawd y Coleg while he was an undergraduate in Bangor during the 1940s. The group was so popular that whenever they sang on the wireless it was said that the streets of North Wales emptied. This experience, at a time when popular entertainment in Welsh was still in its infancy, gave him his first taste of broadcasting. He had a fine speaking voice and debonair good looks that made him something of a charmer in later appearances on television.

His first book proved equally popular. *Y Tri Bob* ("The three Bobs", 1970) is a study of Bob Owen the bibliophile, Bob Lloyd the eisteddfod adjudicator, and Bob Roberts the folk-singer. The rich folk-culture they represented provided him with one of the sources of his patriotism and inspiration as a writer.

All his books contain essays that are admired by aficionados of Welsh prose, a small but gallant band, and his work is sure to find a place in any anthology of *ysgrifau* which may be compiled in the new century.

Robin Williams, broadcaster, essayist and minister of the church: born Penycaerau, Caernarfonshire 3 September 1923; married 1950 Doris Evans (one son, one daughter); died Bangor, Gwynedd 20 December 2003.

The Independent (24 December 2003)

Islwyn Ffowc Elis

Writer who revived the Welsh-language novel

The most popular Welsh-language writer of the 20th century, Islwyn Ffowc Elis, at the age of 29 in 1953, published a novel which captured the imagination of his generation and breathed new life into the writing and reading of Welsh prose.

It was *Cysgod y Cryman* (translated as *Shadow of the Sickle*, 1998), the story of the Vaughans of Lleifior, a farm in upland Montgomeryshire, and the pressures brought upon Edward Vaughan, the father, by the changing social conditions of the post-war period. His son Harri, under the influence of a raven-haired *allumeuse* with whom he becomes involved at university, rebels against the old Liberal values of Edwardian Wales and embraces Communism, and in the novel's sequel, *Yn Ol i Lleifior* (1956; translated as *Return to Lleifior*, 1999), tries to run the farm on co-operative lines.

The Lleifior books were a milestone in the history of the modern Welsh novel as much by virtue of their contemporaneity as by their flowing and inventive style, which, after decades of heavily didactic writing in stiff and sometimes archaic language, delighted younger readers and won for their author the status of a best-seller on a scale not seen since the days of Daniel Owen, who wrote moralistically of chapel culture towards the end of the Victorian era.

In their themes, too, the novels broke new ground. Though set in a rural community, they dealt with characters who represented a modern sense of unease with established ways, while their intimations of Marxism and social rebellion seemed genuinely new and daring.

One of the bravest things they did was to paint a sympathetic portrait of "the good German", the saintly Karl Weissman who, after working on the Lleifior land as a prisoner of war, chooses to stay on after 1945, learns Welsh and eventually, after much tribulation and on the very last page of the latter novel, becomes engaged to Greta Vaughan, Harri's vivacious sister.

Another of Islwyn Ffowc Elis's bold innovations was the odious Englishman Paul Rushmere, a Liverpool surgeon whom Greta marries out of gratitude for his having saved her mother's life: he has no patience with his wife's patriotism and, until his death in a road accident, is the character whom readers most love to hiss.

The novels sold in their thousands and were never thereafter out of print. Adapted for radio and television, abridged for Welsh-learners, and on the syllabus of the Welsh Joint Education Committee for more than forty years, they became classics of modern Welsh literature.

Islwyn Ffowc Elis's publishers, Gomer Press of Llandysul in Cardiganshire, were so encouraged by sales that they began developing their list in search of new readers for a genre which had seemed, in Welsh, to be under threat because of the paucity of suitable material for readers not yet in middle age. The author went on to publish a book a year until the end of the 1950s and, for a while, was able to live as that rare thing in Wales, a full-time novelist

He was born at his aunt's council house in Acton, near Wrexham in Denbighshire, in 1924, but brought up a farmer's son at Glynceiriog in the same county. Like most country children at that time, he spoke only Welsh until the age of ten. After receiving his secondary education at Llangollen, he went up to the University College of North Wales, Bangor, and then – at his father's insistence – trained for the Presbyterian ministry at the Theological Colleges in Aberystwyth and Bala. During the Second World War he was a conscientious objector on religious grounds.

He served as a Calvinistic Methodist minister at Llanfair Caereinion in Montgomeryshire and at Newborough in Anglesey, but was unhappy there and left the ministry in 1956, suffering a breakdown brought on by overwork and a sense of utter failure, or at least an acute awareness that he had no aptitude for it. He was courageous enough to publish an account of this crisis in his denomination's paper, *Y Drysorfa* ("The treasury"), in which he questioned the need for denominationalism and proposed the closure of all chapels and churches in favour of house meetings.

The portraits of the Reverends Tynoro Thomas and Gareth Evans in the Lleifior novels represent the two poles of what a Nonconformist minister can be, the one doctrinally old-fashioned and socially inept, the other well-read, open-minded and eager to meet the world in all its challenging complexity, even to treat Harri Vaughan's atheism seriously. The author left no doubt as to which kind he preferred and had tried to be.

From 1956 to 1963 Islwyn lived in Bangor as a freelance writer and producer of radio programmes for the BBC. He had already won the

Prose Medal at the National Eisteddfod with a collection of essays, *Cyn Oeri'r Gwaed* ("Before the blood runs cold", 1952), in which he first experimented with the rich, limpid style later developed in the narrative of his novels. His seven years in Bangor were something of a psychological victory on behalf of Welsh writers, proving that it was possible to live, albeit precariously, by writing in Welsh.

Always politically active on behalf of Plaid Cymru, he stood as the party's candidate in Montgomeryshire at the general elections of 1959 and 1964 and at the by-election of 1962 caused by the death of Clement Davies, but came nowhere near to shaking the Liberal fiefdom in that constituency.

He played a key role as a press officer in Gwynfor Evans's victory at the by-election in Carmarthen in 1966, when Plaid Cymru won its first seat. He also edited a collection of stories by party members, *Storiau'r Deffro* ("Stories of the awakening"), published in 1959, and did a stint as editor of its newspaper, *Y Ddraig Goch* ("The red dragon").

His nationalism had been awakened when, as a boy he had observed the Welsh of the border areas coming into contact with their English neighbours in the market-town of Oswestry. The boundary between Wales and England, only two miles from his home, had for him an almost mythic significance.

"We in our mountain fastness spoke Welsh," he wrote in a classic essay published in my symposium *Artists in Wales* in 1971: "They on the plain spoke English. We could sing spontaneously in harmony. They could not. We talked of preachers and poets, they of footballers and racehorses. As a boy I was fascinated by the difference."

If there is an anti-English strain in his writing, he was candid enough to trace its source to the teachers who had tyrannised him at school and to quote, in his own defence, the words of D.H. Lawrence: "A writer sheds his sickness in books." He was particularly hurt by not having been taught the history of his own country, a lack which he made up in later life by avid reading.

With his second novel, *Ffenestri Tua'r Gwyll* ("Windows towards the twilight", 1953), he moved into the less familiar world of the arts in which a wealthy, sophisticated, neurotic, sexually frustrated, middle-aged woman dominates and exploits the writers and painters who enjoy her patronage. When it was not so well received, he returned to the people and places he knew best, the yeoman farmers and labourers of Montgomeryshire, and wrote the second Lleifior novel, though not before reviewing *Ffenestri Tua'r Gwyll* in an article entitled "My Unsuccessful Novel".

Other novels followed in quick succession. *Wythnos yng Nghymru Fydd* ("A week in the Wales of the future"), published by Plaid Cymru in 1957, in which a time-traveller visits a future Wales, finding first an utopian society enjoying full self-government and, in another section, a country known as West England in which all traces of Welsh culture have been obliterated by a totalitarian regime, is the most propagandist, though untypical, of all his novels, but it opened up a vein of magic realism in Welsh writing long before it became popular in English.

Islwyn could be acerbic about Wales. With *Blas y Cynfyd* ("A taste of the old world", 1958) he took as his theme the return of a Welshman to the idyllic district of his youth and his gradual disillusionment with its pettiness and hypocrisy. In *Tabyrddau'r Babongo* ("Drums of the Babongo", 1961) he turned to the colonisation of Africa and its implications for other repressed cultures and, always ready to bend the genres, in *Y Blaned Dirion* ("The fair planet", 1968) he wrote the first satirical science fiction in Welsh.

In 1963 Islwyn Ffowc Elis joined the staff of Trinity College, Carmarthen, as a lecturer in Welsh and Drama, but remained in that post for only five years. He then worked as an editor and translator with the Welsh Books Council, but found that having to deal with other writers' manuscripts had an inimical effect on his own work and he went through a painful period in which he wrote very little.

After four more years as a freelance writer, living in Wrexham, in 1975 he took up a lecturer's post at St David's University College, Lampeter, where he was appointed Reader in 1984 and where he remained until his retirement four years later. His students and colleagues found him a conscientious and inspiring teacher, happiest when encouraging young people to write.

A mild-mannered and diffident man, unsure of his success as a novelist and sometimes prickly in face of even the mildest criticism, he was so upset when a colleague of mine at the Arts Council politely enquired as to the progress of a novel for which he had been given a bursary that he abandoned the writing of it, after some 60,000 words, and it never saw the light of day.

He nevertheless persevered with his short stories, collected in the volume *Marwydos* ("Embers") in 1974, with the writing of plays, notably one about Howell Harris, leader of the Methodist Revival in Wales, and the composition of songs, in which he took great pleasure. Some of his lyrics, set to music, are still sung in light entertainment programmes on Welsh radio and television, and his short story "Song of a Pole" has been widely translated. He also made a charming Welsh translation of the *Arabian Nights* and in 1998 published a collection of his highly polished essays and radio talks under the title *Naddion* ("Shavings").

Some critics have taken the view that Islwyn Ffowc Elis, in his attempts to create a wider audience for the Welsh novel by making his work more popular in its appeal, set limits on the literary quality of his writing. That is to underestimate the efficacy of his prose style and the gripping suspense of many of his plots. It is also to ignore the liberating effect he had on other Welsh novelists who, since his day, have taken the form to new heights.

Islwyn was unperturbed by such strictures and, in this connection, fond of pointing to Graham Greene as a writer of "entertainments" which beguiled the reader with their plots and characterisation, as he had set out to do in Welsh. Be that as it may, his books were read for the sheer pleasure of their style by generations of readers and when, in 1999, the first Lleifior novel was voted Welsh Book of the Century, together with its English counterpart, the *Collected Poems* of R.S. Thomas, there was little surprise or envy in literary Wales.

Islwyn Ffowc Elis, writer: born Wrexham, Denbighshire 17 November 1924; Lecturer in Welsh, Trinity College, Carmarthen 1963-68; editor and translator, Welsh Books Council 1968-71; Lecturer in Welsh, St David's University College, Lampeter 1975-84, Reader 1984-88; married 1950 Eirlys Owen (one daughter); died Carmarthen 22 January 2004.

The Independent (27 January 2004)

Nicholas Evans

Painter of coal-mines and miners

The painter Nicholas Evans was unusual in that he did not begin painting until he was in his late sixties and did not exhibit his work until 1978, when he was 71. In that year he held a one-man exhibition at the Arts Council's Oriel Gallery in Cardiff, and was immediately acclaimed as an original painter who depicted his subject matter – the mines and miners of South Wales – in a new and disturbing way.

Whereas painters like Josef Herman and Will Roberts emphasised the heroic robustness of colliers without ever having worked at the coal-face, Nick Evans showed them as victims, their spectral faces ravaged by physical toil and the harsh conditions of work underground which he had experienced as a young man. There is perhaps something troglodytic about his miners, even when they take part in hunger marches or, in scenes that call to mind Stanley Spencer's Cookham, when they ascend in swarms to heaven at the Last Trump, but the painter's sympathy for their lot gives them an iconic power.

Nicholas Evans's show at the Oriel Gallery, which was followed by another at Browse & Darby in London, took the art world by storm. Lawrence Gowing, Professor at the Slade School, compared his work with that of Diego Rivera, the revolutionary Mexican muralist. Every trade union in the country, he wrote in the catalogue, should buy one of Evans's paintings because they tackled the large themes of life and death and portrayed working men with stark realism. The pictures are now in many public galleries, including the Tate Modern and the Glynn Vivian in Swansea, and he exhibited regularly at the Royal Academy's summer show.

His first admirers were surprised to learn that, although he confined himself to painting miners, for the most part, Nicholas Evans had worked underground for only three years. He had left the pits, at his mother's insistence, after his father's death in an accident at the Fforchaman Colliery near Aberdare in 1923, when he was sixteen. He became a railwayman and, in due course, found a relatively safe surface job as a GWR engine driver attached to the coal industry in the Cynon Valley.

His ability to draw was discovered by a teacher at his primary school, who gave him a new pencil and encouraged him to sketch, which he did for a while only to stop because he could not afford to buy paper. He took up drawing again in his sixties as an antidote to a sense of purposelessness he felt after giving up his job. By then the coal industry of South Wales was in terminal decline, but it was as if a lifetime's experience of manual work and the communal memory of the pits were flowing down his arm and seeking expression. He was particularly good at drawing the tools of the colliers' trade, their helmets and mandrels and tommyboxes, the pit-ponies and the timbers which held up the roof.

What began as a hobby became an obsession and his small terraced house in Abernant started to fill up with paintings stacked high in every room. Soon there were so many piled around the walls that once they collapsed on top of him, pinning him down for several hours until he was found by his daughter, Rhoda. It was in collaboration with her that he produced a book about his art, *Symphonies in Black* (1987).

Untrained and painting with his hands and rags on square pieces of hardboard that he bought at a local DIY store and primed with emulsion, he first taught himself perspective and then proceeded to fracture it in a bid to convey the physical and spiritual pain suffered by his former workmates. Their eyes are always half-shut, their noses equine, their hands like shovels, and his palette seems to have had only black, grey, white and a phantasmagorical blue.

In "The Last Bond" the colliers coming up the mineshaft are hardly individuals, because he tended to give the same features to all his faces, and they are pressed against the bars of the cage because they share a common destiny in the claustrophobic environment of the mine. "The men's faces are big," he told the art historian Peter Lord, "because I want to overpower you. I'm shouting at you. Because I'm angry."

If, since they are rooted in a specific social and historical context, there is a political message implied in many of his paintings, there is also a deeply religious dimension. Shortly after his father's death, Nicholas Evans experienced a spiritual conversion and joined the Pentecostal Church, to which he remained faithful for the rest of his life. A lay preacher, he tended to explain his paintings in biblical imagery: the pit of hell, the outer darkness, the fiery coals, the light of the world, and so on.

Many depict religious scenes in an industrial setting. "Entombed – Jesus in the Midst" (1974), now in the collection of the National Museums and Galleries of Wales, shows Christ preaching to miners at their place of work. His figures often strike biblical poses, as in "Carrying out the Dead" (1979) and "Black Avalanche" (1978), in which he responded to the Aberfan Disaster of 1966, where the central figure of a policeman carrying a child's body is surrounded by grieving parents as in a Crucifixion scene.

Nick Evans went on painting until well into his nineties and turned up, cheerful and sociable as ever in his black beret, for the private view of "In His Oils", his exhibition at the Rhondda Heritage Park (on the site of a former mine) in March 2001. The esteem in which he was generally held was reflected in the fact that none of his paintings was priced at under £2,000.

Nicholas Evans, engine-driver and painter: born Aberdare, Glamorgan 10 January 1907; married 1928 Annie Lambert (died 1997; two sons, one daughter); died Abernant, Rhondda Cynon Taff 5 February 2004.

The Independent (5 February 2004)

John Ackerman

Dylan Thomas scholar and biographer

John Ackerman came to prominence as an early critic of the work of Dylan Thomas and did much to lay the foundations for what has since become something of an industry. Ackerman's seminal book *Dylan Thomas: his life and work*, published in 1964, only eleven years after Thomas died in a New York hospital, was a pioneering study that was noted for its critical acumen and balanced account of his life and the circumstances of his death.

It was particularly good on the writer's roots in Swansea, where he had been born and brought up, and in Carmarthenshire, from where his people had come and where he still had relatives, and took as its starting-point his famous description of himself: "One: I am a Welshman; two: I am a drunkard; three: I am a lover of the human race, especially of women." Ackerman examined the extent to which Thomas's poetry and prose were influenced by his Welsh background, arguing that it was more relevant than such passing interests as Surrealism and Freudian psychology. The poet who emerges is not the Dionysiac rantipole of popular anecdote but a religious artist capable of writing 200 drafts of a single poem.

Other biographers, such as John Malcolm Brinnin, had recorded Thomas's calamitous last weeks in America, but John Ackerman pointed to the peculiarly close relationship between the work and early life, bringing to his task a thorough understanding of southwest Wales in the inter-war years.

He visited most of the places with which the writer had been associated, and laid down a number of important markers – for instance, that Thomas, who knew no Welsh, could not have been influenced by Welsh-language poetry – and dispelled several misconceptions about what later commentators have persisted in calling, despite all the evidence to the contrary marshalled by John Ackerman, the "bardic" nature of his role as a poet. Above all, the book was exemplary in avoiding literary over-elaboration and the sensationalism which has dogged Thomas studies ever since.

I first came across John Ackerman in 1970, when he began contributing poems and reviews to my magazine *Poetry Wales*. He went on to publish only one slim volume of verse, *The Image and the Dark*

(1975), but it contained a handful of poems that have ensured for him a place in most anthologies of Welsh writing in English. I recall, in particular, his elegies for Aneurin Bevan, Vernon Watkins and L.A.G. Strong, in which he blended a sense of personal loss with an awareness of more public themes, though he was deeply distrustful of "polite and politic men". His elegy for Bevan (recently voted Welsh Hero of all time) ends with the memorable line: "We fail our heroes, that's what they are for."

When, in 1975, the Welsh Arts Council decided to mount an exhibition in the Sherman Theatre in Cardiff to mark the twentieth anniversary of Dylan Thomas's death, John Ackerman was the obvious choice for curator. The catalogue he put together, *Welsh Dylan*, now a collector's item, was a fascinating album of photographs, manuscripts and other artefacts, many of which had never been seen in public before and on which all subsequent biographies have drawn. John turned up at the reception at which the exhibition was opened by Aeronwy, the writer's daughter, with a Wildean carnation in his lapel, hardly able to contain his delight that so many wished to see the fruits of his meticulous research.

He was born John Ackerman Jones – Wales is a country where the surname Jones can be dropped to no great disadvantage – in the mining town of Maesteg in 1934. His father, a slaughterman and butcher with a stall in Bridgend Market and a van taking meat to outlying villages, soon left his mother and he grew up in the company of numerous aunts; John described his father as "a ruthless, crooked, remote, confident, energetic, and violent man" and his loathing never diminished. The family, being "trade" in a society where almost everyone worked in heavy industry, was comparatively well off and all its members of independent spirit.

His matriarchal grandmother Florence, an autodidact of strong left-wing convictions and literary tastes, presided over a kind of salon in the Lamb, the local pub,where she would address customers on questions of the day before reciting such music-hall favourites as "The Curfew Shall Not Ring Tonight" and "The women of Mumbles Head" and Utopian poems like Tennyson's "Locksley Hall" that speaks of "the Parliament of man, the Federation of the world". It was she who took the boy to London in 1945 to watch, in Downing Street, members of the new Labour administration leaving No 10 for the State Opening of Parliament. John Ackerman was to be a Labour supporter for the rest of his life.

Florence is the heroine of his "fictional autobiography", *Up the Lamb* (1998), which describes with love, sympathy and percipience a resilient, working-class community in which the role of women was paramount. Many of the book's readers were reminded of the auto-biographies of Richard Hoggart and the monologues of Alan Bennett, so much were understatement and a nice sense of humour used to make telling points not only about individuals but the com-munities in which they lived. The book's epigraph is a quotation from Proust: "The true paradises are paradises we have lost."

But although Maesteg was to keep a hold on John's affections, as a gay man who cultivated the campest of manners he found its macho society claustrophic and threatening. After taking degrees at King's College, Westfield College and Birkbeck College at London University, he became an English teacher at St Olave's Church of England School, near Southwark Cathedral, and then lecturer at the Glamorgan College of Education in Barry, and from 1966 to 1984 at Avery Hill College, now part of the University of Greenwich.

He maintained his keen interest in "the Rimbaud of Cwmdonkin Drive" throughout his academic career, publishing *Welsh Dylan: Dylan Thomas's life, writing, and his Wales* (1979), *A Dylan Thomas Companion* (1991) and *Dylan Thomas: the filmscripts* (1995), all three of which were important contributions to our understanding of the writer's oeuvre.

The last book presents a unique portrait of Thomas as a profes-sional writer for the cinema, especially what he called "my war-work" – the documentaries he wrote about London and Coventry during the Blitz. Written to raise public morale, these filmscripts revealed Thomas's political views and promoted an ideal of a more just post-war society of social welfare and full employment.

John Ackerman was a gentle, sociable man who enjoyed friendships with many writers in Wales and London. A bookman to his finger-tips, he had no hobbies except that, on his frequent return visits to Maesteg, he enjoyed nothing better than listening to the choir prac-tice that is still held at the Tyla pub in the nearby village of Llangynwyd every Friday evening.

The book about Dylan Thomas's adventures in the bibulous ambience of Fitzrovia and another about the more ascetic R.S. Thomas on which he had been working for several years had to be put aside with the onset of dementia, and he died in a nursing-home at South Cornelly, near Porthcawl, surrounded by books that he could no longer read.

John Ackerman Jones (John Ackerman), literary critic: born Maesteg, Glamorgan 24 March 1934; Lecturer in English, Glamorgan College of Education 1962-66; Lecturer in English, Avery Hill College 1966-84; died South Cornelly, Bridgend 2 March 2004.

The Independent (11 March 2004)

Eirug Wyn

Iconoclastic novelist and humourist

Eirug Wyn upset the apple-cart of Welsh letters on more than one occasion and, just in case his compatriots were too thick-skinned or too polite to notice, pelted them with rotten fruit until they collapsed with laughter.

His talent was iconoclastic and, to change the metaphor, his favourite target the sacred cows on the mantelpiece of the Welsh Establishment, at which he took pot-shots with all the dark humour at his command. At the same time, his readers had the impression that he dearly loved what he most gleefully castigated and that, like Caradoc Evans, "the hammer of the Welsh", he did it sometimes for sheer fun but more often because he thought his countrymen deserved better. It made for a complex man and a beguiling writer.

Like many who have kicked over the traces in Wales, Eirug Wyn was a son of the manse: his father was a Nonconformist minister in Llanbryn-mair, in the old county of Montgomery. The village has a tradition of Radical dissent and was the home of Samuel Roberts, the great campaigning journalist who, in the 19th century, railed against slavery, English imperialism, capital punishment and the Established Church.

Eirug Wyn was cast in the same mould, except that he put his shoulder to the wheel in the struggle for the Welsh language and its culture. In the 1970s he was a leading member of Cymdeithas yr Iaith Gymraeg (The Welsh-Language Society) and, like so many young people in that confrontational decade, was fined and spent several terms in prison as part of a non-violent campaign to win a greater measure of official recognition for Welsh.

In 1962, as a schoolboy in Deiniolen, Caernarfonshire, where his family had moved, he had listened to the BBC radio lecture by Saunders Lewis in which the veteran Nationalist had called for a movement which would challenge the British state for its failure to grant legal status to Welsh. A few years later, as a sixth former, he decided he would take direct action of his own: he refused to display the L sign on the car in which he was learning to drive, courting prosecution until it became legal to use a D (for *Dysgwr*), a small victory which eventually led to the widespread use of the Welsh version.

On another occasion, in 1971, he caused chaos in court when he protested against being tried in English, making even the judge, policemen and journalists laugh aloud at his surrealist wit.

As a student at Trinity College, Carmarthen, Eirug Wyn (he had dropped the anglicised spelling Wynne) discovered that if you are going to have a revolution it is best not to be too gloomy about it. He was a regular contributor to the satirical magazine *Lol* ("Nonsense"), sharing with his friend Robat Gruffudd, the magazine's proprietor, a distaste for the creaking orthodoxies of Welsh-speaking Wales. Between them they made fun, by fair means and foul, of many eminent Welsh people, publishing blatantly scurrilous articles, mildly lubricious pin-ups and outrageously spoof book reviews that besmirched the reputations of those they wished to belittle. On the other hand, to be lampooned in *Lol* was seen as a sort of accolade and some, affecting insouciance, pretended to complain if they did not regularly appear in its pages.

Unfortunately, when ownership of the magazine passed to Eirug Wyn it led to disaster for his business interests. In 1993 he was taken to court for having defamed a number of directors making programmes for S4C, who were awarded substantial damages that ruined him temporarily. It is said that he could have avoided the outcome if only he had offered to apologise in public but, a headstrong and often wilful man, he refused and faced the consequences.

Among his many commercial enterprises – he was a canny businessman who once had a brisk line in "Welsh watches" – had been bookshops in Carmarthen and Caernarfon, a company that produced Welsh greeting cards and a share in a printing works at Penygroes. He also worked as a television producer with Ffilmiau'r Bont, one of the most accomplished of the many independent companies now flourishing in Wales. But he found greatest delight in writing novels, of which he published fifteen between 1992 and 2009, including four for children.

As a point of honour he did without grant-aid because, in his view, it was patronage dispensed by the tainted hand of the Establishment – by which he meant the Arts Council and the Books Council – for which he reserved his most pungent gall. His books nevertheless sold well, commanding not only admiration among the book-buying public but also respect in academic circles.

Despite his animus towards the great and the good, Eirug Wyn was a genial, sociable man with a wicked sense of mischief, delighting in the fact that he was often mistaken for Eurig Wyn, the Plaid Cymru MEP and prospective candidate for the Ynys Môn seat at Westminster, a confusion which he did nothing to dispel since they shared the same political beliefs. Among his interests were Manchester United, Native Americans and Elvis Presley, about whom he wrote a splendid book in Welsh. He also published a volume of verse under the pseudonym Derek Tomos which is a hilarious send-up of some of our most famous poets.

He came to prominence as a prose writer when he won the Prose Medal at the National Eisteddfod of 1998 with a novel entitled *Blodyn Tatws* ("Potato flower"). To win this once is usually enough to satisfy the *amour propre* of most Welsh writers but Wyn went on to win it again in 2000 with *Tri Mochyn Bach* ("Three little pigs"), perhaps the most entertaining of all his books. He also won the Daniel Owen Prize, the most lucrative award the Eisteddfod has to offer novelists, in 1994 and 2002. The main character in his hardhitting novel *Bitsh!* ("Bitch!", 2002) is a lad employed in a branch of Woolworth's during the 1960s; it pillories the Welsh people for, *inter alia*, their failure to resist the anglicisation of their country.

He wrote in his hospital bed almost until the last, and had the satisfaction of seeing a collection of his short stories, *Y Dyn yn y Cefn heb Fwstash* ("The man at the back without a moustache"), appear just a month before he died.

Eirug Price Wynne (Eirug Wyn), writer: born Llanbryn-mair, Montgomeryshire 11 December 1950; married 1973 Gwenda Pretty (two daughters); died Bangor, Gwynedd 25 April 2004.

The Independent (10 May 2004)

Alun Richards

Prolific writer about the valleys of post-industrial South Wales

Alun Richards was the most talented and prolific of that generation of Welsh prose-writers who came to prominence in the 1960s, just as the industrial communities of the South Wales valleys were beginning to lose the cultural cohesion that had depended on coal and steel and as the Nonconformist chapels started to be turned into bingo halls and supermarts.

Whereas writers of the inter-war generation such as Rhys Davies, Glyn Jones and Gwyn Thomas had been able to write about the life of pit, steelworks, miners' lodge and Sunday School, Alun took as his material a society which was more prosperous, hedonistic and socially mobile, less concerned with religion, politics and working conditions, but still with enough fierce pride in community to distinguish it from the rootless, middle-class suburbia of Cardiff and the leafy villages of the Vale of Glamorgan, some twelve miles to the south. In one of his short stories, "The Scandalous Thoughts of Elmyra Mouth", the pulchritudinous heroine, whose ambitious husband wants them to move down the valley to be near his job as an assistant cameraman with BBC Wales, refuses to do so with the ultimatum, "Travel, you bugger. You'll not move me an inch!"

The view of South Wales in the novels, plays and short stories of Alun Richards, of which there are a great many, is comic, unsentimental, affectionate but scathing in its observation of social pretension and flawed relationships. If many of his stories are set in the male world of rugby club and the roughest of pubs, he is also good at depicting the lot of women involved in failed marriages, adultery and emotional crises arising from their role as homemakers, mothers and often sole breadwinners at a time when male unemployment was casting its shadow in places like Ebbw Vale, Merthyr Tydfil, Aberdare and the Rhondda.

At the heart of his writing is the former mining and railway town of Pontypridd, at the confluence of Taff and Rhondda, where Richards was born in 1929. In his fine autobiography, *Days of Absence* (1986), he described with engaging candour how he was brought up in a strict but loving, comfortable, English-speaking home by his Welsh-speaking maternal grandparents, his mother and father having separated three days after he was born. The identity of his father was kept from him and he glimpsed him only once, his trilby hat silhouetted behind the frosted glass of the front door on the sole occasion he was known to have called at the house.

This experience of being "a fatherless child", in addition to his having a birthmark on his cheek, was the making of Alun Richards as a writer. "I learned at an early age to lie low, to watch, to gauge a mood, to know when it was time to speak," he wrote:

I also learned to listen; to eavesdrop, gathering what bits and pieces of information I could. I listened from corners, behind doors, on tramcars, to hushed voices drifting out of the vestry after chapel, to the gossip of neighbours talking in the street. I kept these phrases to me, hugging them in the secret place.

The acute observation of place and people to be found in his stories had begun even before he went to school.

His time at Pontypridd Boys' Grammar School, one of the best of its kind in the whole of Wales, was marked by rebelliousness and a bare minimum of academic endeavour. "I was thirty-first when I went into the school and I've kept it up," he told his grandmother, still putting a brave face on things. His fraught relationship with E.R Thomas, known to us boys as Piggy, the martinet of a headmaster who served as the father Alun never had, is movingly described in the autobiography. One incident must suffice. Frog-marched into the Assembly Hall to be shown on the Roll of Honour the newly painted name of his uncle, an RAF pilot who had been shot down over Le Havre, he met the teacher's sarcastic jibe "A family of heroes, boy, and what are you?" with the defiant, quick-witted reply, "Alive!" It was a defining moment and thereafter a strange sort of bond grew between the man and boy. From always being in Piggy's bad book, Alun became his Gold Flake Boy, a coveted status because it meant being able to nip out to the shop kept by his grandmother in the middle of the school day and thus choose the lessons he wanted to miss.

After three years at the Monmouth Training College for Teachers in Caerleon, at which he found a place not by virtue of a very ordinary School Certificate but a glowing reference from his old headmaster, Alun served for three years with the Royal Navy, latterly in the rank of Instructor Lieutenant, and so began a fascination with the sea that was to remain with him for the rest of his life. He wrote extensively about ships and sailors, notably in two novels about maritime Swansea, *Ennal's Point* (1977) and *Barque Whisper* (1979), edited *The Penguin Book of Sea Stories* (1977) and *Against the Waves* (1978), and contributed many scripts to the popular television series *The Onedin Line*. For his books about the lifeboat service, he was presented with the Royal National Lifeboat Institution Public Relations Award.

Returning to Wales from London, where he had been a probation officer for three years, he became desperately ill with tuberculosis. He was admitted to the sanatorium at Talgarth in Breconshire where most of his fellow patients were silicotic colliers, many in the last stages of the terrible disease brought on by breathing the dust-laden air of the mines. The two years he spent in hospital as "a witness once more of Homo Sapiens with his trousers down" were a dreadful but enriching experience. Almost blind and left for long periods in a semi-coma as a result of his resistance to streptomycin, he was sustained by the courage, humour and comradeship of the older men in his ward who "kept an eye on him", fed him with bacon from their own plates, placed bets on horses for him, read to him and helped to nurse him back to health. "More than anything," he wrote in an essay for the volume *Artists in Wales* in 1971,

I learned that we are not as different from each other as we would like to believe, and yet each of us is unique... In the last resort, our nationality, race or colour did not matter. We were up against it, all of us had complications of one kind or another, but we made our stand for as long as we could, and one or two of us survived. It was an experience I shall never regret, meat and drink to the writer, whose business it is to make sense of every experience, to shape it in the process, an eternal search for understanding and reasons, and I have been lucky ever since.

From 1957 to 1967 Alun taught English in Cardiff but was then able to become a full-time writer and settle in Mumbles, a seaside suburb of Swansea where his wife was a teacher. He earned his bread and butter by writing for television, including adaptations of Georges Simenon, W. Somerset Maugham and H.G. Wells, and for theatres in Leatherhead, Coventry and Nottingham, though seldom in Wales; his stage plays were published under the title *Plays for Players* in 1975.

From time to time he took fellowships at Universities in Wales and

Australia, and was awarded a Japanese Foundation Fellowship in 1984. But his greatest achievement was in writing the short stories in *Dai Country* (1973) and *The Former Miss Merthyr Tydfil* (1976); his *Selected Stories* appeared in 1995. The most important of his novels are *The Elephant You Gave Me* (1963), *The Home Patch* (1966), *A Woman of Experience* (1969) and *Home to an Empty House* (1974). He also edited two editions of *The Penguin Book of Welsh Short Stories* which were much admired for their quality and range.

A connoisseur of rugby, he published *A Touch of Glory* (1980) on the occasion of the centenary of the Welsh Rugby Union, and in 1984 a memoir of Carwyn James, the rugby-player and coach, a very different kind of Welshman, Welsh-speaking and a staunch member of Plaid Cymru, with whom he had a rare and unexpected affinity. *Carwyn: a personal memoir* reveals his view of Wales, Welsh nationality and the role usually attributed in defining it to the Welsh language, and this in a country where four-fifths of the population are not Welsh-speakers. Welsh had played no part in Alun's upbringing and he tended to bristle when claims were made for it as a badge of Welsh identity, especially in the context of appointments to BBC Wales, an institution against which he invariably fulminated.

His own Welshness was intense and unequivocal, the basis for some of his best writing, but for him it had less to do with language than with the qualities he associated with the industrial, proletarian communities of South Wales: loyalty to family and workmates, warmheartedness, neighbourliness and compassion, a sense of humour in the face of adversity and the absence of deference on grounds of social class. "I am Welsh," he wrote definitively in 1971, "and the rest is propaganda."

Alun Morgan Richards, short-story writer, novelist and dramatist: born Pontypridd, Glamorgan 27 November 1929; married 1957 Helen Howden (three sons, one daughter); died Swansea 2 June 2004.

The Independent (6 June 2004)

J. Gwyn Griffiths

Poet, Classicist and Egyptologist

The immense erudition of J. Gwyn Griffiths, sometime Professor of Classics and Egyptology at the University College of Swansea, was combined with a practical involvement in Welsh politics and a deep attachment to the language and literature of his native Wales.

Although he taught for brief periods at the universities of Cairo, Bonn and Tübingen, it was in Swansea that his academic career was rooted and in the Welsh tradition that he found greatest delight. He was able, moreover, to pursue both with distinction and to move easily between the ancient world and the modern.

He was unusual among Welsh intellectuals in that, despite his academic responsibilities, he preferred a Bohemian way of life that paid scant attention to the bearded orthodoxies and sometimes expressed itself in writing that owed more to the European avant-garde, including Kurt Schwitters, the *collagiste* and Dadaist, than to the conservative niceties of Welsh letters. There was always a whiff of the exotic about him and he could be deadpan and offbeat in the acerbic things he had to say about his contemporaries.

The German influence on him was reinforced when, in 1939, he married Käte Bosse, a refugee from Nazi Germany, who shared not only his literary tastes, including the frank treatment of sexual topics, but also his professional interests. A scholar of Egyptology in her own right, she was for many years Keeper of Archaeology at Swansea Museum and honorary Curator of the Wellcome Museum in the city.

Their first home was at Pentre in the Rhondda Valley. J. Gwyn Griffiths had been born, a son of the Baptist manse, at nearby Porth in 1911 and, after reading Classics at the Universities of Cardiff, Liverpool and Oxford, had his first teaching job at his old grammar school.

In Pentre he and his wife formed a literary circle known as Cylch Cadwgan, the name of a local chieftain after whom Moel Cadwgan, a hill above the town, had been named and which they also gave to their house in St Stephen's Avenue; it was to become one of the most famous literary addresses in Wales. Among the group's members were the young writers Pennar Davies and Rhydwen Williams, both of whom remained close friends for the rest of their lives.

Sharing the same pacifist, left-wing and aesthetic ideals, Cadwgan discussed contemporary trends in European art and literature, arguing in the magazines of the day in favour of liberating Welsh literature from what they saw as the shackles of Puritanism and, more specifically, from the baneful effects of the Nonconformist chapel.

Surprisingly, the principal members of the group returned to the chapel's fold after the Second World War, Pennar Davies as a distinguished Congregationalist theologian, Rhydwen Williams as a Baptist minister and J. Gwyn Griffiths as a staunch, though questioning, member of the same denomination.

Even so, they had opened, if not broken, many windows, delivering a blast of fresh air into the staler corners of the Welsh cultural consciousness, so that J. Gwyn Griffiths, ever the storm petrel, was to look back on the 1940s with fond nostalgia as a time when he had done some of his best work.

The same rebellious spirit was to be found in the pages of *Y Fflam* ("The flame"), a magazine which he helped Euros Bowen edit between 1946 and 1952. Launched partly in response to what Cadwgan thought were the reactionary views of W.J. Gruffydd, Professor of Welsh at Cardiff, a Labour man and editor of the influential journal *Y Llenor* ("The man of letters"), its main aim was to provide a new platform for younger writers who were politically engaged with Plaid Cymru.

Some of the most effective grapeshot aimed at the grey eminence was the work of J. Gwyn Griffiths, but many younger bloods, including the iconoclastic poet Bobi Jones, now himself an elder statesman of the literary scene, had their fling in the pages of *Y Fflam*. It was here, too, that R.S. Thomas made his debut as a Welsh prose-writer of great gravitas and nationalist fire.

Griffiths's own verse was published in five volumes: *Yr Efengyl Dywyll* ("The dark gospel", 1944), the group symposium *Cerddi Cadwgan* ("Cadwgan poems",1953), *Ffroenau'r Ddraig* ("The dragon's nostrils", 1960), *Cerddi Cairo* ("Cairo poems", 1969) and *Cerddi'r Holl Eneidiau* ("All Souls poems", 1981). His poems are sometimes in traditional forms, frequently the sonnet, but the language and metaphors he employed were often too provocative or too obscure for the reader used to the pretty lyrics of the Welsh bucolics.

Patriotic and sometimes propagandist, they take Wales as their theme but in the wider context of the European and classical civilisation in which he was steeped. His poems about Cairo, where he was Visiting Professor in 1968, reflect his profound regard for ancient Egypt while his fifth book, perhaps his most accomplished, was largely written during a sabbatical year at All Souls College, Oxford.

Even so, they range over a huge variety of subjects unconfined by time and place. Catullus rubs shoulders with Howell Harris, leader of the Methodist Revival in Wales, and Gwynfor Evans with Beethoven, while the references are to the Koran, Mithras, Osiris, Wotan, Olympus, the *Madonna degli Alpini*, Hecate, Gentileschi, the Lorelei Rock, the Via Appia and, as if to strain the learning of his most erudite readers to the full, to Champollion – the founder of Egyptology who is credited with having been the first, in 1832, to decipher hieroglyphics. Such a gallimaufry of allusions, together with his fondness for a macaronic style, goes a long way to making J. Gwyn Griffiths the Welsh counterpart of the Scottish poet Hugh MacDiarmid.

The same astonishing multilingual range is to be found in his literary criticism, collected in the volume *I Ganol y Frwydr* ("Into the thick of battle", 1970). Here he tackled the question of whether the writer should be politically engaged, tracing it to Virgil and Martial, and taking in European writers like Moses Hess, Karel Capek and Rilke before examining the pressures on Welsh writers to address issues affecting the moral condition of the nation.

J. Gwyn Griffiths himself left the ivory tower and entered "the thick of battle" on behalf of Plaid Cymru. He stood as the party's candidate on two occasions: in the Gower constituency at the general election of 1959 and again in 1964. He was editor of *Y Ddraig Goch* ("The red dragon"), the party's newspaper between 1948 and 1952, and wrote a number of political pamphlets in which he set out his belief in international co-operation.

During his time at Swansea, where he was appointed Lecturer in the Classics Department in 1946 and given a personal Chair in 1973, he published several scholarly works, beginning with *The Conflict of Horus and Seth* (1960). His editions of Plutarch's *De Iside et Osiride* (1970) and Apuleius of Madauros' *The Isis Book* (1975), the last book of *The Golden Ass*, are both magisterial and brought him a worldwide reputation among scholars in the field.

He went on to write *The Origins of Osiris and his Cult* (1980) and *The Divine Verdict: a study of divine judgement in the ancient religions*

(1991). A selection of his essays was published as *Atlantis and Egypt* in 1991 and his *Triads and Trinity* appeared in 1996.

A full bibliography of his scholarly works, including his contributions to the journal of the Deutsches Archäologisches Institut and to the *Journal of Egyptian Archaeology*, which he edited from 1970 to 1978, is found in the Festschrift edited by A.B. Lloyd, *Studies in Pharaonic Religion and Society* (1992).

J. Gwyn Griffiths strove to marry his classical interests with his commitment to the Welsh language by translating from Latin and Greek. For the Classics Section of the Guild of Graduates of the University of Wales, which he founded in 1951, he edited *Cerddi o'r Lladin* ("Poems from the Latin", 1982), *Cerddi Groeg Clasurol* ("Poems from the Classical Greek", 1989) and a Welsh version of Aristotle's *Poetics* (*Barddoneg*, 1978), which was reissued to his great satisfaction on the occasion of his ninetieth birthday and the Guild's half-centenary in 2001.

Between 1979, when he retired, and 1995, he edited a series of translations for the Welsh Academy, the national association of writers in Wales; it included works by Lampedusa, Zbigniew Herbert, Rilke, Camus, Ionesco, Dürrenmatt, Turgenev, Solzhenitsyn and Galdos, as well as selections of verse from the Gaelic, Irish, German, French, Spanish, Italian, Polish, Russian, Chinese, Persian and Hebrew.

His attachment to his mother-tongue was central to his life's work. During the 1960s, when the Welsh Language Society began challenging the law in an attempt to secure official status for Welsh, he was fined for minor offences on several occasions and was often to be seen at its demonstrations, one of the senior figures in Welsh academic life who backed the robust but non-violent campaign.

A friend of the veteran Nationalist D.J. Williams, who in 1937 had been imprisoned for his part in an act of arson at Penyberth in the Llŷn peninsula, he edited a collection of his stories, *Y Gaseg Ddu* ("The black mare", 1970), and wrote with affection about him.

It was a source of great satisfaction to J. Gwyn Griffiths that his German-born wife, who wrote vivaciously in Welsh, and both their sons, threw themselves into the political and cultural life of Wales with the same gusto. Robat Gruffudd is one of the most enterprising of Welsh publishers and Heini Gruffudd is a tutor in the Department of Adult Continuing Education at the University of Wales, Swansea.

Both are accomplished novelists and deeply involved in the ongoing struggle to win for Welsh the place in the nation's life to which their father devoted so much of his prodigious energies.

John Gwyn Griffiths, writer and classical scholar: born Porth, Glamorgan 7 December 1911; Assistant Lecturer in Classics, University College of Swansea 1946-47, Lecturer 1947-59, Senior Lecturer 1959-65, Reader 1965-73, Professor of Classics and Egyptology 1973-79 (Emeritus); married 1939 Käte Bosse (died 1998; two sons); died Swansea 15 June 2004.

The Independent (18 June 2004)

John Roberts Williams

Editor of Y Cymro *and pioneer of Welsh cinema*

John Roberts Williams was for seventeen years editor of *Y Cymro* ("The Welshman"), the weekly newspaper founded in Wrexham in 1932, which in his time was published in Oswestry and is now owned by North Wales Newspapers in Mold, Flintshire. He was its second editor and, between 1945 and 1962, made it into a popular and authoritative broadsheet reflecting life in Wales in all its aspects.

He brought to the paper a new professionalism learned in his first job with the Herald group in Caernarfon and, in particular, a keen interest in the political scene, both in Wales and the rest of Britain, contributing a witty column that made it essential reading for all with an interest in Welsh affairs. Under his editorship the circulation of *Y Cymro* rose to about 28,000, the highest for any Welsh-language weekly since the golden age of the periodical press in late Victorian times.

The pseudonym he used was John Aelod Jones, and although everyone knew who the writer was (there being few secrets in the small world of the Welsh media), he enjoyed keeping up the pretence that it wasn't him. The subterfuge enabled him the better to avoid being "nobbled", as he once explained to me, by the great and the good who were anxious to be featured in his column, and sometimes not.

He was also a pioneer of the Welsh cinema. While still editor of *Y Cymro*, and with the paper's photographer, Geoff Charles, but pitiably few resources, he directed *Yr Etifeddiaeth* ("The heritage"), a feature film shot in black and white with a CineKodak camera and shown for the first time, with both Welsh and English soundtracks, in Dolgellau during the National Eisteddfod of 1949.

This was not the first Welsh-language talkie – Sir Ifan ab Owen Edwards and John Ellis Williams had made *Y Chwarelwr* ("The quarryman") in 1935 – but it was the first attempt to make a film to the best possible standards of the day and it was rapturously received by audiences throughout North Wales, whether in chapel vestries or in the cinemas of the larger towns.

The film is about the social life of Eifionydd, that district between Porthmadog and Aberdaron on the Llŷn peninsula renowned for the richness of its traditional culture, particularly its music and poetry. John Roberts Williams had been born at Llangybi, near Pwllheli, in 1914 and was a typical man of Eifionydd in his staunch local pride and deep sympathy with his people's way of life.

In his first full-length film he set out to provide documentary evidence of an essentially pre-war culture which he knew was about to disappear for ever. It is seen through the eyes of Freddie Grant, a working-class black boy from Liverpool, who had been evacuated to Llangybi during the war and had learned to speak Welsh, the everyday language of the virtually monoglot community.

Among the vignettes that were captured on camera were a hiring fair at Pwllheli, where prosperous farmers took on their labourers, an open-air sermon by the renegade preacher Tom Nefyn Williams, men working in a wool factory, the Trefor granite quarry, and farm servants living in Spartan conditions in a stable loft – all scenes that would never be seen again. The film had a sonorous, if somewhat florid, commentary by Albert Evans-Jones, the veteran poet known by his bardic name Cynan, but was otherwise silent.

It ended on a cautionary note, with the newly built Butlin's holiday camp on the horizon meant to represent the threat to the indigenous culture of Eifionydd which the film first identified and which the camp subsequently proved to be.

Technically, *Yr Etifeddiaeth* was remarkable for its lighting and the clarity of its images, for the freshness of its observation of everyday scenes and its avoidance of the many clichés so dear to those outsiders who make travelogues about Wales. There were no clog-dancers or women in tall black hats, no harps and no country bumpkins, only the people of Eifionydd going about their daily round in quiet harmony with their neighbours.

It was even more remarkable in that John Roberts Williams and Geoff Charles had no editing machine and had to project the rushes on the wall of their office at *Y Cymro*, which paid them only their expenses in travelling from Oswestry to Caernarfonshire every weekend over a period of two years. John subsequently admitted that the film had many technical faults but remained proud of what was to become a landmark in the history of Welsh cinema.

Compared with *Yr Etifeddiaeth*, his subsequent films were less distinguished. They include a dutiful short about the production of *Y Cymro*, a portrait of the people of Connemara entitled *Tir Na Nog*

("Land of the young") and another, shot in one week, about the visit of a choir from Coedpoeth, near Wrexham, to Madrid, which concentrates more on bullfighting than on choral singing.

John left *Y Cymro* in 1962 and joined the first, short-lived television company Teledu Cymru, as Head of News, but the venture ended within the year in financial catastrophe and amid bitter acrimony. He was then appointed to a post with BBC Wales as editor of the news-magazine *Heddiw* ("Today"), developing it into the first major programme of its kind in the Welsh language.

He made two more documentaries which broke new ground with their eloquent commentaries and subtle camera work. The first, shown in 1970, was *Llanc o Lŷn* ("Young Man from Llŷn"), an affectionate portrait of the poet Cynan which was the first BBC Wales documentary to be shot in colour, followed by its companion piece, *Llanc o Eryri* ("Young man from Snowdonia"), about the writer T.H. Parry-Williams and the influence of landscape upon him.

But by now John had been appointed Head of the BBC's North Wales Department in Bangor, where his administrative duties prevented him from directing any more films. He turned instead to the radio talk, a genre which was to bring him a reputation as an accomplished broadcaster noted for his sardonic wit, deadpan delivery, independent judgement and keen eye for the incongruent in Welsh and world affairs. The effect on his listeners was rather like that of Alistair Cooke writing from America.

He published seven collections of his radio talks between 1984 and 2003, as well as a collection of essays, *Annwyl Gyfeillion* ("Dear friends", 1975), and a volume of short stories, *Arch Noa* ("Noah's ark", 1977), which included a typically self-deprecating review he had written of his own "small but substantial" book and in which, tongue in cheek, he compared it with the novels of Dostoevsky.

The wry humour in his writing, in which some critics detected the influence of Damon Runyon, was deeply rooted in the rich language and raffish characters of the town of Caernarfon. One of them was Wil Napoleon, a real-life portrait of a lovable rogue whose one claim to wider fame was that he had "starred as an extra" in the films *The Inn of the Sixth Happiness* and *The Vikings*, both shot locally.

Pressed to say, in a television programme made about him in 2003, whether he was a member of the Labour Party or Plaid Cymru – he had been associated with both during his student days at the

University College of North Wales, Bangor – John said he saw merit in both but had preferred to remain outside party politics so that he could be "objective" in his reporting, and this was one of the attractive aspects of all that he did. On the same occasion he admitted to having renounced his pacifism and joined the RAF in 1942 but without telling any of his friends, only to be rejected for military service on the grounds that he was deaf in one ear.

In his retirement, John Roberts Williams, a book-lover since his undergraduate days, founded *Y Casglwr* ("The collector"), the magazine of Cymdeithas Bob Owen, a society for book-collectors named after the renowned genealogist and bibliophile Bob Owen of Croesor.

John's autobiography *Yr Eiddoch yn Gywir* ("Yours sincerely"), which appeared in 1990, is an account not so much of his own life (a shy man, he was not much given to writing about himself) but a fascinating commentary on the media in Wales, both print and electronic, over the half-century of his working life.

He was also associated with a group of younger journalists looking into the possibility of publishing a daily newspaper in Welsh. It was a source of great satisfaction that he lived long enough to see *Cymru a'r Byd* ("Wales and the world"), a daily digest of news, launched on the internet by BBC Cymru.

John Roberts Williams, journalist, film director and writer: born Llangybi, Caernarfonshire 24 March 1914; editor, Y Cymro, *1945-62; Head, North Wales Department, Bangor, BBC Cymru 1970-76; editor,* Y Casglwr, *1976- 91; married 1941 Gwendolen Pugh Roberts (died 1969; one son and one daughter deceased); died Caernarfon, Gwynedd 28 October 2004.*

The Independent (30 October 2004)

Jonah Jones

Artist-craftsman in the tradition of Eric Gill

Jonah Jones was a sculptor who, despite a lack of formal training, won a reputation as a master-craftsman in stone and, in particular, as an artist devoted to the word in all its visual forms, from calligraphy to the inscriptions on gravestones. Like Eric Gill, with whose workshops at Pigotts he was briefly associated, and Brancusi, whom he admired more, he was attracted to the religious power of carved stone and was often commissioned to do ecclesiastical work in Wales and England.

For a while a convert to Roman Catholicism, he was fascinated by themes from the Old Testament, especially the story of Jacob – "that great, flawed character" – whose wrestling with the angel is an allegory of man's search for God. Some of his best work, such as the stained glass and carvings he did at Ratcliffe College Chapel and Ampleforth College in 1960 and the Gerard Manley Hopkins window at Loyola Hall near Liverpool, are eloquent expressions of the Catholic faith. For him, as for the Benedictines, *laborare est orare.*

The word, whether biblical or demotic, was the main source of his inspiration. The Trajan alphabet and the graffiti on the walls of the Roman catacombs were both, in his mind, proof that in the human psyche there is a profound desire to make one's mark as a permanent record in a fleeting world, and he believed that the artist, as quintessential man, was best equipped to do what he called "leaving my scratch".

Nor was he in favour of art as a luxury or commodity on which a price could be set, but preferred to make things that took their natural place in the community or landscape, relating them to the genius of the place and always hoping they would come to be accepted as part of the everyday environment.

The sculpture he made in Carrara marble and Welsh slate for the Association of Obstetric Anaesthetists in 1983 and now to be seen at its offices in Bedford Square in London is a good example of his aesthetic principles, as are the lapidary inscriptions to David Lloyd George and Dylan Thomas in Westminster Abbey. In Wales he is remembered as the sculptor of the memorial to the independent Princes al Aberffraw in Anglesey.

Jonah's down-to-earth approach to his art, his belief in the artist-craftsman as maker in a community, had been instilled in him from an early age. Born in 1919 near the pit-village of Washington in County Durham, he was the son of a miner who marched to London in the Jarrow Crusade, and his Geordie upbringing meant a great deal to him, despite his discovery of his Welsh roots.

After leaving grammar school at sixteen, he attended night classes at the King Edward School of Art in Newcastle where Leonard Evetts, author of *Roman Lettering: a study of the letters of the inscription at the base of the Trajan Column, with an outline of the history of lettering in Britain* (1938), introduced him to the art of lettering. He was still struggling to master his craft when the Second World War broke out.

Having undergone some brief training in the Army he volunteered for medical duties with 224 Parachute Field Ambulance, partly because it meant he would not have to bear arms but mainly because he had heard that the artist-craftsman John Petts was already serving with the unit. Jonah had seen, in *The Listener*, an illustration by Petts of one of Dylan Thomas's stories, and was so much taken with it that he felt compelled to contact him. He found him in the training centre at Ringway, where, together with John Ryder, the typographer, they set up a primitive press, printing instructional material for trainee parachutists on purloined paper.

While stationed on Exmoor, Jonah had an "exalted moment" which turned him in the direction of Wales, which his grandfather, a shaft-sinker, had left for Durham some fifty years before. During a walk one afternoon in the company of a homesick Welsh soldier, he gazed across the Bristol Channel and resolved that, come what might, he would somehow find a way of living and working in the land of his fathers. "Romantic idealism, ill-placed, self-indulgent nonsense perhaps," he wrote in an essay in 1973, "but listening to the undiluted boyo who ached with *hiraeth* at my side on that height on Exmoor, I felt a great peace and the beginnings of a longing that was a tap-root."

In the mean while, the war against Hitler had to be won. Although he had been a pacifist in 1939, he came to regard pacifism as an untenable position, especially after his unit landed near Wesel on the Rhine and made its way into northern Germany, as part of the 3rd Parachute Brigade, reaching Belsen in April 1945 shortly after its liberation. What he saw in the camp put him off Germans for the rest of his life and he was never to visit Germany again.

He met his wife, Judith Maro, in the army education centre at Mount Carmel in Palestine in the last phase of the British Mandate there and they had a clandestine wedding in defiance of military protocol. A Hebrew-speaker, she was serving with the ATS but was deeply involved in the Zionist movement that was intent on creating a homeland for the Jews. After the proclamation of the state of Israel in 1948 she was demobilised but found that neither the British nor the Israelis had a place for her, whereupon the Joneses left the country.

Jonah immediately made for Wales and sought out John Petts, who was endeavouring to revive his Caseg Press in a workshop at Llanystumdwy in Caernarfonshire, and the two worked together under the patronage of Lady Lloyd-George until it became clear that in post-war Britain there was little call for the limited editions they had in mind.

The six intensive weeks he spent at Pigotts in Buckinghamshire in 1949 on a small scholarship from the York Trust proved decisive in Jonah Jones's maturing as a sculptor. Gill had died in 1940 and David Jones was no longer there, but from Laurence Cribb he learned how to cut letters in stone and from René Hague, Gill's son-in-law, the finer points of putting lead through the stick.

Returning to Wales, but by now agnostic in religion, he opened his own workshop at Tremadoc on the Llŷn peninsula. His first commission was from Thomas Jones, formerly Lloyd George's private secretary and then President of the University College of Wales, Aberystwyth, who wanted an inscription for the Principal's House. It was followed by lettering for Lloyd George's gravestone at Llanystumdwy and other work which the architect Clough Williams-Ellis put his way.

This was an auspicious start for a sculptor with little academic training but soon afterwards Jonah was struck down with tuberculosis and had to spend the next five years in sanatoria. As part of his convalescence, he turned to the making of busts: among the eminent people who sat for him were Sir Huw Wheldon, John Cowper Powys, Richard Hughes, Bertrand Russell and Gwynfor Evans. He also did the bronzes of the Welsh patriots O.M. Edwards and his son Sir Ifan ab Owen Edwards which stand outside the village of Llanuwchllyn near Bala.

The next seventeen years were spent abroad, first as a teacher at the British School in Rome and then in Belfast and Dublin, initially as an assessor for the National Council for Diplomas in Art and Design at Ulster College. From 1979 to 1978 he was Director of the National College of Art and Design in Dublin and Director of the Kilkenny Design Workshops.

Jonah also wrote two finely crafted novels. The first, *A Tree May Fall* (1980), is about the claims of pacifism on his father's generation and, in particular, the crisis in Anglo-Irish relations after the Easter Rising of 1916, while the second, *Zorn* (1986), deals with the fate of European Jewry. In *The Gallipoli Diary* (1989), a largely autobiographical book, he brought together essays about some of the artists who meant most to him.

Jonah Jones was a genial, unassuming man, never one to push his own work but staunchly committed to his role as craftsman and the power of art to enrich people's lives. The only honour he received was the Queen's Jubilee Medal for service in the arts in 1983. He will be awarded posthumously the honorary membership of the Royal Society of Architects, Wales next week. His last years were spent in Cardiff but, plagued by arthritis, he was no longer able to work in stone.

Leonard Jonah Jones, artist-craftsman and writer: born Washington, Co Durham 17 February 1919; married 1947 Judith Maro (two sons, one daughter); died Cardiff 29 November 2004.

The Independent (2 December 2004)

Glanmor Williams

Pre-eminent and influential historian of Wales

It is not often that a scholar exerts as profound an influence on his field of study as Glanmor Williams, the doyen of Welsh historians, did on his. From 1957 until his retirement in 1982 he was Professor of History at the University College of Swansea, but that fact alone does not account for the paramount role he played in the advancement of Welsh historiography.

He was the pre-eminent historian of Wales, the most prolific and the most authoritative, who made a magisterial contribution to our understanding of religion, language and society in Wales and led, by example, the remarkable renaissance in the writing of Welsh history which got under way shortly after 1945, when he was appointed to a lectureship at Swansea.

Although his interests ranged from the late medieval period to the modern, he paid particular attention to the sixteenth century and the impact of the Protestant Reformation on Welsh life and literature. His *magnum opus* was *The Welsh Church from Conquest to Reformation* (1962), which dealt with the evolution of the Church in the two and a half centuries that followed the Edwardian conquest of Wales in 1282. This book, employing literary and homiletic sources to explore the religious ethos of the period, is one of the fullest studies of the medieval church ever written.

He went on to publish *Welsh Reformation Essays* (1967) and *Wales and the Reformation* (1997), in which he demonstrated how a small group of scholars, seeing in the newly established Protestant Church's use of English a bid to impose uniformity throughout the realm which might harm the largely monolingual Welsh people's chances of acquiring the means of grace, set about translating the Bible, the Prayer Book and a variety of doctrinal works into their native tongue.

The translation of the Bible into Welsh by such scholars as William Salesbury in 1551 and William Morgan in 1588 not only made the language a fit medium for contemporary scholarship but also ensured that the common people, unlike their Celtic cousins in Ireland, Scotland and Brittany, would be literate in their own language for the next four hundred years. The complex story of how the

English and Welsh switched their allegiance from Rome to the Anglican Church is told in Glanmor Williams's books with clarity and an attractively light touch.

In *Recovery, Reorientation and Reformation* (1987), published as part of a series on the history of Wales by Oxford University Press in association with the University of Wales Press, Glanmor presented for the first time a comprehensive account of the two centuries after the disappearance of Owain Glyndŵr, the national hero of the Welsh people, whose revolt against the English Crown between 1400 and 1415 he had already treated in one of the Clarendon Biographies (*Owen Glendower*, 1966) and to which he would return in a larger book, *Owain Glyndwr* (1993).

Once again he showed how the Tudor Acts of Union of 1536-43 not only swept away the outmoded traditions of medieval society, thus allowing the English Crown, supported by the native gentry, to extend its dominion over Wales, but also presented the Welsh with new opportunities for cultural renewal, a process which has continued down to the present.

Language and literature were at the heart of Glanmor's concern to shed light on the concept of Welsh identity as a major subject for historical inquiry, as in *Religion, Language and Nationality in Wales* (1979), in which he examined the roots of cultural and political nationalism in the modern period, with special reference to the industrialisation of south Wales and the growth of a popular press.

Born and brought up in Dowlais, on a hill above the coal and iron town of Merthyr Tydfil, Glanmor Williams received his secondary education at Cyfarthfa School, housed in a mock-baronial castle which had been the home of the Crawshays, the local ironmasters. He was proud of the town's Radical traditions, which included the workers' rising of 1831, of his own working-class origins – his father was a collier and a deeply cultured man – and of the Baptist cause into which he had been born.

His first degrees at the University College of Wales, Aberystwyth, were in History and Welsh, a language which he spoke and wrote with elegance and panache throughout his long career. Some of his finest work was published in Welsh: *Dadeni, Diwygiad a Diwylliant Cymru* ("The Renaissance, the Reformation and the culture of Wales", 1964), *Grym Tafodau Tân* ("The power of fiery tongues", 1984) and *Cymru a'r Gorffennol: côr o leisiau* ("Wales and the past: a choir of voices", 2000) contain many of his most eloquent writings on religion and culture in Wales.

To these themes he brought not only a deep love of his country and an intimate knowledge of its literature but also a calm detachment very different from the polemic of the excitable Marxist historian Gwyn A. Williams, a slightly younger man who, by a curious coincidence, had been brought up a few doors from him (though they were not related) at Pantysgallog, a cluster of streets of which both wrote with affection and great insight. Glanmor Williams rarely showed his political colours, though in an unusually personal essay he once described himself as having more sympathy with Socialism than with Nationalism, but unable to support New Labour.

He was, in his own words, "too British for many a Welsh-speaking Welshman and too Welsh for many an English-speaking one". It was perhaps for this reason that he was appointed to many committees in Wales and England where he was considered to be "a safe pair of hands". He served the federal University of Wales in several capacities, notably as Vice-Principal and Dean of the Faculty of Economic and Social Studies at University College, Swansea, and, from 1986 to 1996, as Vice-President of the University College of Wales, Aberystwyth.

No cloistered scholar, he was also actively involved in the life of the community and the country at large, often as lecturer to local history societies or as after-dinner speaker to learned societies, many of whom relished his fund of anecdotes. He had a nice sense of humour and was not at all pompous or overbearing. Of the Glamorgan History Society and the Gower Society, both of which he helped found, he was among the most zealous members, and for many years he edited their Transactions.

He also edited several massive volumes of the *Glamorgan County History* and served as Chairman of the Board of Celtic Studies, in which capacity he inaugurated *The Welsh History Review* in 1960 and, ten years later, a series of monographs, "Studies in Welsh History", of which he was co-editor. Both these initiatives have enabled scores of young historians to embark on academic careers within and without the University of Wales.

In 1975 Glanmor Williams was appointed President of the Baptist Union of Wales, helping many of the small and dwindling congregations belonging to his denomination. His gifts for reconciling people of opposing views were put to the test during the six years he served as National Governor of BBC Wales and Chairman of the Broadcasting Council for Wales (1965-71), a turbulent period when there was a growing demand for an improved service in the Welsh language. He became a member of the Royal Commission on Ancient Monuments in Wales in 1962 and was its Chairman from 1986 to 1990. On the other side of Offa's Dyke, he represented Wales on the board of the British Library and its Advisory Council

He gave a highly entertaining account of his long and illustrious career in his autobiography, *Glanmor Williams: a life* (2002); which is full of his characteristic insight, generosity and humour.

Glanmor Williams, historian: born Dowlais, Glamorgan 5 May 1920; Assistant Lecturer in History, University College, Swansea 1945-52, Senior Lecturer 1952-57, Professor of History 1957-82 (Emeritus), Vice-Principal 1975-78; FSA 1979; CBE 1981; Chairman, Ancient Monuments Board (Wales) 1983-95; Chairman, Royal Commission on Ancient and Historical Monuments in Wales 1986-90; FBA 1986; Kt 1995; married 1946 Fay Davies (one son, one daughter); died Swansea 24 February 2005.

The Independent (28 February 2005)

Gwynfor Evans

President of Plaid Cymru and the first Welsh Nationalist MP

Gwynfor Evans was the Welsh Nationalist who, in 1980, forced Margaret Thatcher's government to make its first U-turn. The issue was the establishment of a fourth television channel for Wales, to which the Conservatives had first given, and then withdrawn, their commitment. The former MP's declaration that he would fast to death unless William Whitelaw, the Home Secretary, honoured his pledge caused apprehension in London and the mounting tension in Wales was defused only when Nicholas Edwards, the Secretary of State for Wales, eventually announced that the channel, to be known as S4C, would after all be set up.

The steely resolution with which Gwynfor Evans challenged and defeated the Government over its policy for broadcasting in Wales was typical of the man who, from 1945, had been President of Plaid Cymru, the Welsh Nationalist party. He was generally regarded as having been responsible for its growth from a small group of intellectuals, writers, teachers and ministers of religion into the political party which, although largely confined in its electoral strength to the north and west of Wales, to play a key role in the affairs of the country, notably in the National Assembly where, with twelve of the sixty seats, it is the largest group after Labour.

The Government could no longer ignore the party's views and, because there was no doubt that Gwynfor Evans intended carrying out his fast, his stand as its revered leader had to be taken into consideration. The day after the Government's about-turn the words "Gwynfor 1: Whitelaw 0" were painted in bold letters on the Thames embankment opposite Westminster. S4C, which came into existence two years later and is now an integral part of the Government's broadcasting arrangements in Wales, is regarded by many as a monument to one man's vision and courage.

Gwynfor Evans was born in the port of Barry, in the old county of Glamorgan, in 1912. His father, Dan Evans, was a prominent Independent councillor and shopkeeper in the town, and he was brought up in a comfortable, English-speaking, chapel-going home where a portrait of Lloyd George was the family's only concession to party politics. Exasperated by her son's early interest in what she considered the hopeless cause of Welsh Nationalism, his mother once exclaimed: "Oh, Gwynfor, why can't you be like everyone else and become a Liberal?"

It was his reading of Welsh literature while in the sixth form at Barry Grammar School that made a patriot of Gwynfor Evans, but he was more concerned with international affairs, particularly world peace, at the University College of Wales, Aberystwyth, where he read Law, and did not join Plaid Cymru until he was about to go up to St John's College, Oxford, in 1937. After serving his articles in Cardiff, he qualified as a solicitor, but was never to practise, preferring instead to enter a market-garden business which his father had set up at Llangadog in Carmarthenshire, an occupation which would allow him the better to pursue his political interests, virtually on a full-time basis. With the staunch support of his brother Alcwyn, he grew tomatoes there until the severe winter of 1982 put paid to the enterprise.

Christian pacifism was an essential part of Gwynfor Evans's Nationalism. Given an unconditional discharge as a conscientious objector to war, he served from 1939 to 1945 as Secretary of Heddychwyr Cymru, the Welsh pacifist movement which was the equivalent in Wales of the Peace Pledge Union, and during this time came under the influence of George M.Ll. Davies, who worked for the League of Nations. It was this pacifism, passionately upheld by its president after 1945, which ensured that Plaid Cymru – unusually for a Nationalist movement – would set its face against the use of violence as a means of achieving its political goal, which was self-government for Wales.

This stance caused some tension in its ranks during the 1960s, when acts of sabotage were committed by more extreme individuals in protest against the building of English reservoirs in Wales, but it has never been abandoned. Gwynfor Evans spent the first half of his thirty-six-year presidency at the head of a political party which, despite its brilliant tactics, failed in most of its campaigns to win concessions for the land, language and culture of Wales, and made only small electoral progress. Among those campaigns were an attempt to prevent the War Department expropriating more agricultural land on the Epynt mountain in Breconshire and at Trawsfynydd in Merioneth for use by the British army.

The party also pressed for the official recognition of

Monmouthshire as one of the counties of Wales and organised a petition for the granting of legal status to the Welsh language. Perhaps its most serious failure was its unsuccessful attempt to stop Liverpool Corporation building a reservoir in the Tryweryn Valley, although its campaign had the effect of bringing many young people into its ranks in the late 1950s and early 1960s. Gwynfor Evans was always in the vanguard of these campaigns, in which his charismatic personality was a vital factor in attracting others to the cause.

Elected to Carmarthenshire County Council in 1949, he remained a member for the next twenty-five years, often having to face – as Plaid Cymru's only representative – the brutish opposition of the ruling Labour Party. During these years, however, his personal influence grew steadily and he was able, notably as a member of the Court of the University of Wales from 1946 to 1971, to help bring about a number of improvements in such areas as broadcasting and education. He was a member of the British Council's Welsh Advisory Committee from 1947 to 1991. Always arguing in favour of Wales as a national entity, he was among the group of eminent Welshmen who, in 1962, were responsible for setting up Teledu Cymru, the first but short-lived television service broadcasting in Welsh.

Gwynfor first stood as a parliamentary candidate in Merioneth in 1945 but transferred his candidature at the general election of 1964 to Carmarthen, the constituency held by Megan Lloyd George for Labour. His winning of the Carmarthen seat, at a by-election caused by her death and held on 14 July 1966, was a watershed in the fortunes of Plaid Cymru and heralded a new phase in Welsh politics.

Amidst euphoria in Wales, Gwynfor Evans took his seat in the House of Commons as its sole Nationalist member until he was joined by Winnie Ewing of the SNP in the following year. But his first term at Westminster was by no means happy. He was reviled by most Welsh MPs, especially George Thomas (Secretary of State for Wales but not yet Speaker of the House of Commons), and barred from any position of influence. Nor did he relish the rough-and-tumble of Westminster politics, suffering acute stomach pains (on his own testimony) whenever he had to address the House.

Yet, although not a professional politician in the usual sense, Gwynfor Evans was an effective speaker and a dogged propagandist on behalf of the Welsh Nationalist cause. He lost his seat to Labour in February 1970 by just three votes but regained it in October of the same year with a majority of 3,640, only to lose it again five years later.

There was a more private, scholarly side to his character of which those unfamiliar with life in Wales may not be aware. A staunch Congregationalist, Gwynfor was devoted to his chapel and the affairs of the Union of Welsh Independents, which he served as president in 1954. He was also a prolific writer publishing some fifty pamphlets, as well as sixteen books. Among his more substantial works on political subjects are *Rhagom i Ryddid* ("Forward to freedom",1964), *Celtic Nationalism* (with Hugh MacDiarmid, Dudley Owen Edwards and Ioan Bowen Rees, 1968), *A National Future for Wales* (1975), *Diwedd Prydeindod* ("The end of Britishness", 1981) and *Fighting for Wales* (1991).

His characteristic emphasis on tradition, communal values, the culture of ordinary people and the value of the individual, particularly in the small, rural, Welsh-speaking areas, which were at the heart of his Nationalism, is at its most eloquent in his popular history of Wales which appeared in English translation as *Land of My Fathers* in 1974.

It is too soon to attempt a comprehensive assessment of Gwynfor Evans as the leader of Plaid Cymru and his huge contribution to public life must await the historian of post-war Wales who is familiar with all the fields in which he was active. Part of that process will have to take into account the courtesy and immense goodwill he habitually showed even towards his political opponents. I had experience of his eirenic spirit when, in 1995, I was engaged in the translation of his memoirs, which appeared in English as *For the Sake of Wales* the following year. As I sent him each chapter for his approval, he would delete unflattering references to individuals or else find something kinder, more generous, to say about them; he even chose to make out the sunnier side of his old adversary George Thomas.

A reserved man, not much given to the homelier mores of working-class Wales, but one who delighted in the company of his large family and many friends, Gwynfor Evans was pitched into politics not by self-interest (so often a cardinal sin in politicians) but out of a profound concern for the national community of Wales and a vision of the role it might yet play as an independent, non-belligerent member of the family of nations. In 2004, the Welsh public voted him the greatest living politician and fourth in a list of all-time Welsh heroes with Aneurin Bevan and Owain Glyndŵr. He was a great patriot and one of the most distinguished Welshmen of our time.

Richard Gwynfor Evans, politician: born Barry, Glamorgan 1 September 1912; Vice-President Plaid Cymru 1943-45, President 1945-81, honorary President 1982- 2005; MP (Plaid Cymru) for Carmarthen 1966-70, 1974-79; married 1940 Rhiannon Prys Thomas (four sons, three daughters); died Pencarreg, Carmarthenshire 21 April 2005.

The Independent (22 April 2005)

Alun Creunant Davies

First Director of the Welsh Books Council

As first Director of the Welsh Books Council, Alun Creunant Davies played a pioneering role in developing the book trade in Wales, to which he devoted his boundless energy, administrative flair and business acumen. He took up his post, with a staff of one, on St David's Day 1965, an auspicious date for a man who, although never overtly political, drew great strength from his patriotism which, for him, was rooted in the Welsh language and its culture.

Welsh publishing had fallen into the doldrums in the post-war period, with only 234 Welsh-language titles appearing between 1946 and 1951, and fewer than a hundred a year thereafter. The Ready Report of 1951 had concluded that the future of Welsh depended to a large extent on the availability of books in the language and recommended the creation of a fund for the public subsidy of book production by local and central government. Thanks to Alun R. Edwards, the irrepressible Librarian of Cardiganshire, the counties of Wales had begun to provide small grants for the printing of Welsh books, mostly fiction, and a modicum of payment for their authors.

Alun Creunant, as he was widely known in Wales, soon transformed this tentative arrangement by persuading twelve of the thirteen county councils (the exception was Monmouthshire) to make more substantial annual grants to the Books Council. This initiative was followed in 1972 by the Welsh Arts Council's decision to pay for the setting up of four new departments, with responsibility for Design, Editing, Publicity and Marketing and by the Welsh Office's contribution of an annual grant for the subsidy of Welsh book production and some of the concomitant operating costs. The number of Welsh-language titles grew steadily and they were better designed, edited, publicised and marketed than ever before.

The Books Council also expanded rapidly, moving from its cramped offices on the top floor of a building leased from the Farmers' Union of Wales to more spacious accommodation at Castell Brychan, a former Roman Catholic seminary which stands on Constitution Hill, high above the town of Aberystwyth. At the same time the Books Centre, a wholesale distributing warehouse on the Glanyrafon industrial estate at Llanbadarn, on the outskirts of town, which was wholly Alun Creunant's idea, began providing the publishers, booksellers, teachers, librarians and book-buying public of Wales with a fast delivery service that is still the envy of the trade in England, Scotland and Ireland.

Although he was not averse to spending many hours in packing, invoicing and delivering parcels of books to all parts of Wales and the Borders, and was still in this habit long after the Council had its designated staff to carry out such tasks, Alun was determined to implement policies and procedures that would ensure a greater degree of professionalism in what had for long been almost a cottage industry. In this he used his diplomatic skills to persuade those on whom the fortunes of the Books Council depended and was indefatigable in his support for its staff.

None of his colleagues was spared his zeal and there was no such thing as a nine-to-five day, weekends, unsocial hours or holidays. On one occasion, in 1976, I was speaking to the Secretary of the Nobel Committee in the throne room of the Swedish Parliament when a very ornate telephone rang and the call was for me. Alun Creunant Davies wanted to know whether, in my capacity as the Arts Council's Literature Director, I could attend a meeting of one of the Books Council's committees on such-and-such a date. When I said I could, he asked me what the weather was like in Stockholm, told me it was raining in Aberystwyth and then put the phone down. I had to assure my astonished host that the call, though brief, was indeed a very important one. As I was speaking to my compatriot in Welsh, he was none the wiser.

Alun Creunant was born in 1927 at Llansamlet, near Swansea, the only child of a Calvinistic Methodist minister, and went to school in Llandovery in Carmarthenshire. After qualifying as a teacher at Trinity College, Carmarthen, and spending two years in the Army, he was appointed to the staff of Tregaron Primary School and, shortly afterwards, became headmaster at Llangeitho, a small village in rural south Cardiganshire, where he remained for thirteen years.

It was this long association with the county which, in addition to his shrewd business sense, made many people. think of him as a Cardi – a stereotype renowned in Wales for thrift, not to say parsimony, but a nickname he was happy to apply to himself when it suited him. For him, the local was the real, and that meant the Welsh-speaking communities which were nearest his heart. One of the quainter points about the running of the Books Council in its early days, I recall, was that a secretary was sent home early every Friday afternoon because she lived in Llangeitho, where she bought a substantial supply of postage stamps for the week following, thus helping the sub-post office to remain open as a vital part of village life.

Alun served Llangeitho in other ways, too. He ran the local branch of the Welsh League of Youth, teaching the children to act and speak in their native tongue, played a prominent part in the Sunday School and, whenever the need arose, took the services at the Daniel Rowland Memorial Chapel, named after the village's most famous son, one of the leaders of the Methodist Revival. On men like Alun Creunant the traditional culture of Welsh-speaking Wales has long depended and he played his part to the full, in recognition of which the University of Wales awarded him the honorary degree of MA on his retirement in 1987.

He was also active on a wider stage. For five years he was General Secretary of Undeb Cenedlaethol Athrawon Cymru (UCAC), the Welsh teachers' union. He carried out his duties with such vim and efficiency that the wags said the AC in the acronym of the union's name stood for Alun Creunant. Among the public bodies of which he was a member were the National Library and National Museum, the Mid-Wales Development Board and the University College of Wales, Aberystwyth. He served as a Justice of the Peace and Chairman of the North Cardiganshire Magistrates, often exercising an independence of judgement that was usually in favour of the poor and the underprivileged.

As Moderator of the South Wales Association of the Presbyterian Church of Wales in 1979-80, he delivered an address that treated the Church not as something static or hidebound by tradition but as a society of worshippers actively concerned with the contemporary world and ready to adapt to its changing conditions. The re-emergence of Gwasg Pantycelyn, the Connexion's venerable publishing house, was due largely to Davies's efforts on its behalf.

But his main achievement was the establishment of the Welsh Books Council, now, under his successor, Gwerfyl Pierce Jones, one of the most important public bodies in Wales. The first phase of its growth began in 1970 when he and I paid a visit to bilingual Friesland, and in particular to the Book Bang that is held every year in the provincial capital, Leeuwarden. We learned a great deal during that trip and on a subsequent visit to book distributors and publishers in Amsterdam, and brought back a number of ideas which we were able to put into operation almost immediately

I found it easy to co-operate with Alun Creunant Davies, the kindest and most genial of men. For all his caution and attachment to the more traditional aspects of Welsh culture, he was ever ready to experiment and take initiatives if they could be expected to bring about improvements in Welsh publishing and the benevolently central role of the Books Council.

Whenever I go into a bookshop and see the array of books now available in Welsh (more than a thousand new titles a year), together with a wealth of English books from Welsh presses, I think of Sir Christopher Wren and that, in Alun Creunant's case, too, *Si monumentum requiris, circumspice.*

Alun Creunant Davies, arts administrator: born Llansamlet, Glamorgan 31 May 1927; Director, Welsh Books Council 1965-87; married (one son, one daughter); died Aberystwyth 26 October 2005.

The Independent (28 October 2005)

Leslie Norris

Poet and short-story writer who taught at Brigham Young University, Utah

Leslie Norris came to prominence as a poet in the mid 1960s when he started contributing to my magazine *Poetry Wales* and after the publication of his first collection of poems, *Finding Gold*, in 1967. He had been writing verse since his schooldays in Merthyr Tydfil and had already published three small booklets, but he had fallen silent during the 1950s.

The launching of *Poetry Wales* in 1965 rescued his muse and he was to become a regular contributor to the "second flowering" of Welsh writing in English. Even so, he was never a prominent figure in the literary mainstream in Wales, partly because he spent more than fifty years in England and the United States, but more importantly because he chose to live as a "displaced person", at home only in his imagination and the writer's craft.

Among his most anthologised poems are "The Ballad of Billy Rose", about a boxer whom he had seen blinded in the ring, the delicately evocative "Water", set on a farm on the hillside above Merthyr, and "Elegy for David Beynon" in memory of a teacher who, after the coal-tip's slide on to the Pant-glas School at Aberfan in 1966, had been found dead at his desk and, under his arms, the bodies of four children whom he had been trying to protect from the slurry. From all these local incidents Leslie managed to make poems of universal significance and great emotional power.

The town of Merthyr Tydfil, where he had been born in 1921, marked him irrevocably as a Welshman, not so much by language, for he had only a little Welsh, as by an amalgam of local circumstances. Economically depressed but socially vibrant, it was a wondrous place for a young poet, with colourful characters on every street-corner and, beyond Cefn-coed, a hinterland of breathtaking beauty in the foothills of the Brecon Beacons. The lad, bookish and precocious, attended Cyfarthfa Grammar School, housed in the mansion of the Crawshays, the local ironmasters, but learned more, he claimed, from talking to the townsfolk and reading voraciously. He once told me that he had read all of C.M. Doughty's *Arabia Deserta* while mitching from school in the town branch of W.H. Smith's bookshop.

He also claimed to have known the precise moment when he realised he was going to be a poet. It was when a fellow pupil was punished by a brutish headmaster for giving as the opposite of "good", the word "rotten". Leslie pointed out that his friend's father was a grocer and that in his shop they sold good fruit and threw away the rotten; he too was caned for his impertinence. "I became aware then," he told me, "that I knew the English language and the meanings of words better than my headmaster." The smarting pain of this incident was reworked years later in the story "Some Opposites of Good", published in *The Girl from Cardigan* (1988).

After leaving school at the age of seventeen, Leslie took his first job as a rates clerk in the town hall and, two years later, was called up for military service with the RAF only to contract severe blood poisoning within a few weeks, as a consequence of which he was invalided out. Some of his finest poems are elegies for friends killed in the Second World War.

On his return to Merthyr, he worked in a number of uncongenial jobs and read omnivorously, in particular the stories of Glyn Jones, another Merthyr man whom he was not to meet until I introduced them in 1967 but who became his close friend and about whom he wrote an affectionate monograph for the *Writers of Wales* series in 1973.

In 1948, desperate to get out of post-war Merthyr, now changing as the slums were cleared and new light industries took the place of iron and coal, but still a dead-end place for the young and ambitious, he married a Dowlais woman and enrolled as a student at the Teacher Training College in Coventry. He was never to live permanently in Wales again.

From 1952 to 1958 he taught at schools in Yeovil and Bath and was Headmaster of Westergate School, Chichester, then lectured at Bognor Regis College of Education (later the West Sussex Institute of Higher Education, now part of University College, Chichester), where his wife also taught. They lived at Aldingbourne in West Sussex, where the poets Ted Walker and Andrew Young were among their neighbours. The years spent in England were crucial to his development as a poet, if only on account of his reading of Edward Thomas, whose melancholy he shared in large measure and whose response to the rural scene in southern England was similar to his own.

Encouraged by Richard Church, he sent his poems to Cecil Day-Lewis at Chatto & Windus, who published them as *Finding Gold* under the imprint of the Hogarth Press. His reputation was enhanced with the appearance of two more volumes in the *Phoenix Living Poets* series: *Ransoms* (1970) won the Alice Hunt Bartlett Prize in the year of its publication, and *Mountains, Polecats, Pheasants* (1974) was highly praised in the literary press on both sides of the Atlantic. He also began publishing stories and poems in *The Atlantic Monthly* and *The New Yorker*.

Having tried for several years to give up teaching in order to become a full-time writer, in the summer of 1973 he accepted an invitation to be Visiting Professor at the University of Washington in Seattle. So began a long association with American universities which lasted for the rest of his life. On his return to England, he found himself so unsettled by the experience of America that he resigned his Principal Lectureship at Bognor Regis and resolved to earn his living henceforth by his pen.

Even so, he was obliged to take up residencies and fellowships from time to time, notably at Eton in 1977 and at Aston University in the year following. He also made further visits to the US, spending several months on a small island off the coast of Maine, which he celebrated in a sequence of poems which marked the beginning of a new informality in his writing style. In 1978 his first collection of stories, *Sliding* (1978), won the David Higham Prize for Fiction and one of his stories was awarded the Katherine Mansfield Prize.

In Seattle, which he revisited in 1980, he was particularly happy. The post he was given there had previously been held by Vernon Watkins until his sudden death while playing tennis on the campus in 1967. Leslie greatly admired his fellow Welshman's work and had written an MPhil thesis on it at Southampton University, and so he was a natural choice as editor of the memorial volume published by Faber and Faber (*Vernon Watkins, 1906-1967*, 1970).

But it was in Utah, at Brigham Young University, where he first went in 1983, that he enjoyed the greatest status and wrote some of his best work. He was almost immediately made Christiansen Professor of Poetry in the Department of English and, in 1989, was appointed Humanities Professor of Creative Writing.

In the same year he cut his last physical ties with Wales by selling the cottage at Saron in Carmarthenshire which he had owned since the 1950s and from where he had indulged his passion for fly-fishing. Although he talked about returning to live permanently in Wales, henceforth he was only a summer visitor, looking up old friends and attending literary festivals and conferences.

I witnessed at first hand the esteem in which he was held by the Mormons of BYU when, in1991, I was Visiting Professor there. He and I were the only non-members of the Church of Latter Day Saints on the campus and, because I was his friend and compatriot, I shared many of the privileges and friendships which were already his. I was struck, too, by his popularity among students and faculty alike: they flocked to his readings and lectures, bought his books in their hundreds and sought his opinion on their own work at every opportunity with a zeal for poetry which I had previously observed only in Russia.

Apart from his amiable nature and serious approach to the poet's calling I think it was the chaste character of Leslie's work that appealed most to the Mormons. Not only is it fairly conventional in its technique and language, always accessible to the intelligent reader, and so carefully crafted as to allow the singing line to carry it forward, there is hardly any reference to sexual or political matters in it, no preoccupation with vice or crime, and its religious content is not so evident as to offer any challenge to the theology and rituals of their church. His American poems are to be found, for the most part, in *Sequences* (1988) and *A Sea in the Desert* (1989).

Leslie felt at home in Utah, particularly in the valley of the Great Salt Lake, and was able to respond in ways which pleased his hosts, a desert people who like to be flattered on account of their fortitude and single-minded commitment to their church.

In Leslie's last years he turned to writing books for children, including *Merlin & the Snake's Egg* (1978) and *Albert and the Angels* (2000), both published in New York, and, in collaboration with Alan Keele, to translating the poems of Rainer Maria Rilke.

A selection of poems from his dozen volumes appeared in his *Collected Poems* and the stories first brought together in *Sliding* and *The Girl from Cardigan* in his *Collected Stories*, both of which were published by Seren in 1996. Critical acclaim followed: James A. Davies contributed a monograph on him to the *Writers of Wales* series in 1991 and a Festschrift, *An Open World: essays on Leslie Norris* edited by Eugene England and Peter Makuck, appeared in 1994; to the latter book Ted Hughes contributed three poems.

Leslie Norris was a complex man, easily hurt, ambivalent towards his native country, but proud of his calling as a poet, staunch in his friendships and unfailingly generous towards younger poets. If some critics saw him as essentially a poet writing late in the English Georgian tradition, and others complained about his lack of social awareness and his preoccupation with the world of his youth, he stuck steadfastly to his last, content to remain "at the edge of things", that mysterious land where the familiar and the unfamiliar meet, and where his poems and stories had their abundant source.

George Leslie Norris, poet and short-story writer: born Merthyr Tydfil, Glamorgan 21 May 1921: Lecturer, then Principal Lecturer in English, Bognor Regis College of Education 1958-73. FRSL 1974; Christiansen Professor of Poetry, Brigham Young University 1984-2000, Humanities Professor of Creative Writing 1989-2000; married 1948 Kitty Morgan; died Provo, Utah 6 April 2006.

The Independent (10 April 2006)

Kenneth Griffith

Actor and maverick documentary-maker

The actor and documentary film-maker Kenneth Griffith was one of the most distinguished troublemakers of his time. He could exasperate colleagues by his cantankerous manner and stout refusal to compromise his artistic and professional integrity, especially when offered work by those whom he called the "priggish cuckoos" of the BBC's middle management. Even those who were kind to him found he would insist on marching to a different drum.

On one occasion, after he had started rewriting someone else's script so that he would have a bigger part in it, one of the Boulting brothers, who often employed him, was driven to exclaim 'Why are you always so difficult, Kenneth?"

The answer was far from straightforward. Kenneth Griffith was a complicated man and, although he wrote an autobiography in an attempt to explain himself, there was a demon in his personality with which he never came, and never wanted to come, to terms. He had a genuine flair for friendship and could be charming in the company of those whom he respected, but cultivated his reputation as a member of the Awkward Squad most assiduously. He would plough his own furrow whatever the cost – and sometimes it cost him dearly.

The subjects he chose for his documentaries were calculated to upset the British Establishment by virtue of their partisan view of imperial history: Napoleon (he savoured the fact that Boney had struck terror in English hearts); the War of American Independence (he was in favour of it); the Untouchables in India (he argued for their social emancipation and was president of their society); the Anglo-Boer War (he took the side of the Afrikaners); Irish Republicanism (he was a keen supporter of Sinn Fein); the British throne (he thought the House of Windsor had a bogus claim); and so on, in more than two dozen documentaries which are among the most brilliant, and controversial, ever made in Britain. Never one to sit on the fence, he once told Huw Wheldon: "I would never stoop so low as to be objective about anything."

Kenneth Griffith's support for a united Ireland was given fullest expression in his films about Michael Collins, *Hang Up Your Brightest Colours* (1973), and Roger Casement, *Roger Casement: heart of darkness* (1992), in both of which the British government's record in Ireland was roundly castigated. The film about Collins, which begins by quoting his remark "There is no Irish problem, only an English problem", was rejected by Sir Lew Grade at the behest of the IBA and it was to be twenty-one years before the BBC would screen it, after which Kenneth Griffith was taken to the hearts of Republicans in Belfast. A visit to their enclaves in 1993, shortly after the hunger strike that led to the deaths of Bobby Sands and others, confirmed his belief that the British should pull out of the six counties of Ulster, and thereafter he always wore a green ribbon in his coat.

Kenneth Griffith was born in Tenby, Pembrokeshire, in 1921. He attributed his affection for the Irish to the fact that he was Welsh, albeit from that part of Pembrokeshire that had for long been known as "Little England beyond Wales" because it had been settled by Flemish and English weavers soon after the Norman Conquest.

There was an element of guilt in his sense of Welshness, primarily because it was a compatriot, namely David Lloyd George, who had been largely responsible for the partitioning of Ireland in 1922. This feeling was subsumed by his admiration for what he saw as "the true Celtic spirit" – a passionate response to life that has no place for the dry formalities of the English ruling class – and the essence of which he cherished in his Irish friends Tyrone Guthrie and Peter O'Toole.

Apart from his support for Sinn Fein, Kenneth Griffith had no party allegiance, for he had a horror of joining anything. In his autobiography, *The Fool's Pardon* (1994), he described himself as "not a red, but a convinced, though often confused, democrat", and towards the end of his life he did not demur when called "a radical Tory". Yet one of his best documentaries is *The Most Valuable Englishman Ever* (1982), a study of the egalitarian Tom Paine. Nor did he have any time for trades unions: his Equity membership card was stamped "Under protest".

The instinct to be his own man had been ingrained in him from an early age. His parents having separated while he was still a small child, he was brought up at Penally, near Tenby, by his paternal grandparents, staunch Wesleyan Methodists who taught him to question everything. If there was something of the sermon in his films, he gladly acknowledged the influence of the Nonconformist chapel of his boyhood – especially the histrionics of the old-time preachers who, with blazing eyes and fiery tongue, had enthralled and terrified him as a child.

The prolonged absence of his mother left a permanent mark on him. "I have never been able to totally forgive my mother for leaving me; therefore I have never been able to love her," he wrote in his autobiography, adding, "I have a deeply aggressive wariness towards women which has left a trail of domestic disaster behind me." He admitted to having spent most of his life in "an emotional mess": all three of his marriages ended in divorce, although he enjoyed a warm relationship with at least two of his former wives and his five children.

He first entertained hopes of becoming an actor at Green Hill Grammar School in Tenby, where he was encouraged by Miss Evelyn Ward, an English teacher, who remained one of his most trusted friends. His performance in a school play was praised by a local newspaper and he forthwith decided to pursue a career in the theatre. Called to an interview with his headmaster, J.T. Griffith, he was advised to drop the s in his surname because it was a mark of anglicisation, and allowed to leave school before his sixteenth birthday and with no academic qualifications.

In 1937 he made his debut as a professional actor at the Festival Theatre in Cambridge, where Peter Hoare cast him as Cinna the Poet in *Julius Caesar*; he then played Danny in the West Pier Company's production of Emlyn Williams's *Night Must Fall* in Tenby and took a very small part in Thomas Dekker's *The Shoemaker's Holiday*. With bigger parts in *Little Ladyship*, *The Corn is Green* and *Boys in Brown*, he gained experience in treading the boards of repertory theatre.

He had barely had a chance to break into the cinema before the Second World War began. He served with the RAF, mostly in Canada. Often in trouble with the military authorities for minor misdemeanours such as imitating the officers, he used the opportunity to read as widely as he could, though his choice of books was nothing if not unorthodox. On his last visit to Tenby before conscription, he had asked his grandparents to give him, as a farewell present, an English translation of Hitler's *Mein Kampf* so that he could better understand the causes of the conflict in which he was about to become involved, and he may have been the only British soldier to carry that book about with him for the duration. Declared unfit to fly after contracting scarlet fever and now weighing only seven stone, he was invalided out of the RAF in 1942.

He resumed his career in the theatre with Tyrone Guthrie's Old Vic in Liverpool, playing the Chorus in Marlowe's *Doctor Faustus*, but, never at ease with himself as a stage actor, found he preferred the discipline of the cinema. His first screen role had been in *Love on the Dole* (1941) and over the next fifty years he was to appear in more than eighty films. Many are now forgotten – by his own admission, he did a lot of inferior work – but some stand out: *Lucky Jim* (1957), *A Night to Remember* (1958), *I'm All Right, Jack* (1959). *The Lion in Winter* (1968), *The Wild Geese* (1978), *Who Dares Wins* (1982), *Four Weddings and a Funeral* (1994) and *The Englishman Who Went Up a Hill But Came Down a Mountain* (1996).

When he was not playing villains or eccentrics – he claimed passengers would take one look at him in a train compartment and hurriedly leave – he specialised in stereotypical parts as a malevolent Welshman, in which he put on an accent which did not win him many fans in Wales. Even so, as the obsequious Ieuan Jenkins who competes against Peter Sellers' John Lewis for promotion to a sub-librarian's post in *Only Two Can Play* (1962), a film version of Kinglsey Amis's novel *That Uncertain Feeling*, set in Swansea, he made a lot of us laugh.

From about 1965 he began to move away from the cinema to the making of documentaries, partly because they afforded him almost complete control of the medium. His film *Soldiers of the Widow* (1972), about the siege and relief of Ladysmith during the first Boer War, was the first to be made out of his obsession with South Africa. It was followed by an even more hard-hitting documentary, *Black as Hell: Thick as Grass* (1979), about the Impis' attack on the South Wales Borderers' outpost at Rorke's Drift in 1879, in which he played the parts of both British officers and Zulu warriors.

Among other documentaries he made were *A Touch of Churchill, a Touch of Hitler* (1971), a corrosive indictment of Cecil Rhodes; *The Sun's Bright Child* (1975), a life of the actor Edmund Keane, whose memory he revered; *The Light* (1986), a typically one-sided view of David Ben Gurion, Zionism and the creation of the State of Israel; and *But I Have Promises to Keep* (1989), a sympathetic portrait of Nehru that was nevertheless suppressed in India.

In most of these films Kenneth Griffith appeared as himself – hectoring, locquacious, cranky, wild-eyed, combative, tub-thumping, and utterly riveting in the way he delivered his invective and used the camera to maximum effect.

It is inevitable that opinions of the maverick Kenneth Griffith, especially among documentary buffs, will vary widely. Some critics have been perturbed by his taking so many parts in his own productions – Christ, Napoleon, Hitler, and so on. One, writing in *The Times* in 1986, commented that he would not be surprised if Kenneth Griffith were one day to play all the roles in *Gone with the Wind*. Others have taken the sterner view that his documentaries are merely egotistical exercises in polemic and have only negligible cinematic merit.

Despite these strictures, however, it is generally agreed that his work provides a jolt to complacency and invites the viewer to reconsider conventional wisdom regarding some of the less honourable episodes in British colonial history.

Kenneth Griffiths (Kenneth Griffith), actor and documentary film-maker: born Tenby, Pembrokeshire 12 October 1921; married first Joan Stock (two sons, marriage dissolved), second Doria Noar (one daughter, marriage dissolved), third Carole Hagar (one daughter, one son, marriage dissolved); died London 25 June 2006.

The Independent (26 June 2006)

Kyffin Williams

Painter of the iconic mountain landscapes of North Wales

If there is a stereotype of North Wales as a land of mountains, it has much to do with the art of Kyffin Williams who, for more than half a century, painted the rugged landscape of Snowdonia and its people in a style unmistakably his own.

The typical Kyffin picture shows a peak under dark cloud, a lowering sky and perhaps a shepherd, with hazel stick and dog making his way down a rocky slope, or a small farmhouse, its white-washed walls a refuge from the sombre majesty of its setting. The predominant colours are olive-green, slate-grey, ochre and umber, the paint applied lusciously with a palette knife in thick, bold swathes of pigment in which it is possible to take pleasure for its own sake.

Kyffin Williams never tired of painting his native land, or at least those upland parts of it he knew and loved – he rarely ventured into the urban south and never attempted to tackle the industrial landscape of Glamorgan, that other stereotype of modern Welsh painting. He was deeply rooted in Anglesey and Gwynedd, one of the heartlands of the Welsh language, and, although he spoke only English, became its representative artist, just as T.H. Parry-Williams and Kate Roberts were its writers. "I have been extraordinarily lucky," he wrote in the 1971 symposium *Artists in Wales*, "to have been born and reared in such a lovely landscape among people with whom I have so great an affinity."

He was born in Llangefni, Anglesey's market town, in 1918, the younger son of a bank manager and into a family who, on both the spear and the distaff side, had for generations served the Anglican Church as rectors and vicars in the county. Reduced to near poverty by a lawsuit brought against his mother by a malevolent cousin, the family removed in 1925 to Pentre-felin, a village between Criccieth and Porthmadog on the southern side of the Llŷn peninsula, and it was there the boy first had his eyes opened to the grandeur of the Ordovician landscape. "This was a new world," he wrote, "and I loved the melancholic beauty of the mountain storms."

It was a matter of regret for him that his mother, Welsh-speaking but a genteel and highly strung woman, kept him from the village children, with the result that what he learned of the language in later life was only enough to understand the toponymy of the area.

After a spell in a preparatory school at Trearddur in Anglesey, he went to Shrewsbury School, where at the age of sixteen he contracted polioencephalitis which led, two years later, to epilepsy. Even so, having held a job for three years with a firm of land agents in Pwllheli, he enlisted in the Territorial Army with the 6th Battalion of the Royal Welch Fusiliers and, at the outbreak of war, was sent to Northern Ireland.

His military career came to an abrupt halt in the barracks at Wrexham in 1941 when he suffered an epileptic attack. It was there, with an irony the future painter was to relish, he was told by a doctor that he would have to relinquish hopes of returning to land agency because he was "abnormal" and that, as therapy, he ought to take up art. In October 1941 he enrolled at the Slade School of Fine Art under Randolph Schwabe. "They took me in," he said with typical self-deprecation, "because everyone else was away at the war."

At first inept and untutored, and knowing next to nothing about drawing, he was happy at the Slade, relocated for the duration to Oxford and going through one of its less rigorous phases, and found great solace in the use of paint. He began producing pictures in a rough-hewn style not dissimilar to that of his more mature work, and based on what he remembered of his boyhood in North Wales.

The revelation of what art really meant to him came in the library of the Ashmolean Museum when. while gazing at the head of Christ in Piero della Francesca's *Resurrection*, he felt tears rolling down his cheeks. This incident, movingly recounted in *Horizons Hung in Air* and *Land against the Light*, the films made by John Ormond in 1966 and 1978, was to mould his style in that it taught him the vital importance of mood. "It had an incredible effect on me," he said, "because up until then, rather stupidly, I had felt that painting was more or less reproducing the world without getting to any greater depths."

His first and only job was teaching art at Highgate School in London, albeit on a part-time basis, for by now he was set on becoming a professional painter. Living in a dreary room in Bisham Gardens, he managed to survive on soup and kippers cooked by a sympathetic landlady, a Miss Mary Josling, a blind woman who took in lame dogs like him.

"It was in Bisham Gardens," he wrote, "that I first began to draw on my library of memories until I often ceased to be in London as the room became peopled with farmers and sheepdogs, and bounded by stone walls and rocky cliffs." He had found the landscape and figures which were to be his proper subjects for the rest of his life, and shortly afterwards he began painting in Wales.

He gave up teaching altogether in 1973 and returned to Anglesey, where he found a small cottage on the shore of the Menai Straits which was renovated for him at the expense of the Marquess of Anglesey, thereafter his patron and friend, and from which there were splendid views of the mountains of Eryri. On blue-sky days he was usually to be found there; when the weather was overcast, or after snow, he would be out in the mountains with his sketchbook.

Kyffin Williams held his first one-man exhibition at Colnaghi's in 1948 and almost immediately began to enjoy a reputation as the Welsh landscape painter *par excellence*. His inclusion in the Arts Council of Great Britain's *Twenty-five Paintings by Contemporary Welsh Artists*, in the year following confirmed his standing as a major presence in Wales. Further exhibitions of his work were put on in quick succession at the Leicester Galleries, the Glynn Vivian in Swansea, the Tegfryn in Menai Bridge, the Howard Roberts in Cardiff and the Thackeray in London, and over the next few years his work was bought by all the major collections in Wales.

Commissions came his way, too, especially to paint eminent Welshmen such as Sir Thomas Parry, Dr Huw T. Edwards, Sir Charles Evans, Lord Flowers and Sir David Hughes Parry, all stout pillars of the Welsh Establishment which took him up almost as its official portrait painter, so that there is hardly a public institution in Wales which does not have at least one Kyffin picture in its boardroom.

Although the artist preferred his portraits of people to his landscapes, they are not always admired, for it may be that his painterly skills were better suited to the depiction of sky, sea and mountain than to reproducing the features of the great and the good, however distinguished. But some of his women and children have an attractive poignancy and tenderness, while his studies of old country people are done with honesty and sympathy; a selection of them is to be found in his book *Portraits* (1996).

Kyffin was aware of his weaknesses as a painter. Almost as if to escape the confines of what he knew he could do, in 1968, with the help of a Winston Churchill Fellowship, he spent several months in Patagonia, where a hundred years before some 160 Welsh people, fleeing religious, linguistic and political persecution at home, had settled in the salt-dry valley of the Chubut and in the foothills of the Andes, and where several thousand of their descendants are bilingual in Welsh and Spanish to this day. What he brought back was very different from his earlier work in its brighter colours and in its depiction of this arid region and its gaucho people. Most of the gouaches and watercolours he made during the trip were donated, as a valuable pictorial record of the colony, to the National Library of Wales and shown at the National Eisteddfod of 1971. A brief visit to Venice in 1979 again suggested the direction in which his work might have developed if only he had not felt so committed to his native North Wales.

Kyffin was also an accomplished writer. He published two volumes of autobiography: *Across the Straits* (1973),which describes his boyhood and youth, and its sequel *A Wider Sky* (1991), which he dedicated to Lady Anglesey. A superb raconteur, he wrote with panache about the people and places he had known, often movingly and always with wit and compassion. A good selection of his paintings and drawings was reproduced in *The Land and the Sea* (1998).

In one of his many anecdotes, he told how, while out painting one afternoon in Anglesey he returned to his car parked in a narrow lane only to find that it was stuck in the muddy ditch. The noise of the revving engine as he tried to start attracted the attention of a farmer in a nearby field, who promptly helped get the car going again. In gratitude, Kyffin, the most amiable and generous of men, then thrust into the man's hands one of the sketches from which he habitually worked; today it would fetch a thousand pounds in a Cardiff or London gallery. The farmer took one blank look at it, pushed back his cap in bewilderment, roughly folded the paper into eight squares and stuffed it into his back pocket. "*Diolch*," he said curtly, "thank you" – and quickly disappeared through the hedge.

Curiously, given that Kyffin depended so much on official and corporate patronage, he was not averse to expressing acerbic views about such bodies as the Welsh Arts Council, which neglected him for many years, and the ill-fated Centre for the Visual Arts in Cardiff, which during its brief existence in 1999/2000 showed only the work of what he considered the second-rate avant-garde. He was passionately in favour of a National Art Gallery for Wales, which we still do not have, and warmly supportive of the younger painters of whom he approved.

One of his *obiter dicta* was "A painter who pursues success and fashion, chasing after them with the utmost vigour, will, in fact, always be five minutes late". He was able to say this more often, moreover, towards the end of his life when his pictures were fetching high prices and his work had achieved iconic status in Wales. There was a joke about the price of his paintings: "They cost a kyffin lot."

John Kyffin Williams, painter: born Llangefni, Anglesey 9 May 1918; Senior Art Master, Highgate School 1944-73; President, Royal Cambrian Academy, 1969-76, 1992-2006; ARA 1970, RA 1974; OBE 1982; Kt 1999; died Llanfair Pwllgwyngyll, Anglesey 1 September 2006.

The Independent (2 September 2006)

Urien Wiliam

Scholar and writer of popular fiction

Urien William was unusual among Welsh academics in that he wrote for the common reader. He had received his education almost entirely through the Welsh language and insisted on the highest linguistic standards. But his penchant was for writing detective novels, light verse, soap operas, cartoon scripts and books for children.

His uncommon first name – Urien Rheged was king of the Old North (the north-west of England around Carlisle) in the sixth century – was given him by his father, Stephen J. Williams, Professor of Welsh at the University College, Swansea. He was born in the city in 1929.

Like his father, he had a special interest in the grammar of Welsh, and wrote it with precision and a simple elegance that won him many admirers. He published two grammar books and was an acknowledged expert on the finer points of a language that requires a good deal of attention to be written correctly; he believed in reforming the most conservative rules of the written language and making it more flexible and akin to the spoken forms. This interest is shared by his brother, Aled Wiliam, also a writer and translator.

His first degree was in Welsh at Swansea, after which he took an MA in Education and then a doctorate in Psychology at Liverpool University. Refusing to do military service on grounds of conscience, he taught for a few years at Pembroke Dock before taking up a research post at the children's clinic in Colwyn Bay. From Trinity College, Carmarthen, where he had been a lecturer in Welsh, he moved to the Barry College of Education, which later merged with the Glamorgan Polytechnic (now the University of Glamorgan), where until his decision to turn freelance in 1981 he had been Senior Lecturer.

I first came across him in the 1960s at a late-night session of the Welsh Academy, at which he shone as a raconteur and reciter of funny verse. He had an inexhaustible repertoire of *tribannau*, the four-line stanzas popular in Glamorgan in which the last syllable of the third line rhymes with the third in the last line. Aficionados will know of a good example in the opening verse of the song "'Twas on the good ship Venus". Here is another:

Three things I cannot relish:
A woman who is peevish,
To meet a parson without wit
And Llantwit's broken English.

The form is extremely difficult to do in English,though not as difficult as the *englyn*, that other gem of the Welsh alliterative tradition,
but it was from Urien I first heard an *englyn* in French:

Déjà nous sommes à Dijon – jolie ville
   Je la vois en vallon,
  Et viens, Bill, le vin est bon
  Et la bière nous la boirons.

He came to prominence in 1969 when his farce *Cawl Cennin*
("Leek Soup") won the main prize for drama at the National
Eisteddfod; it was followed by *Y Ffin* ("The border") which took the
prize in the year following. The competition was upgraded shortly
afterwards and in 1972 and 1978 he won the Drama Medal with his
plays *Y Llyw Olaf* ("The last prince") and *Y Pypedau* ("The pup-
pet""") – the only playwright to win in successive years.

After turning freelance he was able to work more for radio and television. Perhaps his greatest success, at least in popular terms, was
writing scripts for Wil Cwac Cwac, a winsome duck who is as familiar to Welsh children as Mickey Mouse. The character had been created by Jennie Thomas and J.O. Williams in the early 1930s but Urien
breathed new life into it. He also scripted the soap opera *Coleg*
("College"), about a group of students and staff at a fictitious campus somewhere in South Wales.

Coming as he did from a bookish, highly intellectual background,
and seeing what was happening to the Welsh language outside academic circles, Urien Wiliam chose to join those who strive to extend
the language's domains by writing material that is more entertaining
than educational, and thus he made an important contribution to its
survival as an everyday language that is yet capable of a wide range
of modes and registers. We need quizzes, cartoons and pop songs in
Welsh as much as we need philosophical treatises and historiography.

Among his novels, about a dozen in all, is *Breuddwyd Rhy Bell* ("A
dream too far", 1995), which connects the French landing near
Fishguard in 1797 – "the Last Invasion of Britain" – with the arrival

of French ships in Bantry Bay in Ireland and the part played by Lord
Edward Fitzgerald and the United Irishmen. He also wrote plays for
radio and translated others into Welsh, notably Eugene O'Neill's
Desire Under the Elms.

Urien Wiliam's chief means of relaxation was caravanning. With his
wife and three children he travelled to many parts of Europe, usually finding some place or incident to write about. In one essay, translated as "Hi-ho!" in the anthology *Illuminations* (1998), he gave a
spirited defence of caravanners against the charge of being "middle-
class gypsies", in prose as polished in its style as it was genial in outlook.

*Urien Wiliam, teacher and writer: born Barry, Glamorgan 7 November
1929; married 1955 Eiryth Davies (two sons, one daughter); died
Penarth, Vale of Glamorgan 21 October 2006.*

The Independent (26 October 2006)

W.R.P. George

David Lloyd George's solicitor nephew and poet

The nephew of the Prime Minister David Lloyd George, W. R. P. George was the son of William George, who from 1890, when his elder brother was elected MP for Caernarfon Boroughs, until his appointment as President of the Board of Trade in 1905, enabled him to follow a political career by staying at home in Criccieth to look after the family firm of solicitors – thus providing him with an income at a time when Members of Parliament received no pay.

If it had not been for William George's selfless generosity in supporting the family, which included his uncle the shoemaker Richard Lloyd, a major influence on the young Liberal, Lloyd George would not have developed so early into the consummate politician he became and, without his brother's wise counsel, might have lost contact with the humble background which inspired him in the early stages of his rise to power.

W.R.P. George, like his father a solicitor with chambers in Porthmadog (even at the age of ninety-one he was still practising at William George & Son – his father carried on until he was 101), wrote two valuable accounts of his famous uncle: *The Making of Lloyd George* (1976) and *Lloyd George – backbencher* (1983). The first is based on the brothers' letters and diaries and brings vividly to life the social context from which the Liberal leader emerged as the champion of Nonconformist Wales.

Writing with great insight, he describes how the young Lloyd George, at sixteen the most Machiavellian of articled clerks, carefully laid his plans with a view to making an impact on the local political scene, and how his brother's ambitions in a similar direction were thwarted by the need for him to maintain the family home and business.

The second book deals with Lloyd George's fifteen years as a backbencher and draws on the archive which William George left his son at his death in 1967. It presents a picture of the MP in his slippers, as it were, but also as the angry, ambitious, silver-tongued and frustrated Liberal hungry for power, and attempts to dispel, not altogether convincingly, some of the myths which have accumulated around his private life.

For all his familial piety, W.R.P. George turned his back on the

Liberal Party early in his career and became an active member of Plaid Cymru, which he saw as the heir to the Radical tradition which his father, uncle and cousin Megan Lloyd George had served in their own ways. He was briefly the Vice-President of Plaid Cymru.

Although never persuaded to stand in the party's name at a general election, he served on the County Council, albeit as an Independent among a swarm of Plaid Cymru members, from 1967 to 1996, and was elected Chairman of Gwynedd County Council in 1982. He was one of those who, with the Chief Executive, the late Ioan Bowen Rees, developed the policies designed to maintain Gwynedd as a bastion of the Welsh language.

William Richard Philip George was born at Criccieth (he insisted on spelling it thus) in 1912 and received his education at Friars School, Bangor, and at Wrekin College, Wellington, in Shropshire. After articles, he joined the family firm and, from 1948 to 1975, served as Clerk to the Justices at Barmouth and as a deputy circuit judge of the Crown Court from 1975 to 1980.

Keenly devoted to the cultural life of Wales, he also held a number of honorary posts which included chairmanship of the Assembly of Welsh Counties, an important conduit for autonomist feeling in the Thatcher years. He served as solicitor to the National Eisteddfod and, taking the bardic name Llysor, an old word for "solicitor", as Archdruid of Wales from 1990 to 1993.

He could not have held the last-named post if he had not been a poet of some standing. Having come to prominence by winning the Crown at the National Eisteddfod in 1974 with a poem in the free metres, he published five collections of Welsh verse, namely *Dwyfor* (1948), *Cerddi'r Neraig* ("Neraig poems", 1968), *Grawn Medi* ("September grapes", 1974), *Tân* ("Fire", 1979) and *Dringo'r Ysgol* ("Climbing the ladder",1989). His selected poems, *Mydylau* ("Gleanings"), appeared in 2004.

Among his other literary work, besides plays for radio and television, was *Gyfaill Hoff* ("Dear friend", 1972), an edition of the correspondence of Eluned Morgan, the Welsh Patagonian writer who, after falling under the Pietistic influence of the Keswick Movement, gave up her literary pursuits and channelled her gifts as a writer into letters addressed to friends in Wales, including William George.

W.R.P. George never deliberately tried to make capital out of his family connections, despite looking remarkably like its most renowned member. Of the same stocky build – he was fond of quoting his uncle, "In North Wales we measure a man from the chin up" – and in his later years with the same white mane and pugnacious chin, what he lacked in inches he made up in *gravitas*, putting it to effective use in the neo-druidic ceremonies at the Eisteddfod.

He was also, for many years, the devoted Secretary of the Baptist chapel at Criccieth, the denomination to which his father and uncle had belonged, thus carrying on a family tradition which included total immersion in the waters of the Dwyfor, the small river in which Lloyd George was baptised as a boy and the name of which he took, shortly before his death in 1945, on being elevated to the peerage as Earl Lloyd George of Dwyfor.

As a public figure, W.R.P. George was highly respected for his shining integrity and fundamentally serious approach as much as for his canny way of getting the best out of individuals and institutions alike. Deeply suspicious of the Welsh Office as an essentially undemocratic body, he found immense satisfaction in the creation of the National Assembly for Wales, seeing in it a vindication of all he had stood for during a long career.

His autobiography, *88 Not Out* (2001), is a typically proud but not bombastic study of his celebrated uncle, a rich picture of life in Wales during the greater part of the twentieth century and a percipient self-portrait of one of the most important public figures in the Wales of his time.

William Richard Philip George, solicitor and writer: born Cricieth, Caernarfonshire 20 October 1914; Archdruid of Wales 1990-93; CBE 1996; married 1943 Dora Harley (marriage dissolved),1953 Greta Bogner (one son, three daughters); died Cricieth, Gwynedd 20 November 2006.

The Independent (22 November 2006)

Eirwen Gwynn

Writer on scientific subjects and political activist

Eirwen Gwynn was a Welsh Nationalist whose formidable intellect and forthright opinions were put to the service of Plaid Cymru, the political party which she joined in 1930, only five years after it was founded and when she was still a schoolgirl in the Anglesey market-town of Llangefni.

Her father, a self-trained dentist, encouraged her to read widely and take an interest in current affairs. By the time she was an undergraduate at the University College of North Wales,Bangor, she was a member of the fledgeling party's executive committee and acquainted with its leaders, including Saunders Lewis, Lewis Valentine and D.J. Williams who, in1936, were to carry out an act of arson on the Llŷn peninsula in protest against the Government's decision to build, despite outcry in Wales, an RAF bombing-school on the lands of Penyberth, a house with Recusant associations.

She had seen the flames from the window of the cottage belonging to her parents in nearby Pwllheli and later witnessed the trial of the Three Men of Penyberth at Caernarfon when the jury failed to reach a verdict; the arsonists were subsequently found guilty at the Old Bailey and sentenced to terms of imprisonment.

Eirwen St John Williams was born in the Newsham Park district of Liverpool, among the large Welsh diaspora of that city, in 1916. Welsh was the language of her comfortable home and she was brought up to take pride in her family's roots in north-west Wales. She learned early on to be bold and uncompromising in the face of bullying from pupils and teachers on account of her Welsh identity and considered herself a cut above her monoglot English classmates.

By 1928 the family were living in Llangefni where her father had a practice and where she rebelled against the predominantly English education meted out at the County School. There, while still in a lower form, she was involved in an altercation with an English mistress who had referred to the girls in her class as "Welsh scum", an incident that left its mark on her growing awareness of her own Welshness. She nevertheless did exceptionally well at school and, turning down a place at Cambridge, went up to Bangor to read Physics in 1934.

In Bangor she came out of the shell in which her family's middle-class respectability had confined her, a process in which she was helped by the man she was later to marry, Harri Gwynn, one of the most talented and debonair Bohemians of his generation. On one famous occasion she and Harri, who as President of the Students' Council always insisted on speaking Welsh at its meetings, walked out of a student hop while the band was still playing "God Save the King", much to the consternation of the college authorities.

Her feminism, *avant la lettre*, also dated from this time and from one incident in particular which she never tired of relating. As the only woman in her Honours class, she had to suffer the disparaging remark from a "prejudiced lout" of an external examiner: "What on earth are you doing here?" She blamed him for the fact that she was awarded a degree in the upper second division whereas her lecturers had confidently expected her to get a first.

As the Second World War approached and Saunders Lewis, Plaid Cymru's right-wing and Catholic leader, began showing signs of sympathy with Franco and Hitler, Harri Gwynn and Eirwen St John Williams were among those who formed a new group known as Gwerin ("The common people") which, from within Plaid Cymru, tried to reconcile the principles of Socialism and Welsh Nationalism. The initiative attracted support from a number of leading intellectuals but came to nothing, largely because the patrician Lewis kept an iron grip on the party's ideology and with the outbreak of war it was wound up, its leader, Goronwy Roberts, being elected as Labour MP for Caernarfonshire in 1945.

After completing her doctorate at Bangor, Eirwen St John Williams took a job as Head of the Physics Department at the Grammar School in Rhyl but stayed only a year. Other jobs eluded her, once because the interviewing panel had expected to see a male candidate and were unwilling to accept that a woman could have a PhD in Physics.

In 1942 she married Harri Gwynn, by now working for the Ministry of Supply in Warwick, where she soon joined him, finding employment as an assistant accountant with the Exchequer and Audit Department. In the year following both ministry and department moved back to London, where it was thought the worst of the bombing was over.

Eirwen Gwynn wrote graphically and movingly about the years she and her husband spent in Earl's Court during the Blitz, during which she gave birth to their only child. An English translation of an essay describing their experience of living under aerial bombardment can be found in the anthology *Illuminations* (1998). In it, she explains how a cheerful English woman, a Mrs Newbould, a missionary's widow who had a flat in the same building as the Gwynns, showed exceptional kindness to the young couple and helped them get through a difficult period of their lives.

In 1950, anxious to provide a Welsh-language education for their son, they returned to Wales, taking a smallholding near Rhoslan on the largely monoglot Llŷn peninsula. Neither had experience of raising livestock and conditions there were harsh, with no electricity, running water or telephone, but by dint of hard work they made a success of it, their meagre income supplemented by Harri Gwynn's earnings as a journalist and lecturer; he later became a distinguished broadcaster on the nightly BBC news programme *Heddiw* ("Today") and a well-known poet in the Welsh language.

His wife, too, found a new career lecturing for the Workers' Educational Association and in broadcasting on both radio and television. She was highly articulate in both Welsh and English and soon became known for her trenchant comments on current affairs, especially those touching on scientific subjects, family planning, abortion, space exploration, alcohol abuse, diet, the environment and "the two cultures". Libertarian in her views, she remained in warm sympathy with young people and argued the case for doing away with the sexual inhibitions which had oppressed her as a young woman.

The subject that agitated her most, however, was the Welsh language, particularly its use in the media and schools. She detested slovenly language (whether Welsh or English) and, with a few others, fought long and hard to bring pressure to bear on the broadcasting authorities to ensure that Welsh was not bastardised by the use of English words and that its elegant syntax and rich idiom should not be affected by English usage. For a few years she refused to pay her television licence while the BBC refused to accommodate her views.

She also wrote many books on quasi-scientific subjects, notably *I'r Lleuad a Thu Hwnt* ("To the moon and beyond", 1964), *Priodi* ("Getting married", 1966) and *Bwyta i Fyw* ("Eating to live", 1987), as well as stories and novels such as *Dau Lygad Du* ("Two black eyes", 1979), *Caethiwed* ("Captivity", 1981), *Cwsg ni Ddaw* ("Sleep will not come", 1982), *Torri'n Rhydd* ("Breaking free", 1990) and *Dim ond Un* ("Only one", 1997). More than 1,600 of her articles appeared in journals such as *Y Gwyddonydd* ("The scientist"), *The Observer, The Sunday Times, New Scientist, New Internationalist, The Listener* and *Scientific American*.

Eirwen Gwynn's autobiography *Ni'n Dau: hanes dau gariad* ("Us two: the story of two lovers", 1999), is a straightforward account of her life told with typical candour and clarity but also with animus against those who, in her judgement, had not given her husband his due as a poet. Its penultimate chapter is a discussion of her views on religion in which, unaffected by her husband's Quakerism, she rejects the dogma of orthodox Christianity, unable to reconcile its insistence on a loving God with the horrors that mankind has to suffer, but keeping an open mind on the possibility of a life hereafter.

The Gwynns' son, Iolo ap Gwynn, who teaches in the Biology Department at the University of Wales, Aberystwyth, is a prominent member of Plaid Cymru in Ceredigion.

Eirwen Meiriona St John Williams, political activist and writer: born Liverpool 12 December 1916; married 1942 Harri Gwynn (died 1985; one son); died Tal-y-bont, Ceredigion 25 January 2007.

The Independent (30 January 2007)

Caryl Davies

Historian of linguistic scholarship

Caryl Davies made a major contribution to our understanding of how linguists and antiquarians believed languages came into being, and how they are interrelated, by examining the theories of such scholars as Edward Lhuyd and Sir William Jones regarding the Celtic branch of the Indo-European family. Those of us who can read Welsh consider her principal book, *Adfeilion Babel* ("The ruins of Babel", 2000), to be one of the most erudite and illuminating studies to appear in the language in the last decade or so.

Although the main preoccupation of most Welsh scholars between 1600 and 1800 had been to demonstrate the beauty and antiquity of the Welsh language, they also had a keen interest in language/*langage* and languages/*langues*, so that any approach to an understanding of their motives and conclusions requires a detailed knowledge of the intellectual and scientific background of the age in which they lived. Caryl Davies was thoroughly immersed in the culture of the seventeenth and eighteenth centuries and had several languages at her command, including Russian.

Foremost among the linguists who were examined in her *chef d'oeuvre* were John Davies (*c*.1567-1644), rector of Mallwyd in Merioneth, one of the greatest Welsh scholars of the later Renaissance period, who compiled a famous grammar, *Antiquae Linguae Britannicae* (1621), as well as translating parts of the new Welsh Bible of 1620 from the original languages; it was his assiduous labours in collecting and copying manuscripts which preserved the old bardic vocabulary as the basis for a scientific study of the Welsh language.

Edward Lhuyd (1660?-1709), Keeper at the Ashmolean in Oxford, who embarked on an ambitious scheme to describe all six Celtic languages but died soon after the appearance of the first volume of his *Archaeologia Britannica* (1707), is also given his meed of praise by Caryl Davies, as well as lesser lights like Henry Rowlands (1655-1723), an Anglican priest in his native Anglesey, whose most notorious book, *Mona Antigua Restaurata* (1723), expounds his spurious theories about the origins of the Druids which he fondly locates on the island.

Caryl Davies, while taking such men seriously as the creatures of their age, was able to add a pinch of salt wherever modern scholarship demanded it and sometimes to cut through the thickets of quackery with a billhook expertly wielded.

The leitmotif running through her book is how Welsh antiquaries were able to contribute to the development of linguistic scholarship in Europe and, despite their own shortcomings, helped to nurture a growing awareness among European experts of the Celtic languages and their relationship to other continental languages. The great philologists Sir William Jones ("the Orientalist") and Paul-Yves Pezron figure prominently in her discussion of the European Enlightenment, the movement that united intellectuals of many countries in their quest for the origins of language. If there is one book in Welsh which takes its inspiration from George Steiner's *After Babel* (1975), Caryl Davies's *Adfeilion Babel* is that book; it ends, like Steiner's, in celebrating "the multi-coloured, ever-changing pattern of the world's languages".

Born at Trealaw in the Rhondda in 1926, a daughter of the manse, Catherine Glyn Jones, as she then was, took her first degree in French and Philosophy at the University College of Wales, Aberystwyth, stayed on to do an MA and then moved to Leeds to finish her doctorate; she also studied at Somerville College, Oxford. Already in Leeds was the young poet and Hispanist Gareth Alban Davies, another native of the Rhondda. After their marriage in 1953 the Davieses made their home in Otley in the West Riding of Yorkshire, where they managed to bring up their four children Welsh-speaking. On her husband's retirement from the Chair of Spanish at Leeds University in 1986 they moved back to Wales, settling at Llangwyryfon in the uplands behind Aberystwyth. One of their daughters, Gwen, is married to Simon Thomas, the former Plaid Cymru MP for Ceredigion.

Having spent a year at the Sorbonne, Caryl Davies was fluent in French and among the writers in whom she had an abiding interest was André Gide, whose novel *La Symphonie Pastorale* she and her husband translated as *Y Deillion* ("The blind", 1965) in which the Protestant ethos and the pastor's love for the blind Gertrude are movingly rendered in sinuous Welsh. As Catherine Glyn Davies she also contributed a volume, *Conscience as consciousness: the idea of self-awareness in French philosophical writing from Descartes to Diderot* to the series *Studies on Voltaire and the Eighteenth Century* which was published for the Voltaire Foundation in 1989. Among Russian authors whose work she rendered into Welsh were Chekhov and Tolstoy. Her hobby was the writing of haikus, in both Welsh and English, which were much admired by aficionados of the form.

Caryl Davies was one of those scholars who have made a substantial contribution to the intellectual life of Wales and added lustre to the history of ideas on which the language depends just as much as on soap operas and bilingual road-signs. Her keen intelligence and richly-layered learning, lightly worn, illumined a part of European civilisation to which we the Welsh can justifiably lay claim to belonging.

Catherine (Caryl) Glyn Jones, linguist and historian of ideas: born Trealaw, Glamorgan 26 September 1926; married 1953 Gareth Alban Davies (one son, three daughters); died Aberystwyth, Ceredigion 22 February 2007.

The Independent (17 March 2007)

Elwyn Bowen

Headmaster and historian of rural Breconshire

Elwyn Bowen had the distinction of becoming headmaster of a country school at the age of twenty-one. In 1945 he reversed the usual thrust of Welsh family history by leaving the industrial village of Cefncoedycymmer, now part of Merthyr Tydfil but then in Breconshire, for a headmastership at Beulah, near Builth, deep in the heart of rural mid-Wales. He stayed there for six years, immersing himself in village life and learning the rudiments of schoolmastering which were to stand him in good stead during a teaching career that was to last more than four decades.

In Beulah he discovered a community in which traditional rural crafts and self-sufficiency still flourished and was a witness of their last phase. By the time he left, in 1951, a new economy of consumer goods, mass-produced and shop-bought, had begun to take over and a way of life that had lasted hundreds of years was drawing to a close. His years in the village and at Llwyn Madoc School were described with affection and great insight in *Sweet Beulah Land* (1999).

His own background and upbringing could not have been more different from what he found in sleepy Beulah. He was the great-grandson of a puddler at the Dowlais ironworks, high on the hill above Merthyr, whose daughter was licensee of the Morning Sun inn in the High Street of Cefn.

At the time of the Merthyr Rising of 1831, when workers had taken over the town and raised the Red Flag (a sheet dipped in calf's blood), only to be faced down by the muskets of the Argyle and Sutherland Highlanders, his family, staunch Unitarians, had taken a leading part in the insurrection. The Welsh equivalent of the Peterloo massacre, the episode has assumed legendary proportions and Elwyn Bowen spoke of it as if he had been personally acquainted with Dic Penderyn, who was hanged in Cardiff Gaol on a trumped-up charge of wounding a soldier.

Elwyn was enormously proud of his family's Radical traditions and would recount them at the drop of a hat. The Morning Sun was a rendezvous for ironworkers, miners, colliers, farmers, poets and the local intelligentsia who gathered there nightly for rumbustious discussions in which the attentive boy soon joined. The family attended

Yr Hen Dŷ Cwrdd (The Old Meeting House), a Unitarian chapel where the wounded rioters had been given shelter and medical aid in 1831.

At Vaynor and Penderyn Grammar School, where he went in 1935, he excelled at sports and neglected all other subjects until encouraged by his uncle, a bard-historian, to apply himself to his studies. The result was that he passed his matriculation examinations and entered Trinity College, Carmarthen, in September 1941. Two years later, having barely completed his training as a teacher, he was called up for the Army. Shortly after demobilisation, he was offered a post as a temporary Physical Education teacher at his old school and then, out of the blue and for reasons he was never able to fathom, was invited to go to Beulah.

The village, about fourteen miles west of Builth in the Irfon Valley, and four miles east of the spa town of Llanwrtyd, had about thirty tied cottages and a population of about a hundred. It also had a post office, two shops, a shoemaker, carpenter, wheelwright, nurse, blacksmith, church, chapel, vicarage, inn, woollen factory, corn mill, a school with thirty-eight pupils and a schoolhouse where he was given accommodation.

The entire village and the surrounding farms belonged to the Llwyn Madoc estate owned by the squire, and the new schoolmaster, brought up in egalitarian Merthyr, found it hard to show the deference that was expected of him. In his book there is an hilarious description of a Hunt Ball, to which he had turned up in evening dress and on an ancient motorcycle and at which he was astounded to hear the clipped accents and observe the pretentious manners of the County Set for the first time.

The district was rich in a cultural life which he quickly explored. Llanwrtyd is associated with William Williams of Pantycelyn, the greatest of Welsh hymn-writers, and with Theophilus Evans, historian and grandfather of Theophilus Jones, the county historian of Breconshire. At Llangammarch, high in the Epynt hills, is the home of the Puritan martyr, John Penry, who in 1593 was executed on suspicion of being the author of the Martin Marprelate Tracts denouncing the institution of episcopacy.

Some ten miles along the road to Builth is Cilmeri, where Llywelyn, the Last Prince of independent Wales, is commemorated. All this chimed well with Elwyn's Nonconformist and Radical background and he soon settled down in the village.

But what fascinated him most was that his adopted community was virtually self-sufficient and in this respect had remained almost unchanged for centuries. Its members understood their roles as farmers, craftsmen, servants and labourers in an agrarian economy which, if not flourishing, provided for all their basic needs. These people were bound by obligations of kinship and marriage, as members of extended families and work-groups, co-operating with one another at times of high seasonal activity such as shearing or harvesting, or in sharing horses or implements. The district also had a busy social life centred on chapel and church, and its own eisteddfod and Agricultural Show. In addition, there were strong ties of language, tradition and custom to which Elwyn, as a Welsh-speaker, could appreciate, respect and contribute.

By the time he left the village in 1951 there had been significant changes in what amounted to 'a horse-hoeing husbandry'. The corn mill and the woollen factory had closed, horse-drawn carts were being replaced by tractors and trailers, the wheelwright and blacksmith were almost out of jobs, and the shoemaker reduced to repairing footwear that had been bought in Builth. Rural poverty, much more abject than anything he had encountered in economically depressed Merthyr, was as rife as ever but the advent of a National Health Service in 1947 had alleviated its worst effects. Even so, the greatest source of food was from poaching and pigs and poultry shared the earthen floors of many a home.

In his book, Elwyn describes in loving detail how craftsmen fashioned furniture out of seasoned oak, gambos with a forty-year guarantee, and wheels of elm, oak and ash that would last a lifetime. The making of baskets, shepherds' crooks,crocheted shawls and blankets was more or less a thing of the past. The people had turned to the towns for almost all their material needs.

This theme became the substance of Elwyn's academic career. After Beulah he became Headmaster of his old Grammar School and then moved to a large comprehensive on the Gurnos estate in Merthyr, still one of the most deprived in Wales, but was always able to make time for his research.

For his work into the history of the parish of Vaynor (*recte* Faenor), in which he drew on oral tradition as well as printed sources, he was awarded an MA by the University of Wales in 1981. It was published as *Vaynor: a Study of the Welsh Countryside* (1992), to which Glanmor Williams, the doyen of Welsh historians, contributed a foreword. For a thesis entitled 'Traditional Industries of Breconshire' he was awarded a PhD a few years later and this was expanded and published as *Traditional Industries of Rural Wales* in 2000.

In 1984 Elwyn Bowen received an MBE in the Queen's Birthday Honour list for services to education in Wales and in 1992 he was nominated the Welsh Academy's Historian of the Year. A genial and loquacious man, physically robust until a stroke laid him low in 2002, he was a frequent broadcaster on historical subjects and generous with his time and knowledge in helping younger historians.

Elwyn Bowen, headmaster and historian, born Cefncoedycymmer, Breconshire 6 April 1923; MBE 1984; married 1951 Gwynfa Davies (two daughters); died Merthyr Tydfil 16 March 2007.

The Independent (27 March 2007)

Marion Eames

Author of acclaimed historical novels

The historical novelist Marion Eames was one of the most consummate prose-writers to have taken the matter of Wales as her theme. Her books are admired for their literary quality as much as for the meticulous research on which they were based. She made no concession to those readers who expected the genre to provide mere entertainments or romantic yarns, but produced six novels of high seriousness which are among the finest written in Welsh during the latter half of the last century.

Her first two novels, *Y Stafell Ddirgel* (1969) and its sequel *Y Rhandir Mwyn* (1972), announced the emergence of a new talent which was to reinvigorate the writing of novels on historical subjects, a category still popular among Welsh readers and not only those whose tastes run to bodice-rippers and swashbuckling tales of derring-do.

These novels, translated as *The Secret Room* (1975) and *Fair Wilderness* (1976), and reprinted as Corgi paperbacks, tell the story of the Quaker Rowland Ellis (1650-1731), a member of the minor gentry of Merioneth who joined the Society of Friends in 1672, and of his emigration to Pennsylvania. The name of his old home near Dolgellau, which still stands, is preserved in that of the celebrated Bryn Mawr College in Philadelphia.

Converted by the preaching of George Fox, Ellis was driven out of Wales on account of his religious faith and because he refused to take the Oath of Allegiance to Charles II – Quakers believing that the swearing of any oath is contrary to the teaching of Christ. He joined William Penn's settlement shortly after his arrival in the colony in 1686 and soon became a prominent figure in the community and Philadelphia's representative on its governing body.

Ellis was a man of culture and translated into English, as *A Salutation to the Britains* (1727), Ellis Pugh's *Annerch i'r Cymry* (1721), the first Welsh book to be published in America.

The 'Welsh Tract', of some 40,000 acres and including townships with names like Merion, Gwynedd, Radnor and Haverford, had been promised by Penn to Welsh Quaker immigrants, to be autonomously governed by 'officers, magistrates, juries of our own tongue'.

But the Welsh fell out with Penn after he broke his promise by dividing the Tract between two counties and interspersing them with other settlers, so that its Welsh character was impaired and eventually broken up. The final rupture came when Penn appointed himself the King's Governor in the territory, thus representing the very power which the Welsh Quakers were trying to flee.

Although Welsh continued to be the language of worship in many Pennsylvania meeting houses for another hundred years or so, the Tract gradually lost its identity and many of the Friends either went to live in English settlements or returned to Wales. There is a small exhibition about local Quakers on the square at Dolgellau, for which Marion Eames wrote an explanatory leaflet, and Friends still meet in the town.

The novels, which tell an exciting tale with restraint and great perception, proved a success when televised in serial form by BBC Wales and were among the first costume dramas to herald a new professionalism in Welsh-language television. So authentic were they that it was hard to believe the author had never set foot in Philadelphia.

Marion Eames was born of Anglesey parents at Birkenhead in 1921, but was brought up and educated in Dolgellau, Merioneth, where she attended Dr Williams's School for Girls, notorious in her day for the English education it dispensed. She was to complain in later life that she had received not one Welsh lesson while at school and she felt this lack keenly, but made up for it by voracious reading. Among the foreign writers she admired was Simone Weil, whose book *L'Enracinement* influenced the Welsh philosopher J. R Jones, particularly in his writings about land and language as essential factors in national identity.

After leaving school at fifteen, she took her first job with the county's library service, after which she worked in the library of the University College of Wales, Aberystwyth. She also worked for a few years as an organizer for Plaid Cymru in north Wales and was later appointed editor of *Y Dydd* ("The day"), a weekly newspaper published in Dolgellau. It was her long association with the town that awakened her interest in the early Quakers of the district.

It was in London, where she had gone to study the piano and harp at the Guildhall School of Music, that she met the journalist Griffith Williams, whom she later married. He was already a Quaker and introduced her to the Society of Friends. They returned to Wales on her appointment as a producer of radio programmes for the BBC, making their home at Bonvilston in the Vale of Glamorgan. Among the programmes she made was *Merched yn Bennaf* ("Mainly women"), the Welsh equivalent of *Woman's Hour*.) She also wrote scripts for the nightly soap *Pobol y Cwm* ("People of the valley").

Her third novel was *I Hela Cnau* ("To gather nuts", 1978), in which she dealt with the social causes of the drift of young people from north Wales in search of work in the docks and cotton mills of Merseyside, where the Welsh have for long made up a sizeable part of the population; an English translation appeared as *The Golden Road* in 1990. It was followed by *Y Gaeaf Sydd Unig* ("The winter is lonely", 1982), which is set in the thirteenth century during the reign of Llywelyn ap Gruffudd, the Last Prince of independent Wales.

With *Seren Gaeth* ("Captive star", 1985) she turned from remote history to her own time. This novel concerns a troubled marriage between an academic and a talented music student, and has some resemblances to the real-life relationship between Ernest Jones, the psychoanalyst and biographer of Freud, and his first wife, the young composer Morfydd Llwyn Owen. In particular, it was prompted by a passage from Jones's autobiography *Free Associations* (1959) in which he refers to his wife thus: "Her faith and devotion, so admirable when related to her country and people, were also unfortunately attached to very simple-minded religious beliefs."

Marion Eames's last novel for adults was *Y Ferch Dawel* ("The quiet girl", 1992), in which a young woman, adopted as a child, goes in search of her natural mother and in which the subject of incest is explored.

She also published *A Private Language?* (1997), based on a series of lectures on Welsh literature which she had given, under the auspices of the Workers' Educational Association, to English incomers into the Welsh-speaking heartland of Gwynedd; it was meant as a riposte to a Minister of the Crown who had dismissed the Welsh language as fit only for domestic purposes.

Marion was a shy, softly spoken woman whose mild manner belied a steely commitment to her writing and a clear-eyed view of people and events which, together with her considerable gifts as a writer, equipped her well for the work of writing historical novels. I remember asking her whether she had ever thought of how much money she could have made if she had written her books in English, and receiving a gentle though firm reply to the effect that financial reward meant nothing to her while the Welsh language, in all its rich complexity, was there for her to write in.

Although patriotism was at the heart of her books – she once told me that she had chosen to write about the Quakers because they reminded her of Welsh patriots down the ages who had suffered for their faith – she never allowed propaganda to interfere with her writing, for which reason her novels are all the more convincing in their account of the Welsh people at critical points in their history.

Marion Eames, novelist: born Birkenhead, Cheshire 5 February 1921; radio producer, BBC Wales 1955-80; married 1955 Griffith Williams (died 1977); died Dolgellau, Gwynedd 3 April 2007.

The Independent (6 April 2007)

Gwyn Erfyl Jones

Broadcaster, television executive and writer

It is said, with only slight exaggeration, that the studios, canteens and corridors of BBC Wales are full of ex-ministers and sons of the manse. Gwyn Erfyl Jones, or Gwyn Erfyl as he was generally known, bore out this stereotypical, not to say jaundiced, view of broadcasting in Wales, except that he worked for HTV, formerly Harlech Television, the commercial company set up for Wales and the West of England in 1968. Before joining the company he had served since 1954 in the Congregationalist ministry.

His was the best-known face appearing in HTV's Welsh-language programmes from the Cardiff studios throughout the 1970s. Although he was employed initially as an editor, he became the Cliff Michelmore of Welsh television, presenting several programmes a week and interviewing a great variety of famous people, among them the Italian painter Pietro Annigoni, often with the help of voice-overs and subtitles. He had an interviewing style all his own, a mixture of penetrating analysis, philosophical reflection and sardonic humour that gave his programmes a quality that was much appreciated by viewers wanting intellectual stimulus rather than mere entertainment.

This engagement with ideas, especially those touching on the more numinous aspects of life and death, was central not only to his professional career but to his own outlook as a committed and practising Christian. Not that he was entirely unquestioning or comfortable in his faith. "There are some hymns I can't sing, prayers I can't utter, religious concerns I lose no sleep over," he wrote in an autobiographical essay in 2000, and then, as if to reaffirm his belief in fundamental things, "The only god that dies is the one who is merely an extension of our selves."

He was, too, aware that he belonged to an era that was fast drawing to a close and felt as if he were caught between two worlds and torn apart by them. It was this impatience with outmoded dogma and tension between the spirit and the questing mind that informed many of his programmes. The effort he put into thinking about them was often to be seen etched on his face, so that his delivery was sometimes a touch too ponderous and long-winded.

Among the twelve serious thinkers whom he interviewed in the series *Credaf* ("I believe") which he made for HTV in 1984, shortly after the advent of S4C, the fourth television channel broadcasting partly in Welsh, were Dewi Z. Phillips, Professor of Philosophy at Swansea and chief interpreter of Wittgenstein in Wales, Meredydd Evans, perhaps the finest cultural analyst of his generation, and Dafydd Elis Thomas, now President of the National Assembly and keen Churchman. All responded to Gwyn Erfyl's questions by tackling the weighty issues he raised.

Gwyn Erfyl Jones was born in 1924 on a farm near the village of Llanerfyl in Montgomeryshire from which he took his middle name. He attributed his fondness for good food to his mother's culinary skills, which she had learned while in domestic service in Liverpool, though he never said where he acquired his taste for good wine.

He and his brother slept in a bed over which hung photographs of luminaries of the Calvinistic Methodist pulpit, a popular feature of many homes in Wales until quite recently. In the parlour there was a harmonium on which the boys learned to play the great hymns of Ann Griffiths and Williams Pantycelyn, relishing the words as much as the music. Although staunch in their chapel attendance, the family would take part in the *Plygain*, the early morning carol service held at the church of St. Erfyl on Christmas Day, a tradition still kept in parts of rural Montgomeryshire.

It was little wonder that, as a schoolboy of fifteen, Gwyn Erfyl set his heart on entering the Nonconformist ministry. At the Grammar School in Llanfair Caereinion, where as a virtual monoglot Welsh-speaker he had difficulty in figuring out how the English word for a female fox was 'vixen' and not 'foxess', he eventually excelled at languages, even English, despite a tendency to write it in a flowery style – a charge levelled at some of the programmes he made in 'the thin language'. But he attended a Welsh-language chapel and, although he was still a lad when he first observed its narrowness and hypocrisy, he was called to preach the Gospel of Christ in his mother-tongue.

In 1942, having just sat the examination for the Higher School Certificate, he appeared before an unsympathetic tribunal as a conscientious objector to war on Christian pacifist grounds. He did so with less than total conviction and was duly turned down. "I have my doubts about every absolute standpoint and can always see the value of compromise and the middle way," he later wrote.

For the next three years he served in the Non Combatant Corps attached to the Pioneer Corps, a very underprivileged regiment among whom 'conchies' were extremely unpopular. After basic training, which involved learning how to march but not to carry arms, he was sent to barracks in Carlisle, then to a tank depot near Manchester, and finally to London, where he followed a course for administrators of POW camps.

At the camp in Abergavenny, coming into contact with Italians and Germans for the first time, he took every opportunity to talk to the prisoners, finding in them the essential human goodness that he sought in all men. "Once we venture out from our trenches and walk into no man's land without gun or bayonet," he wrote, "we come to experience the joy of recognition, of reconciliation and of love. It is not a journey for the cynic or the introverted, nor for the proud. It is the Kingdom of Innocence." I think, too, from the conversations I had with him, Gwyn had misgivings about his stand against conscription and regretted some of the things he had believed as a teenager.

After taking a degree in Philosophy at the University College of Wales, Aberystwyth, he lectured in Philosophy, Psychology and Politics at Coleg Harlech, the centre for adult education, but found that the niceties of academic life were not for him. Instead, he worked for a year with the National Coal Board in London and then, in 1954, decided to enter the Congregationalist ministry, answering calls to chapels in Trawsfynydd, Glanaman and Cardiff. His reasons for turning his back on the ministry remain unclear, but may have had something to do with his growing unease at having to preach on a regular basis or perhaps with the difficulty of having to support a wife and four small children on the scant stipend of a Nonconformist minister.

While still in charge of a chapel in Cardiff, he joined Television Wales and the West as a part-time member of the talented team making *Y Dydd* ("The day"), the first serious news programme in Welsh, and when TWW was replaced by HTV, Gwyn Erfyl became a full-time producer and presenter. His career at HTV provided him with ample scope for his gifts as a communicator with philosophical and artistic interests and with a convivial social life that often went on into the small hours in the city's bars and restaurants.

Having made a large number of programmes, some of which won

major prizes, he was promoted to become Head of Documentary, Religious and Arts Programmes at HTV in 1974. Under his supervision the company made programmes such as *Dan Sylw* ("Under consideration") and *Bywyd* ("Life"), which now belong to the golden age of Welsh broadcasting. In 1980, he was promoted to become the company's Controller in North Wales, working from its offices at Theatr Clwyd in Mold. He retired from his post in 1985 but continued to broadcast frequently on S4C.

He published, besides a slim volume of verse, two volumes of essays reflecting his work in television: *Trwy Ddirgel Ffyrdd* ("By mysterious ways",1997) and *Dyfroedd Byw a Cherrynt Croes* ("Living waters and cross currents", 2000). The first of these describes his visits to countries as far afield as Israel, Germany (including Dachau), South Africa, Japan (including Hiroshima), and the Basque Country, all places where he tested his personal beliefs against harsh realities. In the second book he wrote about some of the Welsh writers whom he had known, including Saunders Lewis, Waldo Williams and Alun Llywelyn-Williams, each in his own way presenting a challenge to orthodoxy. Also published here is a thought-provoking analysis of the output and function of S4C in the cultural life of the Welsh nation.

As editor of *Barn* ("Opinion"), the monthly magazine of current affairs, from 1975 to 1979, Gwyn Erfyl succeeded Alwyn D. Rees, who had steered it brilliantly through the tumultuous 'sixties when the young militants of *Cymdeithas yr Iaith Gymraeg* (Welsh Language Society) were calling for a greater measure of official status for Welsh. His editorship was rather more cautious and, like many professional broadcasters, he was careful not to show *parti pris* in the heated debate over the establishment of a Welsh-language fourth channel. S4C was eventually set up by the Thatcher government in 1982, after a threat by Gwynfor Evans to fast to the death if it reneged on its promise, and a new era for Welsh-language broadcasting began of which Gwyn Erfyl took full advantage.

His last years were spent quietly in Bangor and Caernarfon, though he continued to preach from time to time. The University of Wales awarded him an honorary DLitt in 1992 but then, in 1999, his wife, Lisa, with whom he had shared the joys and crises of his spiritual pilgrimage, died suddenly and he was bereft.

Gwyn Erfyl Jones, television producer and HTV executive; born Llanerfyl, Montgomeryshire 9 June 1924; Head of Documentary, Religious and Arts Programmes, HTV (1974-80); HTV's Controller in North Wales (1980-85); married 1949 Lisa Rowlands (died 1999, four daughters); died Bangor, Gwynedd 4 May 2007.

The Independent (5 May 2007)

Ifor Owen

Headmaster and illustrator of children's books

Ifor Owen was devoted to his own small communities in rural north-west Wales, serving them in many capacities but mainly as a primary school headmaster for forty years. He was a gifted teacher who understood the needs of children from Welsh-speaking homes, providing attractive reading material for them and encouraging his staff to help pupils develop their literacy skills in their own language. Besides books, he wrote, illustrated and published the first comic in Welsh, *Hwyl* ("Fun"), the first number of which appeared in 1949 and the last in 1989. It soon became a children's favourite, selling 8,000 copies an issue, and many adults admitted to enjoying it too.

In his concern for the education of Welsh-speaking children Ifor Owen was inspired by Owen M. Edwards, educationist, publisher, and for many years Chief Inspector of Schools in Wales. He revered him as a great patriot whose practical approach to bilingual education had laid the foundations for the growth of national consciousness in the first decades of the twentieth century. Edwards was a native of Llanuwchllyn, where a statue commemorates him at the entrance to the village, and his reputation is kept green in the district, not least through the work of people like Ifor Owen who still maintain its rich culture rooted in the Welsh language. Another influence on him was the renowned bibliophile and genealogist Bob Owen of Croesor, who awakened in him a love of the printed word and image.

An early member of Urdd Gobaith Cymru (The Welsh League of Youth), the movement founded by O.M. Edwards's son, Ifan ab Owen Edwards, in 1922, Ifor Owen played a prominent part in the League's activities and became almost the official designer and illustrator of its publications. In the days before the more professional approach of the Welsh Books Council, he was one of the few who strove to make Welsh children's books more colourful and visually exciting. He also turned his hand to making county maps which featured cameo portraits of the famous men and women who had lived within their borders.

He was born in the village of Cefnddwysarn in Merioneth in 1915. Educated at the Boys' Grammar School in Bala and Bangor Normal

College, where he trained to be a teacher specialising in art and science, he entertained an ambition to teach Art but his father thought Art was "only for girls". Having turned down the offer of a job in Clacton-on-Sea, at the age of twenty-one he was appointed headmaster of the primary school at Croesor, an upland, virtually monoglot community, where he remained until 1948. From then until 1954 he was head of the village school at Gwyddelwern near Corwen and from 1954 to 1976 the first headmaster of Ysgol O.M. Edwards in Llanuwchllyn, near Bala. It gave him particular pleasure to be in charge of a school named after his hero and to live in part of Neuadd Wen ("White Hall"), the large house he had built for himself in the village.

He had begun illustrating books in Croesor while the school was shut by an outbreak of measles. As an illustrator he was always in great demand. The first book he illustrated was *Yr Hen Wraig Bach a'i Mochyn* ("The little old lady and her pig", 1946), after which many commissions from Welsh publishers followed. Among other books were a Welsh version of Collodi's Pinocchio story, *Yr Hogyn Pren* ("The wooden boy") by E. T. Griffiths, and *Hunangofiant Tomi*, by E. Tegla Davies, a classic among Welsh children's tales. In the early 'sixties he turned his hand to designing the sleeves of records produced by the burgeoning pop industry in Wales. An example of his talent as a designer can be seen in the wrought-iron gates of the cemetery at Llanuwchllyn. The amateur drama company which he founded in the village is still going strong.

Many honours came his way. In 1961 he was invested in the White Robe Order of Gorsedd y Beirdd – sometimes said to be the equivalent of the CBE in Wales – and the University of Wales awarded him an honorary MA in 1997. But perhaps the honours which gave him most satisfaction were the prestigious Sir Thomas Parry-Williams Medal, which he received in 1977, and the first-ever Mary Vaughan Jones Award in 1985, named after one of the foremost of Welsh children's authors and thereafter presented triennially by the Welsh Books Council. The Urdd also honoured him and he will be fondly remembered at its annual Eisteddfod which opens on Saturday in Carmarthen. All these awards were for his outstanding contribution to the culture of the districts where his working life had been spent.

A Nationalist by conviction and example, in the late 1950s he was among those who opposed the drowning of the Tryweryn Valley, not far from Bala, to make a reservoir for Liverpool. He was also a staunch member of Cymdeithas yr Iaith Gymraeg (The Welsh Language Society), lending his moral support to the young militants who campaigned for Welsh to be given the official status it now enjoys, often at the cost of their personal liberty. During the Second World War he registered as a conscientious objector and served for many years as a deacon in the Presbyterian chapel at Llanuwchllyn. When, in the 1950s, the extensive Williams Wynn estate passed to the government and was broken up and sold to the tenant farmers, he was secretary of the committee charged with its dispersal.

Ifor Owen was a man in his element at meetings of committees charged with organising or financing local initiatives of a cultural nature. Since the National Eisteddfod depends on support from the district where it is held every year, he served on its Council and was the long-time Chairman of its Art and Craft Committee. He was also a member of the governing body of the National Museum of Wales. But he once told me he also derived great pleasure from sessions of Clwb Llenyddol Pethe Penllyn – the famous literary club that meets in Penllyn, that is to say the district around Llyn Tegid, the lake known to tourists as Bala Lake – where his puckish wit and keen interest in local history were much appreciated.

Ifor Owen, headmaster and illustrator of children's books and periodicals: born Cefnddwysarn, Merioneth, 3 July 1915; married Winefred Jones (deceased, two sons, one daughter); died Dolgellau, Gwynedd 22 May 2007.

The Independent (31 May 2007)

Mercer Simpson

Poet of the East Anglian landscape and critic of Welsh writing in English

Although his roots were in Suffolk, Mercer Simpson felt a close affinity with Wales and the literary affairs of the country where he lived for more than fifty years. He was so often identified with Welsh writing in English that his verse appeared in all the major anthologies and the writers he chose to write about were from the whole canon, from Henry Vaughan to Glyn Jones. As critic, reviewer, editor and poet he made a contribution that was warmly acclaimed by his many friends on the occasion of his eightieth birthday last year.

Even so, it was the scenes of his childhood and early manhood that inspired him most. His first collection, *East Anglian Wordscapes* (1993), which has drawings by Miriam King, is a sequence of twenty poems celebrating places in that 'flat country' between Cambridge, King's Lynn, Great Yarmouth and Ipswich. The book's epigraph comes from an essay by Jeremy Hooker, another English poet living in Wales who is much taken with the sense of place: "Some people who no longer live in a particular place still carry it inside them, and speak from or through it even when they are not speaking about it."

Mercer Simpson was born in Fulham in 1926, the only child of a consultant neurologist, but was sent by elderly parents to King Edward VI School in Bury St Edmunds in Suffolk, in whose Old Boys' journal some of his poems were later reprinted. At the age of eighteen, before the end of the Second World War, he enlisted with the Royal Marines and was identified as officer material, only to find military discipline intolerable and the fatigues incomprehensible: it was a merciful release when he was sent on a Royal Navy short course at Magdalene College, Cambridge. He recalled with relish being informed by his NCO, "Now then, you lot, today is VE Day and you will enjoy it!", before being made to run around the parade ground carrying full packs for an hour or two. After demobilisation he returned to Magdalene to finish a degree in English and the course of his career was thenceforth set.

After training to be a teacher at Bristol University, he moved to Wales for the first time in 1950 on taking up a post as Senior English Master at Monkton School in Cardiff. Many pupils were enthralled by his reciting poetry in the classroom, for he had a stentorian voice inherited, he thought, from his grandfather, also named Mercer Simpson, who had managed the Theatre Royal in Birmingham.

In 1967 he joined the staff of the Glamorgan College of Technology in Trefforest, near Pontypridd, which later grew into a Polytechnic and is now the University of Glamorgan. There he taught Liberal Studies, mainly to students of Engineering among whom this most genial and courteous of men was popular because he was also a canal and railway enthusiast, and a great admirer of Brunel. He was later promoted to Senior Lecturer in the Department of Arts and Language. In 1974 he took a sabbatical and was duly awarded an MA from the University of Wales for a thesis on aspects of English poetry in the twentieth century. Ever after he was rarely to be seen without a tie in the University colours of red, blue and gold. Another sign of his Welsh sympathies was his support for Plaid Cymru at election-time.

Mercer threw himself into Welsh literary life with gusto. A late-flowering poet, he published two more collections of his verse: *Rain from a Clear Blue Sky* (1994) and *Early Departures, Late Arrivals* (2006); a third, *Enclosures and Disclosures*, the proofs of which he showed me from his hospital bed, is to be published before the end of this month.

Although all three books contain poems inspired by places and people in Wales, it was to East Anglia that he most often returned in his imagination. What interested him was life's quiddities, often originating in childhood, usually presented in the context of the natural world and always set in a particular landscape. Many ask questions about the numinous and all may be seen as belonging to the English pastoral tradition. Some of the poems, such as 'Pilgrims to Walsingham', represent a spiritual journey into his own past and a search for religious faith.

It was the Welsh Academy, the national association of writers in Wales, which gave him opportunities to make a contribution to the literary life of his adopted country He served on its committees, edited its news bulletin for five years, read scores of manuscripts, and made himself available to younger writers seeking advice. Equally important work was done for *The Anglo-Welsh Review*, *Poetry Wales* and *The New Welsh Review*, where many of his reviews and articles appeared. But his finest piece of criticism appeared as an introduction to the *Collected Poems* of Glyn Jones in 1996. Here was the mature critic, lucid and and stringent but intent on demonstrating how the long poem 'Seven Keys to Shaderdom' is one of the major achievements of Welsh poetry in English. He also contributed most of the entries on Welsh topics in the *Bloomsbury Guide to English Literature* (1989).

In his younger days Mercer had been an MCC coach and a selector for the Cardiff Schoolboys' XI. At the time of his death he was still President of Pentyrch Cricket Club, a position he had held for more than forty years; he also had a season ticket to watch Cardiff Rugby XV. When his health permitted, he was regular in his attendance at St Bride's-super-Ely in the Vale of Glamorgan, where his wife's family came from, and where he will now be buried.

Mercer Frederick Hampson Simpson, teacher and poet: born Fulham, London, 27 January 1926; Lecturer in Liberal Studies, Glamorgan College of Technology and Senior Lecturer in the Department of Arts and Language, Polytechnic of Wales (1967-81); married 1961 Betty Cook (one daughter); died Cardiff 11 June 2007.

The Independent (22 June 2007)

Ivor Emmanuel

Popular Welsh singer who starred in the film 'Zulu'

Ivor Emmanuel had a moment of fame as the Welsh soldier who, in the film *Zulu* (1963), rallies a handful of men of the South Wales Borderers in their valiant stand against the four thousand warriors of Chief Cetewayo at Rorke's Drift in 1879. If the stars of Cy Endfield's film are Michael Caine, making his debut as an incompetent upper-class officer, and Stanley Baker as the troubled lieutenant who, severely wounded, has to hand over command of the beleaguered outpost to him, it is Ivor Emmanuel, as Private Owen, who inspires the company with a spirited rendering of 'Men of Harlech', the regimental marching tune.

As the Zulu Impis advance wave upon wave, rattling their assegais against their shields and chanting their blood-curdling war-cries, he turns to Baker with the nonchalant comment, 'They've got a very good bass section, mind, but no top tenor, that's for sure,' then bursts into song, the English words of which he had written specially for the film. The musical exhortation notwithstanding, the British garrison is nearly wiped out and saved only when Cetewayo, aware that the Zulus would win at best only a Pyrrhic victory, calls the battle off in salute to the bravery of the combatants on both sides.

The film, based on a story by John Prebble, cost Paramount about 1.5 million dollars and had its world premiere in Johannesburg during the years of apartheid. The distributors later denied that the South African Government invested in the production, but admitted it had supplied manpower and animals. Ivor Emmanuel was among those who were appalled to learn that the Zulus who had taken part in the film were banned from seeing it, the Publications Control Board having deemed it 'unfit for black African consumption'.

In Wales, the heroism of the South Wales Borderers at Rorke's Drift (after which eleven VCs were awarded, the largest number ever given for a single engagement) has become something of a legend, punctured only by the irreverence of the comedian Max Boyce, who retells the story by making one of the soldiers say to Emmanuel as the Zulus relentlessly resume their attack, "For God's sake, Ivor, sing them something they like!"

Ivor Emmanuel was born in the steel town of Margam in 1927 and brought up in Pont-rhyd-y-fen, the industrial village in the upper reaches of the Afan Valley where Richard Burton had been born the previous year. Welsh-speaking and steeped in the eisteddfodic tradition, he sang in chapels and village halls from an early age and, encouraged by his family, soon set his heart on a musical career. He took singing lessons and began to perform with local operatic companies such as the very fine one which was based in Port Talbot in those days.

But like most boys of his time and place, he had to earn his living from mining and at the age of fourteen he went to work underground. His family was shattered when, in 1941, a bomb was accidentally dropped on Pont-rhyd-y-fen by an Allied plane in pursuit of a German bomber during a Luftwaffe raid on Swansea. Both his parents, his grandfather and his two-year-old sister were killed and he and his brother were hurled from their beds into the garden, after which they went to live with an aunt. It was not until a documentary programme was made by S4C in 2001 that he was able to talk about it in public.

After the war, Ivor was a frequent visitor to the West End, where he was enthralled by the American musicals then taking London by storm. He was put up by Richard Burton, who was playing the lead part in *The Lady's Not for Burning*, and it was the actor who gave the young hopeful a start. At his audition for the chorus of *Oklahoma!* at the Royal Theatre in Drury Lane Emmanuel sang 'Some Enchanted Evening', trying hard to make his light baritone voice sound as American as possible.

He spent a year with the show and then another with the D'Oyly Carte Opera Company before returning in 1951 to the Royal Theatre as Sergeant Kenneth Johnson in the smash-hit, *South Pacific* in which an unknown Larry Hagman (later JR in Dallas) also had a small part in the chorus. Further opportunities came his way in a production of *The King and I* at the same theatre and in 1957 as the baseball-player Joe Hardy in *Damn Yankees* at the Coliseum.

Comparisons were inevitably drawn between Ivor Emmanuel and his namesake and compatriot, Ivor Novello, who had charmed the London stage a generation earlier, but despite his matinée looks and heart-throb appeal, 'the boy from Pont-rhyd-y-fen' never quite made it into the same gilded world.

In 1958 he turned his career into television with TWW, the commercial company which had won the first franchise for Wales and the West of England. Its most popular light entertainment programme was *Gwlad y Gân / Land of Song*, in which he was given star billing with the young singer Siân Hopkins, whose sweet voice and girlish freckles chimed attractively with his resonant power and Italianate good looks.

The talent of this pair, despite their having to sing surrounded by a cute kiddies' choir, made the programme, the first live bilingual musical show to be networked from Wales, compulsive viewing for a new generation of viewers. Introduced by Siân Phillips, recently married to Peter O'Toole, it had colourful design, clever lighting and high production values, and did much to enhance the standards and reputation of the medium in Wales.

When the programme was taken off in 1965, Ivor Emmanuel went on to do summer seasons in Blackpool, starring with entertainers such as Shirley Bassey and Morecombe and Wise, and also found work on the *Queen Mary*, sharing the spotlight with Max Jaffa. In the year following he went to New York to play Mr Gruffydd, the fine, upstanding minister in *A Time for Singing*, a Broadway musical version of Richard Llewellyn's novel *How Green Was My Valley*, but it ran for only forty nights, after which his career in musicals was at an end.

Cabaret appearances and pantomime followed, in which his dancing and acting abilities stood him in good stead. For TWW he fronted programmes in which he met, sang and talked to local people in various towns in Wales and the west of England. He proved an adroit interviewer, his winning grin and easy, attentive manner bringing out the best in the people with whom he chatted.

It was during a cruise in the Mediterranean in 1963 that he fell in love with Spain. He bought a villa in the hill-top village of Benelmadena, near Mijas, but the idyllic life of the wealthy expatriate was not to be. His first two marriages failed and in 1991 he lost £220,000, his life's savings, when the Bank of Credit and Commerce collapsed. His friends rallied round and a collection was organised in Pont-rhyd-y-fen by his lifelong friend, Haydn Mizen.

Having decided to settle permanently in Spain, he turned his back on the show-biz world in which he had made his name and lived quietly in the sunshine and within sight of the sea. Homesickness for Wales was gradually overcome and he lost touch with many of his erstwhile colleagues.

So complete was his disappearance from the billings that articles began appearing in the Welsh press that referred to him in the past tense. In 1998 Desmond Carrington spoke of him on BBC Radio 2 as 'the late Ivor Emmanuel', at which tourists started appearing on his doorstep asking to see his grave. As late as 2002 there were messages on the world wide web from fans anxious to know what had become of him.

Now that rumours of his death can no longer be exaggerated, Ivor Emmanuel is remembered with affection and admiration, in his own country and in the wider world, as the soldier who sang 'Men of Harlech' to such stirring effect in that effortless, mellifluous, Welsh voice of his. Not for nothing does the sign near Pont-rhyd-y-fen proudly proclaim (with only slight exaggeration) that the village is the 'Birthplace of Richard Burton, Ivor Emmanuel and Rachel Evans'.

Ivor Lewis Emmanuel, singer: born Port Talbot, Glamorgan 7 November 1927; married 1951, Jane Beazleigh (one son, one daughter, marriage dissolved), 1964 Patricia Bredin (marriage dissolved), 1966 Malinee Oppenborn (one daughter); died Malaga, Spain 20 July 2007.

The Independent (24 July 2007)

Dillwyn Miles

'Mr Pembrokeshire' and Herald Bard

Dillwyn Miles was so closely associated with the county that he was generally known as "Mr Pembrokeshire". He accepted the sobriquet gladly for it reflected his immense pride in having given a lifetime's service as local historian, county councillor and Mayor of Newport, the small seaside town a few miles to the east of Fishguard, where he had been born in 1916. Apart from war service in Palestine, two years at Palestine House in London and a brief spell in Cardiff, he never lived outside Pembrokeshire and his immense energies were devoted to its social, political and cultural life.

He also came to prominence as a member of the Gorsedd of Bards, that august company of neo-druids whose rituals lend colour to the annual ceremonies of the National Eisteddfod. Appointed Grand Sword Bearer in 1959, it was his task partly to withdraw the heavy sword from its scabbard and then sheathe it again, in symbolic reference to the fact that "the Bards of the Isle of Britain are men of peace and bear no naked weapon against anyone".

Promoted to the office of Herald Bard in 1966, he brought to it a stately bearing which suggested that he took it as seriously as was possible for a historian who knew that, in fact, the Gorsedd had been invented in the late 18th century by a wayward genius known as Iolo Morganwg. For Dillwyn Cemais, as he was known in bardic circles, tradition and custom were at the heart of Welsh culture and, as a conservative, he defended them, however spurious their origins, against all detractors.

Dubbed "the druid with the magnificent moustache" by *The Daily Express*, he was sometimes treated by his own countrymen even less reverently, one sharp-tongued critic comparing him to the leader of "a bunch of Bedouin who have lost their camels" – a reference to the white robes and head dresses of the Bards of the Isle of Britain as they parade through the towns in which the Eisteddfod is held each year. The Herald Bard, his authority embodied in the hefty staff he carried, took it all in his stride, convinced that he was doing it for Wales.

One of his first duties after taking up the office was to represent the Gorsedd at the investiture of the Prince of Wales at Caernarfon castle in July 1969, and this he did, amid tight security, with his usual enthusiasm for all things royal and his incorrigible taste for pageantry. His contempt for "the young extremists" who lined the Prince's route extended to the "hooligans" of the Welsh Language Society who were campaigning for greater recognition of Welsh in the public life of Wales.

He had no time for unconstitutional methods and, despite his patriotism, was loth to speak out on behalf of the language, preferring to work for it quietly in his own way, and for this reason he became something of an Uncle Tom in the eyes of those who took a sterner, more radical view. Although he had been an early member of Plaid Cymru, and had allowed his name to go forward as a Labour candidate in the general election of 1945, he sat as an Independent on the parish, district and county councils, generally steering clear of party politics.

One small example of his reverence for royalty must suffice. In 1997, as Herald Bard and responsible for the robes worn by members of the Gorsedd, he refused to acknowledge a letter from a young militant who had stuck the postage stamp upside down on the envelope as a sign of her Republican sympathies. This he took as an insult to the Queen, who as Elisabeth o Windsor is a member of the Gorsedd, and the consequent brouhaha received a good deal of coverage in the Welsh and London press. To the Herald Bard's disgust, the Gorsedd subsequently agreed to accept letters with the stamp inverted.

Dillwyn Miles – his first name was pronounced not with the voiceless fricative lateral ll but as if it had only one l – was the son of the proprietor of the Castle Hotel in Newport and Welsh was his first language. Educated at Fishguard High School and the University College of Wales, Aberystwyth, he was prevented from completing his course in Geography by the breakdown of his health. But well-connected even as a young man, he nevertheless found temporary teaching posts in his native county and, at the age of sixteen, became the unpaid clerk of Newport Parish Council and a burgess of the town three years later, thus beginning his long career in local government. At the outbreak of war in September 1939 he immediately volunteered to serve with the Royal Army Service Corps.

He spent the duration of the war in the Middle East, mostly with

Q branch at British headquarters in Jerusalem, where he was promoted to the rank of Captain, and later in Syria and the Lebanon. In
1942 he founded a Welsh Society, training Arab and Jewish children
to sing traditional songs in Welsh, and helped publish a newsletter for
Welsh soldiers serving in the Middle East. His account of his time in
the Holy Land, published as a chapter in his autobiography, *A
Mingled Yarn* (2000), is notable for the exhilaration he felt at being in
a country with whose history and topography he was familiar, having been brought up in the Sunday School, but also for its description of a pleasant social life apparently far removed from the rigours
of war. Tall, well-built, handsome and sporting that famous brush
moustache, he was something of a ladies' man until, in 1944, he married Joyce Ord, a Canadian who was serving with the ATS in
Palestine.

In 1945 Captain Miles (he used the title after his demobilisation)
was invited by Sir Wyndham Deedes, Chief Secretary of Palestine
under the British Mandate, to apply for the post of National
Organiser at Palestine House, established for the purpose of creating
a better understanding of the British government's commitment,
under the Balfour Declaration of 1917, to setting up a national home
for the Jewish people, and he was duly appointed. Always sympathetic towards the Zionist cause, he threw himself into his work with
gusto, employing his gifts as a public speaker and committee man,
and once again enjoying the social contacts he made and pursuing
his epicurean interests at every opportunity. The attraction of the job
palled after two years, however, as the establishment of the state of
Israel became imminent, and he returned to Wales in 1947.

Again encouraged by Deedes, who was also chairman of the
National Council for Social Service, Dillwyn Miles now resumed his
career in local government, first with Newport Parish Council and
Cemaes Rural District Council, and then with Pembrokeshire
County Council and Haverfordwest Borough Council. The titles of
some of the concomitant offices he held reflect the rich traditions of
the county and, *inter alia*, provided him with opportunities for dress-
ing up: Admiral of the Port, Chairman of the Shrievalty Association,
Burgess Warden of the Gild of Freemen, and so on. He served four
terms as Mayor of Newport, in which office he revived some of the
town's ancient ceremonies such as the Perambulation of the
Boundaries, and in 1951, during the Festival of Britain, took great

pleasure in receiving Princess Marina, Duchess of Kent, who was visiting west Wales as representative of the Queen.

There was nothing he would not do to create favourable publicity for his native place, especially if it involved members of the royal family or some famous personality such as Wilfred Pickles, whose radio programme *Have a Go*, then at the height of its popularity and not short of invitations, was persuaded to visit the county on several occasions during his terms of office.

From 1954 to 1975 Dillwyn Miles was General Secretary of the Pembrokeshire Rural Community Council, in which capacity he had a finger in every pie; after Pembrokeshire was incorporated into the new county of Dyfed in 1974, the post's title was changed to Director of Dyfed Rural Council, and he remained in it until his retirement in 1981. Among his many initiatives were the Best Kept Village Competition, Old People's Week, the County Drama Festival, and the Pembrokeshire Art, Film and Local History Societies. He also represented his county on the committees of the National Association of Local Councils, the Court of Governors of the University of Wales, the Mental Health Review Tribunal for Wales, the West Wales Tourist Association, the Sports Council for Wales, the Prince of Wales Committee, the Dyfed Association for the Disabled, the National Playing Fields Association, and the Council for Small Industries in Wales.

His special interest was in nature conservation. He was Vice-President of the Wales Wildlife Trust, Vice-Chairman of the Pembrokeshire Coast National Park Authority, honorary Secretary of the West Wales Field Society, a member of the Nature Conservancy Council for Wales, and from 1971 to 1980, editor of the magazine *Nature in Wales*; in all this work he was closely associated with R. M. Lockley, the naturalist, until the latter's death in April 2000. The last time I spoke to him on the telephone, in the following December, he asked me in a typically laconic way to guess whom he had in his study. When I failed to do so, he said it was Lockley – he was waiting for the wind to drop so that he could take the island-man's ashes over to Skokholm as a last favour to his old friend.

Most of Dillwyn Miles's publications have to do with the natural or social history of his native county. From 1955 to 1981 he edited *The Pembrokeshire Historian*. His books include *The West Wales Naturalists' Trust and its Nature Reserves* (1975), *The Sheriffs of the County of*

Pembroke 1541-1974 (1976), *The Castles of Pembrokeshire* (1979), *Portrait of Pembrokeshire* (1984), *The Lords of Cemais* (1997) and *A History of the Town and County of Haverfordwest* (1999). His edition of George Owen's *The Description of Penbrokshire*, first published in 1603, is a scholarly work valuable for its preface and footnotes. His last book was an edition of *The Letters of Lt. John George of the Royal Marines* (2002), another Pembrokeshire man.

He also published two books about the Eisteddfod and the Gorsedd: *The Royal National Eisteddfod of Wales* (1982) and *The Secret of the Bards of the Isle of Britain* (1992). His only book in Welsh was *Atgofion Hen Arwyddfardd* ("Reminiscences of an old Herald Bard",1997), which is about his association with the Gorsedd between 1945 and 1996. His autobiography, however, is little more than a plain chronology of his career in which the names of eminent people in whose acquaintance he delighted, particularly if they had titles or important offices, are dropped in almost every paragraph.

Among the honours which came his way was his election as Fellow of the Royal Geographical Society in 1946, of the Society of Antiquaries in 1998 and of the Royal Historical Society in 2000. Many of his friends were dismayed that, given his long record of public service and his great respect for the institution of monarchy, and despite his assiduous cultivation of the Establishment in Wales, his name never appeared in the Queen's Honours list. Perhaps, for Dillwyn Miles, the opportunity to serve his county and country was honour enough.

William James Dillwyn Miles, local government officer, historian of Pembrokeshire and Herald Bard: born Newport (Trefdraeth), Pembrokeshire 25 May 1916; married 1944 Joyce Ord (died 1976; one son, one daughter); General Secretary of the Pembrokeshire Community Council (1954-75) and Director of Dyfed Rural Council (1975-81); died Haverfordwest, Pembrokeshire 1 August 2007.

The Independent (4 August 2007)

Roland Mathias

Poet, editor and critic of Anglo-Welsh literature

As poet, editor, and critic, Roland Mathias made a major contribution to the literature of Wales in English, helping to define and develop it for more than fifty years. His work on the origins and growth of Anglo-Welsh literature, from about the late fifteenth century to the present day, drew its substance and accuracy from his training as a historian, and his literary criticism, of which there is a great deal, blazed a trail down which many others have since ventured. It is no exaggeration to say that, with his friend Raymond Garlick, he was the founding father of post-war Anglo-Welsh literary studies, to which his enormous energies were almost exclusively devoted.

Born on a farm above Talybont-on-Usk in the old county of Breconshire, and in a valley which was subsequently flooded to make a reservoir, Roland was educated at British military schools in Germany, where his father was an army chaplain, and at Caterham School and Jesus College, Oxford, where he took a First in Modern History and played hockey and rugby. Both his parents were Welsh but only his father was Welsh-speaking and the language of his home and education was English. He first became aware of his Welsh identity while reading a boy's adventure novel by Owen Rhoscomyl (Captain Owen Vaughan), but it was many years before he was able to immerse himself in the history and English-language literature of Wales, making it his life's work to read and write about them.

After teaching for a while at schools in England, including the Blue Coat School in Reading and St Clement Dane's in Holborn, he returned to Wales in 1948 as headmaster of Pembroke Dock Grammar School, a post he held for ten years. It was there, a year after his appointment, that he took a leading role in founding *Dock Leaves*, a magazine which, as *The Anglo-Welsh Review* from 1957 until its demise in 1988, was to have a longer continuous existence than any other English-language magazine in Britain, except for *Outposts*. Roland was its editor from 1961 to 1976.

The magazine took as its principal aim the healing of the breach between writers in Welsh and their counterparts whose work was done in English; the literary tag 'Anglo-Welsh' was applied to the latter in order to distinguish between the two camps. From 1958 to

1969 Roland lived in England: he was headmaster of The Herbert Strutt School at Belper in Derbyshire and then of King Edward's Five Ways School in Birmingham. Nevertheless, he strove to establish *The Anglo-Welsh Review* as a journal of the arts in Wales by publishing studies of Welsh composers and painters as well as scholarly articles about aspects of Anglo-Welsh literature which had not, until then, received much critical attention. With no specifically political commitment other than that of Welsh patriot, but with a deep sense of mission and insisting that English-speakers had a part to play in the cultural life of Wales, he sought to strengthen the attachment of writers and readers to the national heritage.

"My writing is anti-cosmopolitan in emphasis," he wrote. "I believe it is important to know and cultivate my own piece of ground. Not to love one's own parish and always to believe in a greater significance elsewhere is not only to deny the well-springs of being but often to miss a natural humanity in the search."

Roland's professional interest as a historian was clearly reflected in the magazine's contents, notably in the many substantial reviews, articles, and editorials which he contributed. His literary criticism has a breadth of outlook, a high seriousness, and a concern with issues rather than with personalities, which put it among the best-informed and most authoritative writing about the culture of modern Wales. His most important books were *Whitsun Riot* (1963), a monograph on Vernon Watkins in the *Writers of Wales* series (1974), a study of the poetry of John Cowper Powys (1979), and an illustrated history of Anglo-Welsh literature (1987). He also edited (with Sam Adams) an anthology of short stories by Anglo-Welsh writers, *The Shining Pyramid* (1970), the Collected Stories of Geraint Goodwin (1976), a volume of essays about David Jones as artist and writer (1976) and (with Raymond Garlick) the definitive anthology, *Anglo-Welsh Poetry 1480-1980* (1984). A selection of his criticism was published under the title *A Ride Through the Wood* in 1985.

The same prodiguous energy is to be seen in his creative writing. His earliest poems, published as *Days Enduring* in 1943, were written at a time when he was suffering the consequences of his pacifist convictions, which he had learned from his mother, and for his resistance to military conscription and refusal to do any kind of war-work: he was twice imprisoned on these accounts. Much of his work draws its strength from the Nonconformist tradition and from his staunch

Christian beliefs. Even the famous sense of guilt associated with that tradition did not inhibit him as a writer: "It shows me a particular vision, a measurement. Out of it I can write," he once commented.

Roland published six more books of poems: *Break in Harvest* (1946), *The Roses of Tretower* (1952), *The Flooded Valley* (1960), *Absalom in the Tree* (1971), and *Snipe's Castle* (1979); his selected poems appeared as *Burning Brambles* in 1983 and his Collected Poems in 2002. His poetry is highly personal, follows no fashion, and in texture and vocabulary showed no great changes over the forty years of its production. Very much to do with Wales and its history, and with specific Welsh landscapes, particularly along the border with England, it is sometimes difficult, usually because of its allusions and erudition, but the reader is always compensated by its honesty, vivid language, and scrupulous craftsmanship. The same qualities went to the making of his short stories, published as *The Eleven Men of Eppynt* in 1956 and collected in 2001.

After his early retirement in 1969, when he settled in Brecon, Roland threw himself into the literary life of Wales which he had done so much to stimulate. He was a member of the Welsh Arts Council's Literature Committee from 1969 to 1979 and the Committee's Chairman for three years. He also served as Chairman of the English-language section of the Welsh Academy, the national society of writers in Wales, from 1975 to 1978. I knew him in both these capacities, but it was while engaged in compiling *The Oxford Companion to the Literature of Wales*, between 1978 and 1986, that I was able to take the full measure of his scholarship and jovial personality. He not only wrote several hundred entries for that reference-book, thus making available the wealth of his learning with typical generosity, but also served as consultant to the editorial board, saving us from many an error of fact and judgement.

When, in 1985, Roland suffered a stroke, it seemed as if a line had been drawn under one of the most varied, prolific, and influential careers ever enjoyed by a writer in post-war Wales. But in 1992, to the delight of his many friends, he began once again to write, and in 1996 published his last book of poems, *A Field at Vallorcines*.

It was a remarkable achievement, and testimony to the resolute character and extraordinary ability of a good man and a fine writer. His memory is honoured by the Roland Mathias Prize which, in a last act of generosity, he endowed a few years ago.

Roland Glyn Mathias, poet, editor, and critic: born Talybont-on-Usk, Breconshire 4 September 1915; headmaster, Pembroke Dock Grammar School (1948-58), The Herbert Strutt School, Belper, Derbyshire (1958-64), King Edward Five Ways School, Birmingham (1964-69); editor, Dock Leaves, later The Anglo-Welsh Review (1961-76); Chairman, the Welsh Academy (1975-78) and the Literature Committee of the Welsh Arts Council (1976-79); 1944 married Mary (Molly) Hawes (died 1996, one son, two daughters); died Brecon, Powys 16 August 2007.

The Independent (17 August 2007)

W. S. Jones

Dramatist who mixed absurdist theatre with village-hall farce

W. S. Jones was unique among Welsh dramatists in that he wrote not in the literary language employed by major playwrights such as Saunders Lewis but in his own rich dialect that was so peppered with English expressions that some critics thought it a debased or pidgin form. The effect on the educated Welsh-speaker's ear was as barbarous as that of a strong Geordie accent on an Oxbridge don's. Much of the comedy in his plays springs from his deft use of this racy, demotic Welsh and the laughter often depends on seeing his characters slip on verbal banana-skins. His plays do not have plots so much as an anarchic humour that drives the action along to its unexpected, sometimes preposterous climax.

Wil Sam, as he was affectionately known in a land where the surname Jones is as common as blackberries, was unrepentant about using English phrases for theatrical effect, delighting in the unease this habit produced in his audiences and among critics of more traditional taste. To deplore it, he argued, was to miss the point: English, for him, was a foreign language, rather like French is for Del Boy, and he enjoyed hearing his characters misuse it at every turn. To make it seem even more outlandish, he habitually spelt English words in a Welsh way, as in 'cyt ddy comic' and 'sgersli belîf it', and would often complain he was in trouble with the 'England Refeniw'.

His most famous character was his *alter ego*, Ifas y Tryc (Evans the Truck), a bowler-hatted, wing-collared, moustachioed carrier who would lean a while on his trolley and, with lugubrious features and deadpan manner, deliver his pungent opinions on any subject under the sun. The part was brilliantly played by the actor Stewart Jones who made his name as the homespun philosopher whose horse sense was capable of demolishing anything and anyone, particularly the high and mighty, with special animus reserved for pompous officialdom or the overbearing English visitor. 'Britannia rŵls ddy Wêls' was one of his many catch-phrases that have been grafted onto the Welsh language. One of his few tropes than can be easily translated is 'I'm not saying anything – what I'm saying is ...', which became his hallmark. A selection of his monologues, as waspish as any of Alan Bennett's, is to be found in the paperback, *Ifas y Tryc* (1973).

If Wil Sam wrote more or less as he spoke, it was because he had a keen ear for local idiom and believed that, instead of artifice in art, the dramatist should rely on his own voice and the everyday plebeian speech of his own community. This talent is best displayed in his short plays, a selection of which was published as *Deg Drama Wil Sam* (1995), with an introduction by the distinguished writer Emyr Humphreys, who admired his work and collaborated with him on more than one occasion.

Wil Sam had the knack of introducing symbolic devices into his plays and this led some critics to relate them to the Theatre of the Absurd. Mixed with village-hall farce, there are indeed faint echoes of Beckett, N. F. Simpson and Ionesco, but his genius was comic rather than tragic. Despite his fondness for tramps and other social misfits and the location of his plays in a barber's shop, on a rubbish heap or in a ramshackle farmhouse, it was not uttermost despair but the hilarious absurdity of human existence that concerned him most. The appeal of his plays is none the less for that.

For him the local was the universal. He was born in 1920 at Llanystumdwy, the village on the Llŷn peninsula where Lloyd George was brought up. His father was in sail and his mother, before her marriage, had been a maid in the household of Sir Wilfred King, a minister at the Board of Trade. One of Wil Sam's many anecdotes recounted how, in 1912, his mother had taken a telephone call for her employer in which news of the sinking of the *Titanic* first reached London.

The boy had almost no formal education. 'I was a dunce at school,' he wrote in his autobiography, 'but I had enough in my head to know how much of a dunce I was.' Like his brother Elis Gwyn Jones, a talented painter and teacher, Wil Sam spent the whole of his life in Eifionydd, a district of Gwynedd renowned for its thriving cultural life, where he found work as a mechanic at various garages. At the outbreak of war he registered as a conscientious objector on religious grounds and was ordered to work in food distribution, which he did for the duration.

One day, while delivering milk from the back of a lorry, he persuaded an old woman to sell him three dilapidated bicycles, which he then repaired and sold for a small profit. Thus began his love of anything on wheels. Machines of all kinds, but especially cars and motor-bikes, provided him with boundless delight and he became an expert at restoring them, eventually owning his own garage in Llanystumdwy. This was no chrome-and-glass affair but a place where local people, and some from far and wide, would come to chat with him about machines and racing, as well as books, the theatre and issues of the day, in much the same way as country folk had gathered in the village smithy in times gone by. He was as frequent a visitor to the Isle of Man, Silverstone and Le Mans circuits as he was to the Dublin, Liverpool and London theatres.

He began dabbling in writing as a young man, sending humorous short stories and satirical poems to local eisteddfodau and then, whether they won or not, having them broadcast on radio. In 1962 he shared first prize for a short play at the National Eisteddfod held in Llanelli. But the greatest stimulus was Theatr y Gegin, an amateur drama workshop opened in Cricieth in 1963, for which he began writing plays and where he met actors, producers and other writers. Among the productions in which he was involved were plays by Chekhov, Shaw, Synge, Frisch, Pinter, Osborne, Friel and Albee, all in Welsh translation, as well as work by Welsh writers, including his own. He always maintained that he wrote primarily for his own community and saw his work as a means of bringing about social regeneration and cultural renewal, and for that he had to write in the language of the people he knew best.

In 1976 the theatre, like so many amateur enterprises, went dark. It was already facing financial difficulties because some of its actors, notably Stewart Jones, had left for more lucrative work in television, but now Cricieth town council, which suspected it of being a hive of Nationalist activity because several of its members had taken part in protests against the Investiture of the Prince of Wales in 1969, claimed it wanted the building for other purposes. The workshop's last production was *Dinas Barhaus* ("Abiding city") by W. S. Jones.

The writer now found he had a reputation as a playwright of immense power and output but no local theatre in which his work could be adequately performed. Undaunted, he turned to radio and television. Soon more and more commissions came his way, so that he was able to give up his garage and go to live as a full-time writer in the nearby village of Rhos-lan, though keeping up his interest in cars and motor-bikes and often writing about them. His seminal lecture on the state of Welsh theatre, *Y Toblarôn*, was delivered in 1975, a selection of his stories, *Dyn y Mwnci* ("The monkey man"), was published in 1979 and his important play, *Y Sul Hwnnw* ("That Sunday"), in 1981.

A genial but self-deprecating man, Wil Sam steered clear of all academies, was never taken up by the literary establishment in Wales, was awarded no honours and would not have allowed his work to be translated into English even if that had been feasible. He played his part in the campaigns of *Cymdeithas yr Iaith Gymraeg* (Welsh Language Society) and in defending the Llŷn peninsula from the effects of tourism and English in-migration but was not comfortable on any political platform. Even so, one of his favourite sayings was, 'The Welsh language isn't a dish of trifle to be kept in a dark place', and in his plays, properly considered as his life's work, its poetry can be heard at its most rumbustious.

William Samuel Jones, motor-mechanic and playwright: born Llanystumdwy, Caernarfonshire 28 May 1920; married 1950 Dora Ann Jones (two daughters); died Bangor, Gwynedd 15 November 2007.

The Independent (26 November 2007)

Susan Williams-Ellis

Ceramics designer and co-owner of Portmeirion Potteries

The distinctive designs of Portmeirion Potteries, now sold in gift shops in some thirty-four countries, were the work of Susan Williams-Ellis who, with her husband Euan Cooper-Willis, founded the company in 1960. It grew from small beginnings after they had bought a run-down pottery-decorating firm in Stoke-on-Trent called A. E. Gray Ltd, for which she had provided some designs. They were produced exclusively for sale at Portmeirion, the Italianate village near Penrhyndeudraeth in north-west Wales which had been created by her father, the renowned architect Clough Williams-Ellis. A year later, the couple bought a second firm, Kirkham's Ltd, which was equipped for the manufacture of pottery, and so she was able to start designing shapes as well as surface patterns. Some of her designs from this early phase such as 'Moss Agate', 'Gold Diamond', 'Talisman', and 'Tiger Lily' are now collectors' items. Within a few years the Portmeirion company had gained a reputation as an innovative force in British ceramic design.

Susan Williams-Ellis was born, in the house of the art critic Roger Fry, at the epicentre of the Bloomsbury set in 1918. Her parents counted Frank Lloyd-Wright, Augustus John, Lytton Strachey, Rudyard Kipling, and Virginia Woolf among their friends. She studied Ceramics with Bernard and David Leach at Dartington and then spent four years at Chelsea Polytechnic, where she was taught by Graham Sutherland and Henry Moore, but left without a certificate. On being awarded an honorary MA by Keele University in 2005 for her services to the industry and the town of Stoke-on-Trent, she pointed out, modestly and ruefully, that she had never failed an exam in her life because she had never taken one.

Her innate feeling for three-dimensional form, however, and for artefacts that were both functional and aesthetically pleasing, was well developed and it never failed her. Also in 2005, together with Gillian Ayres, Terence Conran and Ralph Steadman, she was made an honorary Fellow of the University of the Arts, London.

During the late 1940s and early 1950s she and her husband, who had studied Mathematics at Cambridge and worked part-time as a stockbroker in the City, lived an almost self-sufficient life on their farm in Wales. They had met after her brother Christopher, who had been Euan's room-mate at Cambridge, was killed in action before Monte Cassino in May 1944. To supplement their income Susan took on some book illustration, worked as a draughtswoman for the Air Ministry and taught at Dartington and St Martin's School of Art in London. The couple's interest in pottery was awakened while keeping a small giftshop at Portmeirion where they observed what people bought as souvenirs of their holiday in Wales. Besides giftware, Susan designed tableware and cookware, all produced to fit comfortably into the domestic kitchen.

By dint of hard work and commercial acumen, the Portmeirion company went from strength to strength, despite three major recessions and several shifts in consumer taste. The 'Botanic Garden' pottery designs introduced in 1972 were immediate best-sellers and put the firm on a sound financial footing for the first time: the set, consisting of about thirty floral designs and incorporating leaf borders and intertwined butterflies, was one of the most typical, and popular, designs ever made by Portmeirion. In 1979 the company rented a factory in Penrhyndeudraeth known as the Crochendy ('Pottery'), at which ceramics were hand-painted. But the main premises remained in Stoke-on-Trent, where new machinery, warehouses and a loading bay were built. A shop was opened in Pont Street in London. The firm also started trading in the United States, now its largest single market where sales exceed $20 million. In 1989 Portmeirion Potteries bought the Crown Windsor site in Stoke-on-Trent, re-equipping it as a casting plant, and in the same year the company was presented with the Queen's Award for Export. In 1995 Anwyl Cooper-Willis, one of the founders' daughters, was appointed Marketing and Design Director; another daughter, Menna Angharad, is a designer and Siân Cwper, another daughter, is a well-known peace-campaigner. Their son, Robin Llywelyn, is Managing Director of Portmeirion Village and a novelist of immense talent who has opened up new vistas for the writing of fiction in the Welsh language.

Susan Williams-Ellis , very much the driving force behind the family firm from the start, was never content to rest on her laurels. Besides ceramics, she designed textiles, furniture, rugs, table lamps, trays, candles and jewellery, all in a style recognisably her own and with an appeal not unlike that of Laura Ashley's fabrics. Her private passion, revealed only when the BBC made a documentary about her in the early 1990s, was for the underwater world of coral reefs. From the Maldives to Hawaii, from the Red Sea and Tahiti to the Great Barrier Reef, she recorded marine life with the help of a snorkel and fins. Often in the water for hours on end, she drew what she saw on waterproof board and plastic paper, and later transferred the images onto a textured board using acrylics. An exhibition of her underwater work was shown at the Plas Glyn-y-Weddw gallery on the Llŷn peninsula in 2002, when she was in her eighty-fourth year. Among her other interests were gardening and the abundant wild life of the corner of north-west Wales made famous by her distinguished father and her own talent as a designer and businesswoman.

Susan Caroline Williams-Ellis, ceramic designer: born Guildford, Surrey 6 June 1918; married 1945 Euan Cooper-Willis (one son, three daughters); co-owner Portmeirion Potteries Ltd 1960-2007; died Portmeirion, Gwynedd 27 November 2007.

The Independent (29 November 2007)

John FitzGerald

Carmelite priest and poet in his adopted language

The remarkable achievement of John FitzGerald, a Carmelite of Irish parentage but brought up in England, was that he learned Welsh and made it the language of his religious, intellectual and social life. He was not alone in this, for the Catholic Church has had, in Wales, more than one luminary not born within the Welsh tradition, especially people of Irish stock such as Father Daniel Mullins, sometime Bishop of Menevia, who have made distinguished contributions to the life of their adopted country. John FitzGerald was unusual for having, besides his priestly vocation, an interest in literary matters and a talent for writing verse of a very high order.

Born in Ludlow in 1927 to parents from County Kerry, he spent his childhood in Chesterfield and Sheffield. At the age of thirteen he was sent to board at Coleg Mair, a small Catholic seminary housed in Castell Brychan, high above the town of Aberystwyth. There he had his first Welsh lessons in a class taught by none less than Saunders Lewis, the eminent man of letters and Nationalist who, in 1937, had lost his lecturer's post at University College, Swansea, after serving a gaol sentence for his part in an act of arson at Penyberth on the Llŷn peninsula, where an RAF bombing school was under construction.

In 1940 Lewis was living a little to the south of Aberystwyth and, shunned by all except the Church to which he was a convert and the political party, Plaid Cymru, which he led, was eking out a living as a journalist and part-time teacher at Coleg Mair. John FitzGerald remained in close touch with Lewis until the latter's death in 1985, dedicating his first book *i SL am agor drws a ffenestri* ('to SL for opening a door and windows'). He shared Lewis's political views but steered clear of his right-wing intransigence.

From 1942 , when he took the name John, to 1948 he was a novitiate with the Carmelites in Ireland, and was to serve with the White Friars for the rest of his life. At University College, Dublin, he began by reading Welsh in the Department headed by Professor John Lloyd-Jones who advised him to switch to Greek and Latin, which he did, graduating with a first in Classics in 1946. He kept up his Welsh, however, by borrowing books in the language from Lloyd-Jones.

Having decided to remain in the Order, he pursued further studies in Dublin for another four years and was ordained priest in 1951. There followed a year studying Theology in Rome and three reading Classics at Christ's College, Cambridge, where he came into contact with many Welsh-speakers at convivial meetings of the society known as Cymdeithas y Mabinogion.

He returned to live in Wales in 1956 on his appointment to the staff of Coleg Mair at Tre-gib near Llandeilo in Carmarthenshire. He had already written poems in English but now he turned to Welsh, mastering not only the rich idioms of Carmarthenshire but also, in the company of local poets, the intricate rules of Welsh prosody. His first successful poem in Welsh, '*Calan 1960*' ('New year's day 1960'), written after listening to Professor Bernard Lovell deliver the Reith Lecture, attempts to address the immensity of the cosmos.

After three years the college was moved from Llandeilo to Cheltenham where he taught Philosophy to Carmelite seminarians until 1964. In that year he was appointed Chaplain to Catholic students at the University College of Wales, Aberystwyth, and six years later to a lectureship in the Department of Philosophy. In 1988 he was a member of the panel which produced a new translation of the Bible into Welsh. His brother Gregory also served as Chaplain in Aberystwyth.

Ecumenical in outlook, and not always in full agreement with his Church, he counted many Anglican and Nonconformist clergymen among his friends, all of whom responded to his sunny temperament and intellectual abilities. On radio and television he was often to be heard, in his own quiet way, debating questions of the day and sometimes the most complex philosophical questions about life and death. After Vatican II he set about translating devotional texts into Welsh. He put Welsh-speaking Catholics in his debt by translating (with Patrick Donovan) *Llyfr Offeren y Sul* ('A book of Sunday service', 1988) and by founding *Y Cylchgrawn Catholig* ('The Catholic magazine'), which he also edited for ten years.

Having retired in 1992, he was once again made Chaplain but was obliged to quit this work in 2004 to assist in the parish of Llanelli. The move from Aberystwyth, where he had many friends of all faiths and none, and especially from the work of the Chaplaincy in which he delighted, was particularly painful but, obedient as ever, and after only a day's hesitation, he cheerfully took up his new work because it was his duty to do so.

He published two volumes of verse, *Cadwyn Cenedl* ('A nation's chain', 1969) and *Grawn Gwirionedd* ('Grapes of truth', 2006), though the second contains all the poems in the first as well as about thirty others. Here is the englyn which serves as an epigraph to his first book:

Iaith wâr Sir Gâr a gerais – iaith dirion,
    afradlon, hyfrydlais.
    Rhan a chartref a gefais
    yn ei swyn, a minnau'n Sais.

('It was the civilized tongue of Carmarthenshire I loved, a happy language / prodigal and mellifluous. / I had a part and a home / in its spell, and me an Englishman.')

Many other poems, as might be expected, are devotional, though he also found inspiration in the natural scene, in people, in music, and in *jeux d'esprit* as in the poem '*I'm gwraig*', in which he addresses his 'wife', adding in a note: 'Perhaps I should note that I'm not married'. Even when contemplating the numinous he found there was reason to ask difficult questions, for there was nothing complacent about his faith, and in this he may be compared with that other priest-poet, R. S. Thomas, though he had nothing of the latter's bleak fascination with 'the untenanted Cross'. He was particularly attracted to the work of Thomas Aquinas.

Besides Welsh, John FitzGerald learnt Irish and a little Basque, and translated from Greek both ancient and modern, including Aristotle's Nicomachean Ethics and poems by Sappho and Cavafy. On the occasion of Gwynfor Evans's victory in the Carmarthen by-election of July 1966 he began a poem of thanks with the words, 'Lord, everlasting Father of all nations, almighty God, we know you aren't a member of any political party...' before asking that the Welsh be woken to sing His praise.

Although he always described himself as English by birth and Irish by parentage, John FitzGerald chose to be Welsh by virtue of his attachment to the language and people of Wales. He was certainly among those who have woven the thread of Catholicism into the fabric of Welsh life. Father Fitz, as he was known to his students, or

Ieuan Hir ('Tall John') in literary circles, had a puckish sense of humour, an infectious grin and chuckle, and a merry twinkle in his eye. One came away from a chat with him feeling that here was a man who was serenely happy in his faith and steadfast in his love for humankind. The last time I saw him was on the field of the National Eisteddfod, at a stall run by members of Y Cylch Catholig ('The Catholic circle'), where he was to be found every August without fail.

Of our conversation I recall the relish with which he told me about the beauties of Euskara, the Basque language, and how he was slowly acquiring it. For the last ten years of his life he had visited the Basque Country, staying with a community of Franciscans and learning to speak and write verse in Basque.

Like all Carmelite brothers in the Province of England and Wales, he is to be buried at Aylesford, the White Friars' ancient religious house in Kent.

Michael John FitzGerald, Roman Catholic priest and member of the Carmelite Order: born Ludlow, Shropshire 3 February 1927; ordained priest 1951; Catholic Chaplain, University College of Wales, Aberystwyth (1964-70); Lecturer in Philosophy (1970-2004); priest, parish of Llanelli (2004-07); died Carmarthen 28 November 2007.

The Independent (11 December 2007)

Aled Rhys Wiliam

Scholar, broadcaster and poet

Aled Rhys Wiliam was the son of Stephen J. Williams, for many years Professor of Welsh at Swansea, who was an authority on medieval Welsh literature and a descriptive grammarian of the language. Like his brother Urien, who became a dramatist, and his sister Annest, who is a professional translator, he was brought up to revere the structure of Welsh and to speak it not only correctly but with due regard to its flexibility and mellifluous qualities. As a translator and commentator he excelled by virtue of his grasp of the literary language and his ability to express the most complex concepts in clear, cadenced idioms. If there is a Welsh equivalent of Received Pronunciation – the language of the public schools, though with different social connotations in Wales – then Aled Rhys Wiliam had it and used it admirably.

He was born in Llandeilo, in rural Carmarthenshire, in 1926 but brought up in Swansea and educated at the Gwendraeth County School in the industrial part of the same county. At University College, Swansea, he read Welsh, Latin and French, and also studied at Basel in Switzerland and at Trinity College and University College, Dublin. After two years as a teacher with the Army Educational Corps between 1947 and 1949, he began research into the Welsh Laws under Professor Idris Foster at St Catherine's, Oxford. He learned German in order to read Celtic scholarship in that language, as well as Russian and Japanese.

His main interest was the 'Venedotian Code' of the Laws now known as the Iorwerth texts after the name of a lawyer mentioned in them. They form an important part of the Laws of Hywel Dda whose writ ran throughout most of Wales until the Edwardian Conquest of 1282 and even down to the Act of Union of 1536. They reveal the favourable legislative and social climate created in Gwynedd under the aegis of Llywelyn ap Gruffudd, the ruler known as Llywelyn Fawr ('the Great'), and offer a wealth of detail about how the Welsh language had developed as the medium for a legal system of great sophistication. His edition of *Llyfr Iorwerth* ('The book of Iorwerth') was published in 1960, earning him a doctorate and the prestigious Hywel Dda Prize from the University of Wales. He also published

The Book of Cynog: a Medieval Welsh Law Digest (1990).

Aled Rhys Wiliam began his career in 1954 as an assistant editor with *Geiriadur Prifysgol Cymru / A Dictionary of the Welsh Language*, the first standard dictionary of Welsh to be based on historical principles, on which work began in 1921 and which is now available in four hefty volumes. Although the Welsh counterpart of the *Oxford English Dictionary*, the *Geiriadur* differs in that it serves both as a monolingual Welsh dictionary and as a bilingual Welsh-English dictionary. Housed at the National Library in Aberystwyth, it is an ongoing project which attempts, by means of regular supplements, to keep up with a changing world and its effects on the language. Aled Rhys Wiliam was one of the many scholars associated with its progress over the years.

After moving in 1956 to Cardiff, where he lectured at the Cardiff College of Education in Cyncoed, Wiliam – his father gave the original Welsh surname to all his children – made a new career as an announcer and presenter with BBC Cymru. Among his duties were reading links for the news and introducing the features programme *Heddiw* ('Today'), for many years the BBC's flagship production in the Welsh language. From 1964 to 1994 he provided an English translation of the ceremonies of the National Eisteddfod in whose arcana he was expert. He was admitted to the White Robe of the Gorsedd of Bards in 1975.

From 1969 to 1982 he was Director of Audiovisual Media at Salford University, but then returned to Wales and settled in Rhyl, on the north Wales coast, where he began writing verse in the traditional metres. Soon mastering *cynghanedd*, the complex rules of prosody dating from early medieval times in which many Welsh poets still write today, he suddenly came into public view in 1984 as winner of the Chair, one of the premier prizes at the National Eisteddfod. His winning poem, entitled '*Y Pethau Bychein*' ('The small things'), a reference to St David's injunction to his followers to 'do the little things which you have heard from me and which I have shown you', was written under the pseudonym Carpe Diem and praised by the adjudicators for its intellectual rigour and classic mastery of the art.

His wit and erudition were also put to good use as a member of the Tegeingl (north-east Wales) team of poets who competed on the popular radio programme *Talwrn y Beirdd*. It is regrettable that this highly accomplished poet, who began writing late in life, published only one book of verse, namely *Cywain* ('Garnering', 1995), which includes his magisterial poem of 1984.

Aled Ioan Rhys Wiliam, scholar and poet: born Llandeilo, Carmarthenshire 4 December 1926; Chaired Poet of the National Eisteddfod of Wales 1984; married 1954 Meiriona Williams (one son, three daughters; marriage dissolved); 1980 Ann Owen (two step-daughters); died Rhyl, Denbighshire 1 January 2008.

The Independent (8 January 2008)

Alun Hoddinott

Composer of prodigious energy and fluency

Alun Hoddinott was one of the few Welsh composers whose work is well known outside Wales and one of the most versatile and prolific British composers of all time. He wrote in a wide variety of forms, and at such an astonishing rate that one wag among his compatriots famously referred to him as the only composer in Europe who could write music faster than it could be played. His prodigious energy went into the making of operas, symphonies, sinfoniettas, sonatas, concertos, oratorios, fugues, motets, film music, dance suites and cantatas, as well as a large number of chamber, vocal and choral works. This Protean fluency and versatility prompted none less than Sir Charles Groves to draw a comparison between Hoddinott and Haydn.

Perhaps Hoddinott's most popular success was his first opera, *The Beach of Falesá*, based on a story by Robert Louis Stevenson with a libretto by Glyn Jones, which was given its premiere by Welsh National Opera at Cardiff New Theatre in 1974. It marked a new phase in his work with its more frequent use of instruments in extended solo roles, sharp-etched dramatic outbursts and a deepening of orchestral colour appropriate to the atmosphere of its romantic subject.

Among his later operas were *The Magician* (1976), with a libretto by John Morgan (for HTV); *What the Old Man Does is Always Right* (1977); *The Rajah's Diamond* (1978) and *The Trumpet Major* (1981), the last-named based on a novel by Thomas Hardy, on both of which he collaborated with Myfanwy Piper. His last work in this genre was *Tower* (1999), inspired by the colliery of that name at Hirwaun, the last deep mine in South Wales which, threatened with closure, was bought from the National Coal Board and successfully run by its workers until 2008.

Alun Hoddinott was born in 1929 in the mining town of Bargoed, at the top of the Rhymney Valley, where his father was a teacher, and brought up in Pont-lliw, near Swansea, after his father took a post there. The family was not especially musical but the boy showed an early interest in composition and started taking violin lessons at the age of four. Educated at Gowerton Grammar School, he won a composition scholarship to University College, Cardiff, graduating in 1949. While still a student he wrote an overture, a symphonic suite for orchestra, a cello concerto and several string quartets, together with songs and choral works; all these were performed publicly and some were broadcast, but were later withdrawn and are not listed as part of his oeuvre.

After studying privately for a few years with the Australian composer Arthur Benjamin, Alun joined the staff of the Cardiff (later Welsh) College of Music and Drama in 1951. His first success as a composer came in 1954 when his *Clarinet Concerto No. 3* was performed at the Cheltenham Festival by Gervase de Peyer and the Hallé Orchestra under Sir John Barbirolli. In 1953 he was awarded the Walford Davies Prize for composition and in 1957 he won the Arnold Bax Medal, the first of many triumphs in a long and illustrious career.

Cheltenham was to be the scene of several Hoddinott premieres in the years that followed, among them the *Harp Concerto* of 1958, the *Symphony No. 2* of 1962 and the *Piano Concerto No. 3* of 1966. These early works displayed what came to be recognised as an identifiable Hoddinott sound consisting of a darkly brooding lyricism, cumulative in its effect until the tension is broken and dispersed in a series of jaunty *scherzi*. The sound is sometimes said to be 'Celtic' but that is a somewhat old-fashioned view of Celtitude, though the colour, scintillating effects, fiery outbursts, and sheer panache of Alun's music may well qualify for the epithet.

He moved to the Music Department of his old college in 1959 and became Professor of Music there in 1967, a post he held until his retirement twenty years later. He often wrote in response to commissions from Music Festivals. The cantata, *Dives and Lazarus*, was composed for the Farnham Schools Festival and performed there in 1965 with the Welsh National Opera Chorale. The text is a version of the folk-tale of Dives, the rich man who goes to Hell, and Lazarus, the poor man who goes to Heaven, but cast in the mould of Stravinsky's *A Sermon, a Narrative and a Prayer*, that is to say it is a short homily about Good and Evil and their rewards, with the musical style suitably stripped down for children.

His *Variants for Orchestra*, performed by the Royal Philharmonic Society in 1966, and *Night Music*, performed by the New Philharmonia Orchestra in the year following, signalled a change of direction which owed something to the Polish school represented by Lutoslawski and Penderecki. Even so, the influence of Bartók and Hindemith was still apparent in the slow nocturnal movements and the more general aspects of line, rhythm and structure.

The most admired work of Alun's middle period was *The Sun, the Great Luminary of the Universe*, which was first performed at the Swansea Music Festival in 1970 by the London Symphony Orchestra conducted by Vernon Handley. The work takes its title from an apocalyptic passage in *Portrait of the Artist as a Young Man*, each section corresponding to a sentence in Joyce's prose. The structure is again cumulative, the tensions marked by contrasts of explosive sound followed by what the composer called 'massive silences'. Thematic ideas are taken from Bach's *Es Ist Genug* and the famous '*Dies irae*' motif is heard in shadowy outline at the climax, with a coda bringing the whole to a quiet close. It is a nocturnal piece, reflecting the composer's lifelong habit of writing during the hours of darkness.

Similar features are to be heard in Hoddinott's symphonies, though not at the expense of linear construction, which continued to hold a central place in his musical thinking. Long melodies, often supported by a repetitive oscillation of two adjacent harmonies, reminiscent of both Sibelius and Berg, lend the scores a powerful lyricism and a fugal quality.

The work is complex, but the complexity is never arbitrary, for it is born of an ability, or compulsion, 'to see the world from varying angles, to explore the interaction of separate forces, to reshape material in the light of other events'. Among the composer's favourite techniques up to about 1970 was that of the palindrome, even the double palindrome, in which a sequence of notes is stated and then restated in reverse order. It is to be heard at its most effective in his *Oboe Concerto* (1955) and *Piano Concerto* (1960), where it is used with a twelve-note line centred on a key note.

The same technical virtuosity is demonstrated in his concertos. A violinist by training, Alun composed directly onto an orchestral score, without the intermediate use of a piano outline, but with an acute awareness of instrumental colour as a creative stimulus. The *Piano Concerto No. 2*, written in 1960, is scored for an orchestra of double woodwind, brass, percussion and strings. The *Concerto for Horn and Orchestra* was written in 1969, by which time he had become increasingly interested in the colouristic potential of the percussion section.

As Head of the Music Department at Cardiff, one of the largest in the United Kingdom, Alun Hoddinott played a major role in introducing audiences to the work of modern composers. From 1976 the Cardiff Festival of Twentieth Century Music, of which he was founder and Artistic Director, commissioned and performed new works by Britten, Tippett, Walton, Messiaen, Maxwell-Davies and many others – more than two hundred in all. The Festival has done much to awaken public interest in modern music in Wales, a country in which the amateur and folk traditions have for long reigned supreme.

There is nothing folkloric in Alun Hoddinott's music, and most critics have perceived in it a Mediterranean light rather than anything specifically Welsh, but he did use Welsh material in some of his works, often drawn from the visual arts and literature. The neo-Impressionistic *Landscapes* (1975), for example, was derived from '*Eryri*', a poem about Snowdonia by T. H. Parry-Williams, while *Roman Dream*, *Ancestor Worship* and *An Apple Tree and a Pig* were inspired by poems by his friend Emyr Humphreys. Between 1950 and 1976 Alun wrote incidental music for radio plays and films, including works by Dannie Abse, Lorca, Saunders Lewis, Christopher Fry, Anouilh, Browning, and Gwyn Thomas.

Although firmly rooted in Wales, Alun Hoddinott travelled widely, especially to southern Europe, and to the USA as visiting professor and composer-in-residence at Universities in Texas, Kansas, Oklahoma, Nebraska, Columbia and Guelph, Ontario. In 1989, his sixtieth year, his long association with the London Symphony Orchestra bore magnificent fruit in *Noctis Equi* (Opus 132), a poem for cello and orchestra, inspired by the haunting line in Marlowe's *Doctor Faustus*, '*O lente, lente currite, noctis equi*'. This work, which was first conducted at the Barbican by Rostropovich, is generally thought to be Hoddinott's finest composition.

Some critics, however, may prefer his *Fourth*, *Fifth* and *Sixth Symphonies*, his *Horn Concerto*, any of the *Piano Sonatas*, the choral symphony *Sinfoni Fidei*, or even the lighter but no less important *Welsh Dances* and the *Quodlibet on Welsh Nursery Rhymes*. It is difficult to choose from among a vast output of about 300 works, but at least the composer was well served by his recording companies, which included Argo, Decca, Lyrita, Nimbus and Oriana, so that his music is now available to a wide audience. He was fortunate, too, in having the financial support of the Welsh Arts Council throughout his career.

Among the works he wrote during the 1990s were *A May Song* (Wales Garden Festival, 1992), *Gloria for Chorus and Organ* (Tenby Festival, 1992), *Wind Quartet* (Gower Festival, 1993), *Missa Sancti David* (Fishguard Festival, 1994), *Three Hymns for Mixed Chorus and Organ* (North Wales Music Festival, 1994), *String Quartet No. 4* (Machynlleth Festival, 1996), *Sonata No. 6 for Violin and Piano* (Lower Machen Festival, 1997) and *Grongar Hill for baritone, string quartet and piano* (Beaumaris Festival, 1998). If that is to mention only a few among many, at least it suggests the extent to which the work of Alun Hoddinott, which baffled its first audiences in Wales, has now been accepted as a rich component in the musical life of the nation.

He was honoured at the opening of the Wales Millennium Centre in 2004 and wrote a minute-long fanfare for the wedding of the Prince of Wales and Camilla Parker Bowles in 2005. Shortly before he was taken ill in 2007, he finished his last major work, *Taliesin*. Also in 2007, in acknowledgement of his long association with it, the BBC Welsh National Orchestra named its new home at the Millennium Centre Neuadd Hoddinott, due to be opened in 2009. On the night before he died, the world premiere of his last string quartet was performed at London's Wigmore Hall.

A genial and convivial man, though single minded and sometimes ruthless in his commitment to his art, Alun Hoddinott was generous and hospitable towards other composers and music-makers. His wife, Rhiannon, a Welsh-speaker, was his translator, collaborator and amanuensis. At their homes in Lisvane, a leafy suburb of Cardiff, and later in Three Crosses, on Gower, they entertained their many friends in lavish style, delighting in the company of other artists and wide-ranging, late-night talk accompanied by good wine and loud laughter.

Alun Hoddinott, composer: born Bargoed, Glamorgan 11 August 1929; Lecturer, Cardiff College of Music and Drama 1951-59; Lecturer, University College of South Wales and Monmouthshire (later University College, Cardiff) 1959-65, Reader 1965-67, Professor and Head of the Department of Music 1967-87 (Emeritus), Fellow 1983-2008; Professor and Head of the Department of Music, University College, Cardiff 1967-87;

Alun Hoddinott

Artistic Director of the Cardiff Festival of Twentieth Century Music 1967-89, President 1990-2008; Governor, Welsh National Theatre 1968-74; CBE 1983; married 1953 Rhiannon Huws (one son); Hon. DMus.; died Swansea 12 March 2008.

The Independent (14 March 2008)

The following obituaries by Meic Stephens have also appeared in *The Independent:*

Bruce Griffiths, *30 January 1999*
Howard Winstone, *3 October 2000*
Lyn Evans, *7 December 2001*
Goronwy Daniel, *20 January 2003*
Phil Williams, *13 June 2003*
Ronan Huon, *28 October 2003*
Dennis Coslett, *21 May 2004*
Emrys Evans, *21 July 2004*
Gordon Parry, *6 September 2004*
Anthony Lewis, *11 November 2005*
Peter Law, *26 April 2006*
Alun Menai Williams, *8 July 2006*
G. O. Jones, *14 July 2006*
J. A. Davies, *27 February 2007*
John Clement, *7 June 2007*
Tasker Watkins, *10 September 2007*
Ray Gravell, *2 November 2007*

Five of his obituaries have appeared in other newspapers:

John Ormond, *The Guardian, 9 June 1990*
Will Roberts, *The Times, 18 March 2000*
Huw Weekes, *The Guardian, 12 February 2001*
Peter Prendergast, *The Guardian, 22 January 2007*
Grenfell Jones, *The Guardian, 13 March 2007*